*The Neurotic Behavior
of Organizations*

The
NEUROTIC BEHAVIOR
of
ORGANIZATIONS

Uri Merry, Ph.D
George I. Brown, Ed.D

gestalt institute of cleveland press

*Published and Distributed by Gardner Press, Inc.
New York & London*

Second Printing 1990

Gardner Press, Inc.
19 Union Square West
New York, NY 10003

All foreign orders except Canada and South·America to:
Afterhurst Limited
Chancery House
319 City Road
London N1, United Kingdom

Library of Congress Cataloging in Publication Data

Merry, Uri.
   The neurotic behavior of organizations.

   Bibliography: p.
   Includes index.
   1. Neuroses—Treatment. 2. Gestalt therapy.
3. Organizational behavior. I. Brown, George Isaac.
II. Title. [DNLM: 1. Behavior. 2. Organizations.
3. Psychotherapy. HD58.7 M573n]
RC530.M464 1985   155.9'26   85-20558
ISBN 0-89876-116-6 (Gardner Press)

PRINTED IN THE UNITED STATES OF AMERICA

DESIGN BY SIDNEY SOLOMON

Contents

PREFACE

> "My University degree and my background are in Chemical Engineering. But over 90% of my time during my business career has been spent in dealing with people, motivating people, understanding people, appealing to people—and, finally, trying to unite people in pursuit of our goals." Robert Goizueta, CEO, Major Corporation, in *Forbes Magazine*, April 30, 1984.

Recent reports on the status of business schools have urged the addition of a greater "human factor" orientation. These reports stress the need for learning about motivation, communication, negotiation, and relationships. And two recently highly popular books, *In Search of Excellence* by Peters and Waterman and *Megatrends* by John Naisbitt, stress the importance of human factors in business and other organizations.

These are just partial evidence of the importance of the human factor in what happens in the systemic interaction (1) of individuals within organizations, and (2) between the individual and the organization, and (3) of how individuals, individually and collectively, affect the organization's structure and functioning. The reification of organizations or the attempts to solve their problems in a purely rational way often neglect this factor at high cost.

Furthermore, just as individuals can exhibit neurotic behavior or worse, so can organizations. This book examines that condition for both organizations as a whole and their parts, as well as the roles individuals and groups play in these neuroses.

Gestalt therapy is a major school of individual therapy known for its power, efficiency, and effectiveness. As a "human factor" systems approach, it provides a rich repertoire of interventions with individuals that can be directly applied to organizations and their subsystems. Its different perspective equips the manager, consultant, theoretician, or change agent with ways to conceptualize and comprehend the complexities of organizations better, and also supplies fresh systems approaches to work with the difficult and confusing problems that emerge in the task and maintenance functions of an organization.

Most important, this book presents the first systematic treatment of organizations from a Gestalt perspective, directed to both those who work from within organizations and those who are outside consultants. Although most would agree that an understanding of organizational pathology is important, little attention has been paid to such pathology when it is pervasive. Organizational development consultants often focus on troubled parts of an organization, but when there are significant patterns of overall dysfunctional organizational behavior, less seems to be known about what happens to the organization. In this book we make an arbitrary operational distinction of degree between organizations exhibiting dysfunction, herein called neurotic organizational behavior, and declining organizations. When distortions of reality have reached such a magnitude within the organization that it begins to deteriorate functionally, we have a declining organization. A distinction between neurotic organizational behavior and declining organizations is made (1) to highlight the fact that usually neurotic organizational behavior can be relatively more easily dealt with than can be the situation of a declining organization, and (2) if unattended, neurotic organizational behavior can grow, leading to the creation of a self-destructive, declining organization.

To help explain what happens to organizations as systems with neurotic, dysfunctional conditions, the authors draw upon the theory and methodology of Gestalt therapy. Gestalt therapy has already demonstrated itself to be a powerful set of interventions and theory that sometimes dramatically change individual neurotic behavior. In addition, it has been used as a working systems approach in a variety of other professional contexts such as education, medicine, and law. The authors believe Gestalt therapy holds great promise when adapted for use in understanding and working with organizations. Its use, however, is not intended to replace other organizational theories, but to provide an alternative perspective.

The authors provide a combination of expertise in the fields of organizational behavior and Gestalt therapy. One of the authors (Merry) has been an organizational development consultant for 15 years, working with communities, industries, schools, and a variety of institutions. He has developed a wide range of approaches to help organizations and has written a book on these. Along with teaching organizational behavior and development at both under-graduate and graduate levels, he has developed and facilitated numerous workshops for managers and top executives of organizations and is involved in training and teaching organizational consultants.

The other author (Brown) originally studied with Fritz Perls, the founder of Gestalt therapy, and later served as cotherapist with him. He is on the editorial board of *The Gestalt Journal*, and has written a number of articles and books related to the use of Gestalt therapy. He teaches Gestalt therapy and organizational leadership in a graduate school at the University of California, and for 15 years has led training workshops throughout the world. He also serves as consultant to the Organizational Designs in Communication group.

The two authors, with their interest in each other's work, over a period of five years have collaborated in bringing these two together. Originating from needs to find a way to understand dysfunctional organizational behavior as a phenomenon and to do something about dysfunction, the authors explored the potential in creating analogies from Gestalt therapy theory and practice with individuals for organizations.

On the theoretical level, the work helps fill a gap in organizational theory. On the level of practice, it provides a new perspective for managers and others who have to deal with dysfunctional phenomena. Managers whose organizations and subsystems are fundamentally healthy will find here ways to keep them along with ways to deal with what we term neurotic organizational behavior as it emerges. In the academic field, the book may be used as a text in courses on organizational theory, organizational behavior, management, and the like. It can be of help to consultants, organizational development practitioners, and others who need to assist organizations struggling with neurotic manifestations. This book will also be of special interest to the many practitioners in the field of Gestalt therapy who wish to work with organizations. And it could have direct application to family systems as well as other organizational structures.

Overall, the book represents an attempt to understand how organizations can decline as a result of neurosis, as well as exhibit a less intense but more prevalent form of neurotic organizational behavior. In defining these phenomena, it describes their characteristics, their symptoms, and conditions under which they develop, the various stages of their development and their effects on organizational functioning, and the mechanisms organizations use to maintain delusions. All these are done within the perspective of Gestalt therapy and overall systems theory.

The book is divided into two parts. The first part consists of three chapters that describe neurotic organizational behavior and declining organizations—their characteristics, differences, and dynamics. The second part of the book explains these phenomena in depth from a Gestalt therapy perspective with suggested procedures.

Most of the case studies used are true, with names and circumstances changed to preserve anonymity.

In sum this book is an attempt to provide an understanding of common forms of organizational pathology. It opens a whole new domain of organizational study and exploits the as yet mostly untapped potential application of Gestalt therapy at the organizational level.

The Neurotic Behavior
of Organizations

NEUROTIC ORGANIZATIONAL BEHAVIOR AND DECLINING ORGANIZATIONS

CHAPTER 1

THE CHARACTERISTICS OF DECLINING ORGANIZATIONS

OVERVIEW

There are similarities between individual neurotic behavior and declining organizations. The chapter describes the background and methods of collecting data on criteria that identify declining organizations. The organizations studied here were less than a handful of companies that were caught in a vicious circle of recurring crisis. The study resulted in a list of 15 identifying characteristics. These were later subsumed into an abbreviated and more workable list of seven criteria.

In the study there seemed to be much similarity between the criteria identifying declining organizations and the symptoms of neurotic individual behavior, as described in the literature, and in particular in Gestalt therapy. The first published studies on organizational neurosis also described symptoms bearing much resemblance to the symptoms found in declining organizations. Declining organizations appeared to be a subset of disintegrating organizations among a larger set of organizations that displayed neurotic organizational behavior. *The declining organization was an orga-*

nization displaying neurotic behavior to a degree that was leading to organizational decline. Neurotic organizational behavior by itself appeared to be a more widespread and less severe form of neurotic behavior in organizations.

CRITERIA OF DECLINING ORGANIZATIONS

Telboard produced synthetic wallboards for the building industry. Almost from its foundation it began having troubles. The running-in period was one of intense squabbles and conflict at the top management level. Many things went wrong and managers blamed each other for the mishaps. After some time production went up, but again a series of labor disputes caused a decline. Many products were defective and customers complained of low quality. The shop floor climate was one of dissatisfaction, cynicism, and low morale. Interpersonal tensions and group conflicts were rife throughout the company. Capable professionals who had an option left. The company's self-image was very, very low, and all attempts to change things had failed. Periodically a crisis would break out, thus worsening matters. Telboard was a "declining organization."

In 1979, the Applied Social Research Institute decided to create a project team to collect data and come up with recommendations on how to deal with what we termed "declining organizations." These were a small number of organizations that, in contrast to the majority of well-functioning organizations of their kind, for years had been having extreme difficulties in functioning effectively. They were called declining organizations because they all had recurring, worsening crises. They seemed not to react to the usual organizational development intervention strategies and approaches developed by the Institute. The condition of some of these organizations was becoming precarious, with dwindling production, decreasing membership, and ever-growing financial losses.

It was felt that particular attention should be devoted to the study of these organizations and attempts should be made to characterize them by describing what was distinctive about them in contrast to other organizations, along with understanding the conditions that led to their development. By increasing understanding there was a hope that approaches could be developed that would help them break out of the vicious circle of their recurring crises and allow them to renew themselves.

The members of the project team (which included one of the authors) were experienced organizational development consultants who had spent years consulting with organizations, specifically with declining organizations. The team collected the data by individually interviewing consultants and others who had experience and expertise in consulting with and assisting the organizations being studied.

The outcome was an agreed-upon list of criteria of declining organizations. This list had two sections. The first part was an initial attempt to trace the conditions under which these organizations developed. The second part was a list of criteria that covered all the "symptoms" that had been observed. The following 15 items, later developed by the involved author, are based on the list of criteria of these organizations.

1. Feelings of organizational inadequacy.
2. Lack of energy, low motivation.
3. Interpersonal and intergroup conflict.
4. Much individual frustration and unhappiness.
5. Low morale.
6. Negative selection in membership.
7. Decreasing outputs and inputs.
8. Disagreement on organizational goals and values; norm disruptment.
9. Inability in cope with everyday problems.
10. Inability to plan ahead.
11. Breakdown in communications, feedback, and monitoring.
12. Recurring intensifying periods of crisis.
13. Breakdown of leadership.
14. Neglect of physical facilities.
15. A failure script.

A SHORTER LIST OF CRITERIA

There is difficulty in dealing with a phenomenon that is described by 15 criteria. It, therefore, seemed advisable to develop a shorter, more manageable list of criteria that would miss nothing of the essentials found in the longer list. Distilling the 15 criteria makes a shorter list of six major categories. All criteria found in the longer list can be subsumed under one of the wider categories found in the shorter list. An example would be lack of motivation, low energy, individual frustration, and unhappiness, all subsumed under a wider category of "organizational climate." The abbreviated list is as follows:

1. *A failure self-image.*
   (1) Feelings of organizational inadequacy.
   (15) A failure script.

2. *A low-energy climate*
   (2) Lack of energy, low motivation.
   (5) Low morale.
   (4) Much individual frustration and unhappiness.

3. *Breakdown of communication*
   (3) Interpersonal and intergroup conflict.
   (11) Breakdown of communication, feedback, and monitoring.

4. *Disagreement on goals and values; norm disruption.*
   (8) Disagreement on organizational goals and values; norm disruption.

5. *Organizational dysfunctioning*
   (7) Decreasing outputs and inputs.
   (9) Inability to cope with everyday problems.
   (10) Inability to plan ahead.
   (14) Neglect of physical facilities.

6. *Deteriorating condition*
   (13) Breakdown of leadership.
   (6) Negative selection in membership.
   (12) Recurring intensifying periods of crisis.

To this list was added a seventh criterion, which had led to identifying these organizations. That criterion was the organization's tendency to maintain its dysfunctional life-style despite its self-defeating character. All attempts to assist the organization in breaking out of its dysfunctional patterns seemed to be of no avail. Organizational consultants, who attempted to help the organization change its patterns and renew itself by returning to healthy functioning, found that their efforts produced few results. The gamut of interventions and strategies developed in applied behavioral science seemed useless in dealing with the phenomena of these organizations. A seventh criterion was therefore added to the abbreviated list, *the difficulty of changing these patterns.*

Here is the shorter list with more details of the items of which it is composed.

1. *A failure self-image*
   a. *Feelings of organizational inadequacy*

   Members of the organization are aware of their organization's inability to function effectively. They speak about it among themselves and tell outsiders about it. They say, "We can't solve our own problems," "We are in a mess, that is how things are with us." Members describe their organization in negative terms such as "failure," "sick," "mess." They compare their own organization's inadequacy and inability to deal with its problems with other organizations that are seen as successful, adaptive, coping, and so forth. Sometimes the descriptions are accompanied by what appears to be an almost hopeless, cynical attitude. The organization's self-image is one of failure, inability to cope with problems, and incapability of the organization to be responsible for itself.

   b. *A failure script*

   The organization seems to be caught in a failure script. It is as if the organization is predestined to fail in every project it attempts. It even appears as if it chooses ventures and policies that are sure not to succeed. The organization sees itself as inadequate, and like a self-fulfilling prophecy proves this to itself by repeatedly failing in all it does. The organization appears to have created a fantasized self-image of inadequacy and failure and is building its reality through the negative filters of this image. It appears to be caught in a vicious circle of creating a negative organizational reality out of a negative self-model. It then justifies the model by the negative reality it has created. The model feeds into organizational reality and reality reinforces the model of failure and inadequacy. All attempts to help the organization escape from its failure script appear to fail. It is as if the organization is doomed to a deteriorating process of decline and disintegration.

2. *A low-energy climate*
   a. *Lack of energy, low motivation*

   The atmosphere of the organization is lethargic. There is a very low level of energy and motivation. Nothing seems to be worth investing energy in. People ask: "Why trouble yourself? Nothing will come of it." Years of abortive attempts to "get things going" have led to disillusionment, withdrawal, and apathy. There is an air of boredom and tiredness in everything. People seem to be unable to be motivated by anything. It appears as if all the surplus energy in the organization has been drained out, possibly by internal bickering and manipulating and by abortive coping in the past. It seems as if lack of trust in each other inhibits investing energy in cooperative efforts to improve conditions.

b. *Low morale*

The low energy, lack of motivation and unhappiness seep through into the norms of organizational behavior and affect the climate of the organization. People stop caring in performing their organizational functions. They miss meetings or come late. In meetings that deal with organizational business, they behave skeptically, and are uninvolved and uncommitted. Many matters are not taken care of, and no one tries to do anything about this. People stop making an effort and become accustomed to things not working out, services not being given as they should be, decisions not implemented. People say: "Things are hopeless. We can't get anything done." Innovation and experimentation with new ways, methods, and approaches cease. Low achievement, an attitude of not caring, and a measure of hopelessness characterize the atmosphere.

c. *Individual frustration and unhappiness*

People talk about individual frustration and unhappiness. They may say: "I'm not getting anywhere here." "Life is miserable." "There is nothing to look forward to." "I feel boxed in." They often express feelings of not being valued and of not being able to develop their potential and capabilities. Some say: "I feel small here." "You are not appreciated here." "You cannot develop yourself under these conditions." There is much discontent and dissatisfaction. The inability of the dysfunctioning organization to satisfy individual needs adquately leads to increasing frustration and more pressure to do something about them. Some withdraw to a passive stance. Many people seem as if their vitality has burned out; they live hopelessly and regret their life in the organization.

3. *Breakdown of communication*

a. *Interpersonal and intergroup conflict*

People seem to have lost trust in each other and treat each other with suspicion, and often with a measure of hostility.

They make scapegoats of each other and blame each other, as individuals or as groups, for their plight. People say: "If we had less of them, things would be different around here" or "They always want everything for themselves but are not willing to do anything for others" or "Since they have come, things have gone from bad to worse." Barriers of suspicion and hostility develop between people in different departments, or of different age, background, education, seniority, status, or occupation. Newcomer groups are often made the scapegoats for increasing frustration. In their everyday interaction, people often become critical, evaluative, sarcastic, and hurtful to each other. There is much tension between people in leadership positions and between leadership and rank and file. Formal and informal groups close their ranks against other groups that seem hostile.

b. *Breakdown in communication, feedback, and monitoring*

Communication between people and between sectors of the organization becomes disrupted. Increasing distrust, hostility, and conflict lead people and groups to withdraw from each other, to decrease interaction and the flow of communication. Departments and groups barricade themselves against other departments and groups. Communication is guarded, filtered, and partial. Important information is not transmitted or is distorted in transmission between horizontal sections of the organization and laterally between rank and file and management. Internal and external feedback mechanisms dysfunction. As people communicate less with each other, and do so with distrust, they become increasingly wary about communicating to others about the effects of the latter's actions. The necessary flow of information is not taking place. The organization runs into increasing difficulties in monitoring what is happening inside it and outside it, in the relevant environment.

4. *Disagreement on goals and values; norm disagreement*

a. *Disagreement on organizational goals and values; norm disruption*

Agreement as to the organization's mission and its goals and values is disrupted. Different sections of the organization, different groups, different departments, and people with different characteristics (age, education, origin, etc.) have different priorities with respect to what they want the organization to achieve and disagree about the values by which to evaluate goals. Leadership loses the ability to define the organization's mission, goals, and central values in a way that will be accepted by most of the people in the organization. There is no unifying mission to which peple can commit themselves. Organizational life loses meaning and significance. These differences express themselves in the disruption of norms, thus affecting everyday behavior in the organization. Accepted ways of doing things are undermined. In all areas of life in the organization, there are deviations from accepted ways of behavior. The organization has difficulty dealing with these and maintaining the fabric of work, living, interaction, and relationships. It becomes more and more difficult to engender cohesive, cooperative action around common organizational objectives. Organizational rites and traditions that once inspired emotional and spiritual identification lose their meaning for most people. The disruption of accepted norms leads to severe deviations in behavior that border on the extreme. The periodic disclosure of this wracks the declining organization with a new scandal.

5. *Organizational dysfunctioning*
  a. *Decreasing outputs and inputs*
    The lack of energy and motivation, the low morale, the conflicts, and negative selection all have effects on the organization's inputs and outputs and the ratio between the inputs and the outputs. At a certain stage the organization's dysfunctioning affects its core production processes and decreases productivity and outputs. Work efficiency and effectiveness go down and low outputs, quantitatively and qualitatively, become the norm in the organization. Inability to generate solutions to problems engendered by inevitable environmental changes and internal disorganization decreases the organization's adaptibility. Lack of innovation blocks raising production with new approaches and methods. Dwindling financial resources make investment in new technology difficult. Loss of talented and capable people decreases the organization's ability to deal with its declining productive ability. Decreasing outputs lead to decreasing inputs. A state of decline develops, with outputs exceeding inputs and the organization eating up its reserve resources.
  b. *Inability to cope with everyday problems*
    The organization has difficulty dealing efficiently and prac-

tically with its regular business. It loses its ability to function in a manner that allows it to cope with everyday problems. The low energy, low morale, low motivation, conflict, disagreement on goals, disruption of norms, and communication breakdown all undermine the organization's ability to cope with new situations satisfactorily. The organization's decision-making structure ceases to function effectively and matters are not dealt with efficiently and on time. Decisions that should have been made at the middle levels flow to the top, which, in turn, suffers from decision-making overload. The organization's low morale reflects its ineffective functioning and amplifies the ineffectiveness.

c. *Inability to plan ahead*

The organization appears to be caught in a crisis management mode. It deals with problems only when they reach crisis proportions and no longer can be ignored. The decision-making bodies are busy "putting out the fires" that are constantly starting. Typically they might be involved in finding a replacement for someone who is leaving, or with a breakdown in some facility, a conflict disrupting organizational life, a scandal, the loss of an income source, and so on. Dealing with these everyday occurrences takes all the time and energy of the organization and its decision makers. There is little left to devote to planning for the future. The feeling is that turnover in personnel, everyday disruptions, and the fact that many decisions are not carried out make planning ahead unfeasible. The organization does not plan ahead; it has no long-term goals, no strategic planning, no scenario of its future development, and no priorities among its objectives. Trends developing in the environment that may seriously affect the organization or provide it with opportunities are ignored. The organization lives from moment to moment, with no eye for the future.

d. *Neglect of physical facilities*

Physical facilities, which are the property of the organization, show signs of neglect and apathetic treatment. Buildings, gardens, and work equipment bear the marks of lack of care and maintenance. Organizational facilities that were created to serve people's needs, such as dining areas, recreational facilities, and libraries, appear neglected and the related services slovenly. Breakdowns in equipment because of a lack of suitable maintenance are common. The apathy, hopelessness, low morale, and disintegrative tendencies of the organization find their material expression in the outward appearance of the physical facilities of the organization.

6. *Deteriorating conditions*
a. *Breakdown of leadership*

Many of the capable people have left the organization. New people with talent and managerial capabilities are not joining the organization. New leadership is not being trained. The authority of existing leadership is undermined. Management at all levels becomes poorer and poorer. The organization loses its ability to attract or develop new leadership and capable professionals and specialists to help the management. Tensions among leaders increase and often turn into intense conflicts between different groups backing different leaders. Stronger people try to build their own dominions out of their teams or departments. The organization may disintegrate into very loosely coupled, uncoordinated, competing, and conflicting little kingdoms, each fighting for its share of the diminishing pie.

b. *Negative selection in membership*

Many people want to leave the organization. If they have alternatives, and conditions favor a move, they do so. The organization loses its most capable, talented, energetic, and skilled people, as these are generally the ones who find it easier to move to another organization that can utilize their talents. Some of the more capable people may try to change things. But after a number of abortive attempts, which are blocked by the organization's avoidance patterns, they give up and seek their fortune elsewhere. Younger people, with less seniority and therefore less investment, are among those who leave the organization. Newcomers, who have fewer commitments and also other options, leave as well. The organization has difficulty attracting new capable, talented people, and it is unable to keep those it has. The selection is a negative one. Those who are young, talented, innovative, energetic, creative, and capable leave. The older people, who have greater seniority and fewer options, remain. New blood does not flow in to energize the system.

c. *Recurring, intensifying periods of crisis*

The organization seems to be caught in a cycle of recurring, intensifying crises leading in a direction of organizational deterioration. Periodically matters come to a head and the organization passes through a serious crisis that worsens its general condition. The crisis may be connected to a transition period in the organization's life cycle (e.g., institutionalization). It may be regularly connected to a specific season of the year (e.g., people planning to leave at year end). It also may be unconnected to any cycle or regularity, but result from a particular occurrence, such as a serious breakdown or a heavy financial loss. Whatever the triggering event, the crisis takes its toll. Many matters come to a head, the stress level in the organization goes up, and the entire system becomes disrupted by the intense fluctuations. The organization, feeling much stress, sometimes looks for outside help, financial, consultative, or otherwise. Whether alone, or with help, the organization does something to alleviate the immediate cause of the crisis, or it subsides on its own after a time. This may be followed by another period of relative quiet until the next crisis breaks out. The new steady state reached by the organization after a crisis may often be at a lower level of organizational health, functioning, and adaptivity. The crises repeat themselves at an accelerated rate each time, thus worsening the organization's condition.

Sumarizing the foregoing gives the following abbreviated list of criteria:

1. Failure self-image.
2. Low-energy climate.
3. Breakdown of communication.
4. Disagreement on goals, values, and norms.
5. Organizational dysfunctioning.
6. Deteriorating condition.
7. Difficulty in changing these patterns.

Most of the people in the community were over 60 years old; almost all of the young people born in Haydrew had left it for better prospects. The two major industries in the community were a fruit-canning plant and a plastic injection factory, both of which had great difficulty finding workers in the area.

Haydrew saw itself as a failure and people who lived there described it thus: "We have no hope." "We always messed things up." "This place never had any luck." "Whoever has initiative or talent moves out of here."

The community council hardly functioned, and its members did not trust each other. Decisions were seldom made, and when made were not implemented. Funds were scarce, and this could be seen in every aspect of public facilities. Everything looked shoddy and uncared for.

The place was wracked with hostility, fights between different factions, family feuds, and conflicts of all sorts. Every now and then, a new scandal would break out over some form of corruption, bribery, or some other ugly incident.

There had been a number of times in Haydrew's history when a few people had decided to change things by taking matters into their own hands. But these attempts always failed. Now people had resigned themselves to their fate. Energy had ebbed out of the place. The climate was one of lack of hope, low energy, nothing to look forward to. Hope was gone.

DECLINING ORGANIZATIONS AND NEUROTIC ORGANIZATIONAL BEHAVIOR

A number of factors suggested the possibility that the seven-factor list developed as criteria for identifying declining organizations could be generalized to a wider class of organizations. In other words, these criteria were not only the property of a small number of companies in crisis, but could be used to identify and describe other organizations that appeared to be suffering from similar difficulties.

The symptoms seemed to be very close to what at the individual level would be described as neurotic behavior. The following from a standard text (Coleman, 1972) illustrates some points of similarity.

The common core of neurosis is a maladaptive life-style, typified by anxiety and avoidance. Basic to this neurotic life style are: (1) faulty evaluations of reality and the tendency to avoid problems rather than cope with them—the neurotic nucleus; and (2) the tendency to maintain the life-style despite its pathologic self-defeating nature—the neurotic paradox. (p. 218)

Perls, the originator of Gestalt therapy, refers to a similar configuration of symptoms when describing neurotic individual behavior. In dealing with a *failure self-image*, Perls writes about the neurotic living in a world that is out of touch, and therefore progressively hallucinatory, projected, and otherwise unreal. Perls

(1980) describes how the neurotic is "lacking the support of self-esteem" and is "in a constant need for external support" (p. 99). He "is busy nagging, disapproving of himself."

A *low energy level* is typical of a neurotic. Perls describes how all the person's energy is "drained in neurotic functioning" and there remains "no surplus for integration and self-organizing" (p. 111). He also writes about (Perls, 1976) the neurotic's boredom and low energy—"energy becomes smaller and smaller" (p. 12).

Perls sees one of the functions of therapy as dealing with *the breakdown in communication* and the splits and conflicts within a person's personality. The neurotic needs to renew genuine contact and to assimilate the parts of the self he or she is avoiding. It is necessary to integrate warring parts of one's personality, such as the "top dog" and the "underdog." Genuine communication between and acceptance of the parts of the self that have disowned each other must be renewed. Perls notes the *conflict of goals and values* in the neurotic's behavior. He sees the neurotic as being in a state of confusion, unable to decide what his or her needs were and incapable of assigning priorities to the needs. The neurotic is in a state of existential crisis.

Perls (1980) further sees the neurotic as being in a *dysfunctional state* using "outmoded ways of acting" and being "tortured about the future because the present is out of his hands" (p. 44). The neurotic "consults the therapist because he hopes to find in him the environmental support that will supplement his own inadequate means of support" (p. 45). The neurotic cannot function effectively because "his homeostasis is not working properly" (p. 45).

The *deteriorating condition* of the neurotic is noted by Perls (1976). The "ability to cope with the world becomes less and less" (p. 12). Perls (1980) suggests that "when the individual is frozen to an outmoded way of acting, he is less capable of meeting any of his survival needs, including his social needs" (p. 26). The neurotic "is lacking, to a marked degree, one of the essential qualities that promote survival-self support" (p. 46).

And finally, Perls (1980) points out how *difficult* it is for the neurotic *to change dysfunctional behavior patterns*. The neurotic's "means of manipulation are manifold" and can be used with whomever attempts to assist in changing the neurotic behaviors. They are used to frustrate all approaches to change the neurotic's patterns; "his manipulations are directed towards preserving and cherishing his handicap, rather than getting rid of it" (p. 47). Perls recognizes that an organization can be neurotic like an individual. In some frequently quoted paragraphs, he (1980, pp. 26–27) attempted to differentiate between a healthy society and a neurotic one.

What struck us was that the seven symptoms found in declining organizations seemed to be very similar to those found in neurotic individuals.

A survey of the organizational literature revealed that, although not sufficiently researched and established theoretically, organizational neurosis was beginning to be recognized. Organizational theorists with a psychoanalytic background (e.g., De Board, 1978; Kets de Vries, 1982) were using the concept "neurotic organization," or the "neurotic behavior of an organization," for phenomena that appeared to be similar to the symptoms on the list of declining organizations. Two studies—one (Harvey & Albertson, 1971) developed on the basis of clinical observation, and the other (Kets de Vries & Miller, 1982) based on broad empirical research—deal directly with "neurotic organizations," and report phenomena similar to those described in the abbreviated list. Other studies of organizational pathology describe organizations with many of the seven symptoms (e.g., Levinson, 1972; De Greene, 1982). The organizations are not defined as neurotic but their description is close to that of declining organizations.

Clinical observation, discussions with other organizational consultants, and a survey of the literature on organizational pathology, crisis, and so forth (e.g., Miller, 1978; Levinson, 1972; Fink et al., 1971; Smart & Vertinsky, 1977; Whetten, 1980; Robbins, 1983) all lead to the conclusion that it might be advisable to distinguish and differentiate between two kinds, or two levels, of neurotic behavior in organizations. One level, henceforth called declining organizations, is that described by the abbreviated list of seven criteria. These appeared to describe an advanced stage of organizational neurosis that had deeply affected the entire organization. The organization was having difficulty functioning effectively, and it seemed to be in a process of decline marked by recurring periods of crisis.

Another form, or level, of neurotic functioning appeared to be more widespread among organizations, but not as deeply pathologic as that in declining organizations. This was named "neurotic organizational behavior" and was differentiated from declining organizations.

Organizations displaying neurotic organizational behavior do evidence some of the symptoms of declining organizations, but generally in a lighter form—the neurotic behavior may be only in a department or other subsystem. They do not necessarily have a failure self-image. This is replaced by some other form of reality distortion, by delusion or fantasy. Organizations that display neurotic organizational behavior need not be in a condition of decline. The organizational dysfunctioning has not spread to a degree that is leading to organizational disintegration. Such organizations appear to have repetitive patterns of pathologic, seemingly unchangeable behavior, involving a false representation of reality in the organization or a subsystem. This definition of neurotic organizational behavior will be dealt with in detail in Chapter 2.

While further study may find this to be imprecise or inexact, at this stage of knowledge a declining organization will be regarded as a much more severe form of neurotic organizational behavior, which, in turn, is causing organizational decline. The definition used here will be: *A declining organization is an organization with a negative self-image in which neurotic organizational behavior has reached such a magnitude and depth that the organization is in a process of decline.* In this definition, and throughout this book, "organization" will refer to both an entire organization, such as a manufacturing company, and to any of its subunits, such as a department or team. This definition stresses two elements: (1) A declining organization belongs to the set of organizations that display neurotic organizational behavior. (2) Within that set of organizations, a declining organization belongs to a subset that has a negative self-image and the neurotic organizational behavior has reached such proportions that it is propelling the organization in the direction of decline. "Decline" will be used as a state of a dissipative system as described by Adams (1975):

Dissipative systems can, however, manifest different states, depending on the relative input-output ratio:
(1) in expanding systems, input is greater than output;
(2) in declining systems, output is greater than input;
(3) in steady states, input is equal to output. (p. 128).

A declining organization therefore is an organization that is displaying neurotic organizational behavior to a degree that the organization's outputs are regularly greater than its inputs.

The major part of this work will deal with organizational neurosis: the conditions under which it develops; the various forms it takes; and the way it affects organizational functioning.

PROPOSITIONS AND DEFINITIONS

★ Declining organizations may be identified by the following seven criteria: (1) a failure self-image; (2) a low-energy climate; (3) breakdown of communication; (4) disagreement on goals, values, and norms; (5) organizational dysfunctioning; (6) deteriorating conditions; and (7) difficulty in changing these patterns.

★ A declining organization is an organization with a negative self-image in which neurotic organizational behavior has reached such a magnitude and depth that the organization is in a process of decline.

★ Neurotic organizational behavior is repetitive patterns of pathologic, seemingly unchangeable, organizational behavior, involving a false representation of reality.

These definitions and propositions are based on clinical observation from a variety of sources. They are in need of more extensive research.

CHAPTER 2

NEUROTIC ORGANIZATIONAL BEHAVIOR

OVERVIEW

In this chapter we define neurotic organizational behavior and elaborate on the definition by examining each part of it and comparing it with similar phenomena.

Neurotic organizational behavior patterns tend to recur. We contrast these with forms of organizational dysfunctioning, and we also explore the provocative question of whether neurotic organizational behavior is on the increase.

The definition of neurotic organizational behavior as a form of organizational pathology and its relation to organizational effectiveness are clarified. The pitfalls of a pathologic model of organizational functioning are described.

The difficulty of dealing with and changing neurotic organizational behavior and the "vicious circle" quality of neurotic organizational behavior is included in the next section.

Neurotic organizational behavior is defined as an organizational-level phenomenon in contrast to an individual-level phenomenon. This difference is clarified and a first attempt is made to draw up a list of distinctions between individuals as systems and organizations as systems.

The chapter ends with a clarification of the difference between distortion of reality in neurotic organizational behavior and the concept of organizational myth.

A DEFINITION OF NEUROTIC ORGANIZATIONAL BEHAVIOR

Kertog was a medium-sized company that produced rubber fittings used in other industries. Kertog believed that its success lay in the quality of its products. This belief persisted even when the use of newly discovered synthetic material instead of rubber became a feasible alternative for many of the factories to which Kertog supplied its products. Kertog could have opened up a new line of production to supply fittings, which, while much cheaper, were of a sufficient standard to satisfy the needs of many of its customers. But Kertog's slogan was: "Quality Before Anything Else." Management at all levels colluded in taking a stand against using the new material and investing in a new production line. When one customer after another began to buy from competitors who used the cheaper material, the story told in Kertog was, "They will return to us when they find out what quality they are getting."

Many loyal customers, who needed both the higher quality goods of Kertog and the cheaper product, appealed to Kertog to begin producing the cheaper product in addition to its high-quality products. But it seemed as if Kertog could not change its self-image as a high-quality producer. Loss of income led to management trying to decrease costs by cutting fringe benefits and layoffs. The work climate in the industry became one of tension and conflict. Consultants were called in but their report recommending a move toward creating a second line of cheaper products was ignored. A changeover of management occurred, but no change in policy took place. Kertog persisted in making only quality products, and was eventually taken over by another company.

Neurotic organizational behavior will be defined as (1) repetitive patterns of (2) pathologic (3) seemingly unchangeable (4) organizational behavior, (5) involving a distortion of reality. In this definition "organizational" refers either to the organization *as a whole or to one of its parts*, such as a management team or a department.

The different parts of this definition deserve clarification.

1. *Repetitive patterns.* The behavior is not one-time behavior, a "one-shot error" of judgment, but a recurring pattern of behavior persisting over a meaningful time period. Nor is it a single adjustment to an environmental deterioration or disaster. It is a configuration of behaviors occurring over a long time frame and emanating from the organization itself.

2. *Pathologic.* A part of the organization is not in a state of healthy functioning. Some of its variables are beyond their ranges of stability, or the costs of keeping them within the ranges of stability are significantly increased. Part of the organization is malfunctioning, although the organization as a whole might be functioning well in many areas.

3. *Seemingly unchangeable.* The neurotic organizational behavior is not a state that is amenable to regular adjustment processes. The organization seems to be unable to change the pattern of behavior that is causing it trouble. Sometimes the organization is aware of the relationship between its behavior and its malfunctioning, sometimes not. In either case, when it recognizes the link and when it does not, the organization appears to have difficulty pulling itself out of the pattern it has developed. The organization seems to be caught in a vicious circle from which it is unable to extricate itself.

4. *Organizational behavior.* Differing from a phenomenon at the individual level, this is not an action a person can take without the collaboration of others. Instead it is a collective phenomenon at the organizational level. The behavior emanates from the interdependence and interaction of people as well as subsystems as components of an organization. These are patterns of behavior of the organization, not of individuals.

5. *Involving a distortion of reality.** The organization, or more precisely, members of the organization in their organizational context, are not in touch with important aspects of what is really happening inside the organization or in its environment. The collective phenomenon of the organization has distorted reality and replaced it with an imaginary, fantasy-based distortion of reality. The organization has created an intermediate zone of illusion between itself and the world.

As will be demonstrated throughout this work, the definition of neurotic organizational behavior, as given here, is derived from analogies developed from Perls' descriptions of neurotic individual behavior. In many places throughout his work, Perls refers to the repetitiveness, pathology, seeming unchangeability, and fantasy-like qualities of neurotic individual behavior. Perls uses the term "neurotic" very often. He calls many behaviors neurotic, but makes no attempt to develop a systematic definition of neurotic individual behavior. The definition given here for neurotic organizational behavior is an attempt to develop a systematic definition using analogies from the rich mine of ideas developed in Gestalt therapy.

Pathologic organizational behavior takes many forms. Scott (1981), De Greene (1982), and Miller (1978) have detailed the variety of forms pathology may take in organizations. Neurotic organizational behavior is one of these. It is a special kind that consists of repetitive patterns, of seemingly unchangeable organizational behavior, involving a false representation of reality.

How widespread, prevalent, and damaging neurotic organizational behavior is relative to other forms of organizational pathology is a matter for research. It is probably unique in that it is more difficult to deal with through the usual rational forms of treatment and consultation that are of help in confronting other forms of organizational pathology. How widespread neurotic organizational behavior is at this stage can only be a matter of speculation. It appears to be becoming more common today but there is no empirical evidence as yet to support this proposition.

As a Repetitive Pattern of Behavior

Neurotic organizational behavior is a repetitive pattern of behavior and not a single reaction to environmental depletion. Ultimately neurotic organizational behavior is rooted in the difficulty of organizations or their subsystems in adapting to a changing environment. But this does not mean that neurotic organizational behavior develops automatically in an organization as a result of a decline in environmental conditions. Organizational textbooks abound with examples of organizations that did not adapt to, and were unable to survive in, a worsening environment. A marked decline in markets, because of product obsolescence, can hand a fatal blow to an industry. Industries connected with the stage coach years ago, the vacuum tube some years ago, and the record industry today all have faced environmental situations that could lead to crisis, bankruptcy, and organizational demise. In these cases a severe decline in environmental conditions placed the organization's adaptive and survival capability in jeopardy.

But all of these examples may have nothing to do with neurotic organizational behavior. The change in conditions was real, not an organizational fantasy. Although the industries' adjustment and adaptive steps did not save them, they may not have been neurotic. It is not in these situations, in particular, that neurotic organizational behavior develops. There is no evidence that recurring patterns of pathological organizational behavior necessarily develop from environmental deterioration.

Neurotic organizational behavior is a recurring pattern of pathologic behavior and not a deterioration in organizational effectiveness resulting from an incorrect decision or a mistaken policy. Management may evaluate information invertly, or make a decision or initiate a policy that can have extremely negative consequences for the organization. As a result the organization may pass through a difficult period of crisis and struggle for survival. This does not mean that it is suffering from neurotic organizational behavior. It means that a wrong decision was made and the organization is suffering as a consequence.

The repetitive patterns of neurotic organizational behavior are not a necessary reaction to environmental deterioration, nor are they necessarily the aftermath of an incorrect decision or policy. The repetitive patterns of dysfunctional behavior persist over time under differing environmental conditions and organizational decisions and policies.

> The machine maintenance department in the plant was in need of some kind of major change. All the departments in the factory complained that they could not get service from it, and when they did get service, it was given in such a way that they did not want to ask for it again. We were requested by the plant manager to try to do something about this, and he had arranged for us to meet with the foreman in charge of the service department. Our meeting with the foreman, and later with others in maintenance, gave us the picture maintenance had of the rest of the plant.
>
> They saw most of the people who worked with the plant's machinery as irresponsible, undependable, careless, and arrogant young people, who were not interested in taking care of their equipment and neglected essential checkups—leading to endless breakdowns. And "as they don't care a bit, we are not going to let them walk over us. They won't exploit us."

We checked the plant statistics and found no increase in the rate of breakdowns in equipment. What we did find was a doubling in size of the factory and the machines without any increase in the size of maintenance. They had twice the work and were rushing about trying to repair all that had to be taken care of. The same group of ten old-timers was trying to service double the machines. They were stretched beyond their limits, unable to meet all expectations, and were exasperated and frustrated. They refused to add young people to their team; they had not kept up with the new maintenance technologies; and they had not advanced in their technical knowledge and ability for the past 15 years. They were unhappy and angry with themselves, and projected this on others in the factory. They had developed a delusion that they were high-quality technicians and "the only one's who really cared about things over here." They closed themselves to the messages they were receiving from others and ended all attempts of management to give them consultative or technical help and guidance.

Under similar environmental conditions, one organization might be healthy and another might display neurotic organizational behavior. The behavior emanates from the organization itself. Environmental conditions may be positive, yet an organization can keep repeating its pathologic patterns of dysfunctional behavior. Clinical observation supports the proposition that under similar conditions one organization may be functioning effectively and another displaying neurotic organizational behavior. While the etiology of the neurotic organizational behavior phenomena lies in the dynamics of the organization-environment field, the responsibility for choosing the neurotic pattern and maintaining it lies on the organization.

Eric Jantsch (1975) describes organizations as purposeful systems. Purposeful systems formulate and select policy objectives, goals, and targets, whereas deterministic systems, for example, only pursue prescribed targets. They are inventive in the sense of changing their structure through internal generation of information, in accordance with their intensions to change the environment.

Organizations have choices, they are not predetermined. As purposeful systems organizations bear the responsibility for their choices. The organization always has the decision to persist with the neurotic pattern or to adopt a healthier mode of functioning.

These remarks pertain to a single organization in its particular environment. They may, however, distort the overall picture. Organizations as a whole are affected by their environments, and if the environment encourages neurotic organizational behavior development, the chances of neurotic symptoms developing will increase. This is not contradictory but complementary to a natural-selection perspective on organizations, such as that of Hannan and Freeman (1977), or to McKelvey's evolutionary view that adoption to a changing environment explains organizational differences, and thus change and evolution. The percentage of exposed organizations displaying neurotic organizational behavior will probably tend to increase if environmental conditions encourage this. This is very similar to the phenomenon of shell shock. The percentage of shell shock among soldiers increases in wartime battle conditions. The soldiers experiencing the shell shock had the potential for a breakdown, but this probably would not have surfaced under normal peacetime conditions. The aggravated stress of battle increased the number of breakdowns (Merry & Arnon, 1973).

A tentative proposition is that environmental conditions are today being aggravated in a direction that is encouraging the development of neurotic behavior in more organizations—that is, neurotic organizational behavior is probably more prevalent today than in the past, and might be on the increase. There is no empirical support for this proposition, and it may not be easy to verify. Whetten (1980) marshals much evidence to support a proposition of increasing organizational decline. But this is not proof of neurotic organizational behavior increase. The organizations may have disintegrated and dissolved for reasons other than neurotic organizational behavior. De Greene (1982) substantiates an increase in organizational crises. But this again is only an indication.

The proposition is built on a deduction from the basic propositions regarding the etiology of neurotic organizational behavior. If such behavior generally develops in situations where the organization has difficulty adapting to environmental change, when adaptation becomes more difficult, neurotic organizational behavior might be more widespread among organizations. It is proposed that the increasing rates of environmental change, turbulence, complexity, and interdependence are making adaptation more difficult. Thus the interaction between the organization and the environment takes place within the context of a constantly changing field—which might be increasing organizational neurosis.

Pondy and Mitroff (1979) warn against a control systems model of organizations that regards the environment as "a source of disturbance to be adapted to instead of the source of 'information' that makes internal organization possible" (p. 12). They see an open system as being at such a level of complexity "that it can maintain that complexity only in the presence of a throughput from a differentiated environment" (p. 13). If the organization attempts to decrease environmental diversity, its own internal structure will deteriorate. Pondy and Mitcoff suggest that "an organization is unable to maintain internal complexity *except* in the presence of environmental diversity. Surplus complexity is simply not possible for this view, but shortage is."

While probably accepting the overall thrust of these passages, other scholars of organizations would differ with the last statement. The increasing rate of change and surplus complexity might seem to be possible, and even prevalent, in terms of organizations' adaptive capability.

De Greene (1982), in analyzing the increasing prevalence of crisis in organizations, writes: "System complexity has begun to transcend human capabilities to bring out human limitations. This trend continues in accelerated form today" (p. 12).

These descriptions give some indirect support to the very tentative proposition that with the increasing turbulence of today's environment, neurotic organizational behavior might be on the increase. But this proposition cannot be accepted until it has empirical support. Other factors may be working against the increase of neurotic organizational behavior. For example, if with the changing work force there develops a trend of more voluntary mobility between work organizations, this might decrease the pressure cooker situation in which neurotic organizational behavior develops. Therefore, until empirical data are forthcoming, no validated proposition may be made as to the increase in neurotic organizational behavior in organizations.

As an Organizational Pathology

A variety of terms has been used in the organizational literature to depict organizational dysfunctioning or aspects of organizational dysfunctioning. Such terms include: ineffectiveness, inefficiency, stress, strain, crisis, pathology, ill health, nonadaptive, maladaptive, maladjustment, disintegrative, failure, decline. While many terms are used, there is no commonly accepted agreement on their meaning in the organizational context, and also no conceptual framework that attempts to integrate them.

Neurotic organizational behavior is defined in this work as a form of organizational pathology. The relationship of neurotic organizational behavior to some of the other terms used to denote organizational dysfunctioning will be clarified throughout. At this stage it will suffice to review the meaning of organizational pathology.

The *American College Dictionary* (1962) defines pathology as (1) the science of the origin, nature and course of diseases; and (2) the conditions and processes of diseases. Patho means "suffering," "disease," and "feeling."

Probably the most systematic attempt to deal with organizational pathology is that of Miller (1978), whose definition of pathology will be used in this work. Miller writes:

Any state of a system is pathological in which one or more variables remain for a significant period beyond their ranges of stability, or in which the costs of the adjustment processes required to keep them within their ranges of stability are significantly increased. (p. 81)

Miller points out that steady states may be disturbed "by malfunctioning of subsystems or components or by unfavorable conditions in the environment or suprasystem" (p. 81). If they are prolonged too long, they may exhaust the adjustment processes with which the system attempts to cope with them.

The categories of organizational pathology Miller describes are: (1) lack of matter-energy inputs; (2) excesses of matter-energy inputs; (3) inputs of inappropriate forms of matter-energy; (4) lack of information inputs; (5) excesses of information inputs; (6) inputs of maladaptive genetic information in the template; (7) abnormalities in internal matter-energy processes; and (8) abnormalities in internal information processes.

In Miller's terms neurotic organizational behavior probably belongs to the category of pathology called abnormalities in internal information processing. He writes about "blockages or distortions in information flows and inadequate two-way feedbacks, especially across boundaries between subsystems or components . . ." (p. 710). Category 4—lack of information inputs (awareness deficiencies)—may also be at the heart of the problem. In research with families conducted by the Center for Intimate Systems of the Gestalt Institute of Cleveland, the focus on the awareness side is seen as the key to dealing with contact and energy issues. Neurotic organizational behavior will be defined here as a form of pathologic organizational behavior. This will mean that, for a significant period, the behavior is causing organizational variables to be beyond their ranges of stability or the costs of adjustment have significantly increased.

In choosing a model based on pathology, it is well to be aware of some of the pitfalls. Being aware of the weaknesses of a model can decrease the danger of being affected by them.

A pathologic model may inadvertently create an image of a static, homeostatic "healthy" state from which the pathology deviates. The dynamic, developmental aspects of human systems may be overlooked. The healthy state may be seen as some norm that does not change at different stages of the organization's development. It may be seen as being the same among different organizations. This viewpoint ignores the fact that organizations, like individuals, change, develop, and can actualize their potential. What may be a healthy norm at one stage of an organization's development may be a regression at a more developed stage. Pathology must always be seen in terms of a deviation from the present *dynamic* state of the organization, and not as a measure of a certain preconceived mode of functioning.

Another weakness of the pathologic conceptualization is that it does not address the case of the organization that is permanently functioning at a very low level of effectiveness and exploiting very little of its inherent potential, while not deviating from its regular state. In this kind of organization, pathology needs to be operationalized in terms of deviation from potential functioning and not from regular functioning.

A third pitfall of the pathology model is imaging the organization as an inactive, passive object that is being acted upon. The proactive, responsible, self-organizing, purposeful, self-realizing aspects of organizational existence may be overseen or deemphasized. In this mode the organization may be seen as not being responsible for its plight. The environment, or whatever else may be blamed for the organizational pathology and consultants, as in the medical model, may be expected to put things right and guide the organization back to wellness. In neurotic organizational behavior, it is extremely important to stress, as in Gestalt work with individuals, the responsibility of the organization for its present and future functioning. While a natural disaster or an economic slump can severely damage an organization, the final responsibility for the organization always rests with itself.

It must be clearly emphasized that though there is pathology in the organization, the organization as a whole may be functioning well. *In neurotic organizational behavior, the pathology has not as yet meaningfully impaired total organizational functioning. Total organizational dysfunctioning occurs in declining organizations.*

Neurotic Organizational Behavior and Organizational Effectiveness.

The problem of relating neurotic organizational behavior as defined here to organizational ineffectiveness is that it is not clear what organizational effectiveness or ineffectiveness means. A survey of theories and research in the area of effectiveness depicts a state of disagreement and confusion as to the definition of effectiveness. Some analysts have defined effectiveness with one criterion such as productivity, while others use a multivariate model. Some researchers place the emphasis on internal effectiveness in the sense of internal integration. Others see effectiveness in terms of external adaptation to the environment. Some theoreticians use a short-term criterion for effectiveness, such as member satisfaction; others use a medium-range or long-term criterion, such as organizational survival.

Possibly one of the clarifying attempts to integrate some of the different viewpoints of effectiveness was to relate them to a time dimension. Gibson and colleagues (1976) have suggested the following model of organizational effectiveness and the time dimension.

	Time		
	Short-Run	*Intermediate*	*Long-Run*
Criteria	Production Efficiency Satisfaction	Adaptiveness Development	Survival

Production	=	The ability of organization to produce the quantity and quality of output the environment demands.
Efficiency	=	The ratio of inputs to outputs.
Satisfaction	=	Refers to that of participants and customers.
Adaptiveness	=	The extent to which the organization responds to internal and external changes.
Development	=	The measure of the organization's investment in enhancing its capability.
Survival	=	The organization's capability of surviving in the long run.

In examining neurotic organizational behavior in relation to these criteria, it appears to be related more to the short-run pole of the continuum; in particular, to satisfaction and efficiency but not to production. Declining organizations seem to be related also to the long-run pole, specifically to survival. An organization displaying neurotic organizational behavior may be functioning well as a whole and need not endanger its survival. On the other hand, a declining organization is often on the road to disintegration, decline, and demise.

It needs also to be restated and emphasized clearly that not all of the criteria of organizational effectiveness need be related to neurotic organizational behavior. An organization may be ineffective in a variety of ways without exhibiting neurotic organizational behavior. An organization's efficiency may deteriorate, or its members' satisfaction be frustrated because of faulty management, outdated technology, declining markets, and many other causes.

Chapter 9 on the disruption of contact and withdrawal, and Chapter 10 on the disruption of the task and maintenance cycle, will both deal with organizational dysfunctioning and ineffectiveness in relation to neurotic organizational behavior.

Its Seemingly Unchangeable Quality

One of the specific characteristics of neurotic organizational behavior that contributes to differentiating it from other forms of organizational pathology is the difficulty of changing it. It is not easy to deal with. Kets de Vries and Miller (1982) write that it is deeply ingrained and resistant to change.

Organizations displaying neurotic organizational behavior are difficult to help by the usual array of approaches and interventions used in the course of organizational consulting and development. Writing about neurotic organizational pathology, Kets de Vries and Miller (1982) suggest that "it is unlikely that they can be adequately addressed by management consultants who have a standard bag of tools" (p. 40). They propose that "organizational change agents will be effective only if they get at the roots of dysfunctions. But this might be very difficult if problems are so deeply ingrained and so broadly manifested" (p. 40). Harvey and Albertson (1971) propose that the neurotic organization's members may express anger or resentment toward, or lavish praise on, the consultant trying to help them, persist in holding on to their inadequate and dysfunctional coping responses, and even exert a tremendous amount of collective energy in trying to maintain them. The authors appear to be referring to what we would term a declining organization.

It was, in fact, this "unchangeable" quality of declining organizations that brought them to our attention. A number of unsuccessful attempts to help declining organizations suggested that this was something different. Many of the real difficulties facing organizations may be alleviated in a constructive, creative problem-solving mode. The problem is diagnosed and brought to full awareness in the organization, alternative options of dealing with it are generated and evaluated, energy is mobilized for action, decisions are made, actions are implemented, and structures are created to ensure implementation and evaluation.

Neurotic organizational behavior is not as problematic as a declining organization but still may not be responsive to a rational approach, even when it is participative, experiential, and grounded in the feelings and values of the organization's members. The organization seems to be incapable of dealing with its neurotic behavior in an effective way. The blockage may take place at any of a number of points: awareness raising, energy mobilization, decision making, or action implementation. These points of blockage and their effects will be detailed in Chapter 10. It appears as if the neurotic organizational behavior patterns are not easily dealt with by the regular intervention approaches of organizational development and organizational consultancy.

Harvey and Albertson (1971) write: "Just as it is with a neurotic individual, the neurotic organization is its own worst enemy" (p. 775). Perls (1980) writes: "The neurotic's problem is not that he cannot manipulate, but that his manipulations are directed towards preserving and cherishing his handicap, rather than getting rid of it" (p. 47). While this is more clearly applicable to a declining organization, it also has relevance to neurotic organizational behavior.

In neurotic individual behavior, one is caught in a double bind that creates a vicious circle from which it is extremely difficult to extricate oneself. The person is trapped in a painful reality. "He feels that he is in an existential crisis—that is, he feels that the psychological needs with which he has identified himself and which are as vital to him as breath itself, are not being met by his present mode of life" (Perls, 1980, p. 44). The person has taken refuge in avoidance, by substituting a fantasy for parts of reality. A variety of neurotic mechanisms are used to support this process (see Chapter 6 on neurotic mechanisms). These mechanisms assist in maintaining the delusion and filter out feedback and other information that might undermine the possibility of continuing with the delusion. The person does not wish to face the responsibility of dealing with the unhappy condition, and avoids this by substituting fantasies for reality and developing mechanisms that maintain the fantasies. In this way the vicious circle is closed. In order to deal with the pathology, the person needs to face reality and take responsibility. But the pathology, and its forms and mechanisms, were developed precisely not to face reality and not to take responsibility. So the person is caught in a double bind. If awareness develops of how the person is blocking reality, he or she might have to face the unhappy predicament and take responsibility. But this is not desirable, and so the neurosis persists, painful and distressing as it may be.

At the organizational level, with neurotic organizational behavior, very similar processes seem to be taking place. The members of the team or organization have developed a mechanism to avoid the responsibility of confronting an unhappy organizational condition that appears to be unchangeable and from which there seems to be no personal refuge. As will be detailed in Chapter 7, the organization makes use of neurotic mechanisms to ensure the maintenance of its dysfunctional delusions.

The organization is caught in the same double bind as the neurotic individual. If the organization's members were to become aware of the organizational delusions and how they were blocking reality, they might have to confront this reality. But it was precisely to avoid this responsibility that the fantasy was developed. In discussing *dysfunctional* organizational myths, Bradford and Harvey (1970) write that they are "deeply rooted in the belief and perceptual structures of the organization, and are difficult to isolate and identify, and even more difficult to root out." They permit the members of the organization "to be passive, dependent, and ultimately irresponsible in coping with organization problems" (p. 4).

It is, therefore, not by chance that the organization that displays neurotic organizational behavior is not amenable to the regular approaches of organizational consulting and development. That approach would attempt to increase awareness of the gap between what "is" and what the organization "wants" or "desires." By clarifying and bringing to awareness the elements that could bridge this gap, generally energy would be mobilized that would lead to the implementation of action to close the gap. But the organization displaying neurotic behavior is doing all it can to avoid confronting the situation. The neurotic mechanisms assist the organization in manipulating its environment to avoid taking responsibility for itself and attempts to help it. As Harvey and Albertson suggest: "Organization members are implcitly or explicitly collaborating with one another to maintain the status quo" (p. 773). They can do this in a variety of ways: they may block awareness raising, or energy mobilization, or decision making, or action implementation. The ways in which they do this are detailed in Chapter 10 on the disruption of the task and maintenance cycle.

As Organizational, Not Individual Behavior

Neurotic organizational behavior is not the same as neurotic individual behavior. Harvey and Albertson (1971) write:

Organizational neurosis stems from *collective* dynamics unique to the organization. Thus organizations develop social norms and standards, neurotic in character, the breaking of which by individual members results in the application of social pressure to conform. (p. 698)

Neurotic organizational behavior is not a characteristic of all the people in the organization. A department may be behaving neurotically; other departments may be functioning well. In other organizations to which they belong, the same people can maintain healthy functioning relationships (Harvey & Albertson, 1971). In their family, or in any other social environment, they can function in a completely different, adaptive manner. The neurotic organizational behavior is a pathologic pattern of behavior connected to a specific organization or part of an organization in a particular set of circumstances. The members of the organization, upon meeting each other in a different setting, behave and relate differently, and are often aware of doing so. New people who join the organization are caught in the neurotic pattern of relationships; if they do not leave, they adjust to it and conform to it (Kets de Vries & Miller, 1982). At later, more developed stages of neurotic organizational behavior, in declining organizations, there may develop a relationship between neurotic organizational behavior and the proportion of neurotic individuals in the organization as the result of a sieving process that may filter out healthier elements of the population. Perls (1980) describes it this way: "A society containing a large number of neurotic individuals must be a neurotic society; of the individuals living in a neurotic society, a large number must be neurotic. (p. 26)

The phenomenon Perls describes seems to be more typical of

declining organizations than of organizations displaying neurotic organizational behavior.

Neurotic organizational behavior is a collective or social phenomenon and not an individual-level phenomenon. Like all special phenomena, it is expressed through the behavior of individuals, and individuals are thus the entry points for system change. The system to be focused on is the organization, team, or department of which individuals and groups are components. It is not the individuals who are parts of the personality or body. When one person has a fantasy, it is an individual's fantasy. When a number of people have similar fantasies, but do not communicate them to each other, and they do not affect the pattern of their interaction, the fantasies are still fantasies of individuals. When people in a group have fantasies that they communicate to each other and their behavior and interaction as a group are affected, this is a collective phenomenon at the group level. When the fantasy of a group or a category of members is communicated to other individuals and groups in the organization and it affects their behavior as an organization, it may be called an organizational delusion. An *organizational delusion is a collective phenomenon at the organizational level.*

In neurotic organizational behavior, the fantasy is shared by groups, by categories of people, and sometimes by all of the organization's members. The content of the fantasy is the organizational reality, and is not about the individuals who are holding the fantasy.

An individual seems to be able to maintain a distorted picture of self despite impinging reality and contrary feedback. But it is difficult to maintain a distorted image of a shared reality without the support of others in the organization. And it is extremely difficult to maintain a distorted idiosyncratic image of organizational reality in the face of contradicting images and the pressures of organizational norms, culture, and demands for conformity. The possibility of maintaining a fantasy about organizational reality increases when it is shared with others who have the same fantasy. People are able to believe in the meanings they have invested in reality if sufficient others share this attribution with them. Ironically, an individual who actually perceives reality and expresses this conflicting perception within an organization that is experiencing neurotic organizational behavior could be subject to sanctions by others in the organization.

People in organizations attempt to close the gestalt of pressing unsatisfied needs by substituting fantasy for reality. The fantasy is an illusory gestalt closure. This can be done by people collaborating and supporting each other in creating, developing, and maintaining the organizational fantasy.

The neurotic organizational delusion, like the myth, serves as a framework within which to attribute shared meaning to activities and events, and serves as a basis for coordinated behavior. The problem is that it is a distortion of reality and therefore pathological. The organizational delusion is a collective phenomenon—an expression of organizational behavior and not the summation of individual fantasies.

From a systems theory viewpoint, individuals and organizations are both systems, but on a different level of phenomena. The distinction between levels, as Miller suggests, is "derived from a long scientific tradition of empirical observation of the entire gamut of living systems." Miller (1978) points out that:

This extensive experience of the community of scientific observers has led to a consensus that there are certain fundamental forms of organization of living matter-energy. Indeed the classical division of subject matter among the various disciplines of the life or behavior sciences is implicitly or explicitly based upon this consensus. (p. 25)

He suggests these characteristics as identifying each level and differentiating between it and other levels: (1) physical proximity of its units; (2) similar size of its units, which is significantly different from the levels above and below; (3) similarity of its constituent units; (4) common fate of its units; and (5) distinctive structure and process of its units.

While these characteristics differentiate between systems at different levels, they do not make explicit the specific differences between individuals and organizations. No commonly agreed-upon list of this kind exists in the literature. The following is a tentative list developed from a variety of sources, including Boulding (1968), Miller (1978), Pondy and Mitcoff (1979), and the authors' own observations. It is impossible to deal with these items in detail or to validate them here. A number of the items refer to both groups and organizations.

1. Historically organizations come into existence later than individuals.

2. Physically organizations are larger than individuals.

3. Cooperation is an emergent quality of groups and organiza-

tions and by definition is not found at the individual level.

4. Technological achievements with matter-energy and information processing are an emergent property of organizations.

5. Groups and organizations may control larger territory than individuals.

6. Groups and organizations versus individuals may mobilize a greater amount of physical energy, manipulate ability to alter the environment, and manufacture artifacts.

7. Groups and organizations may, relative to the individual, command more effective adjustment processes against stress.

8. Groups and organizations versus individuals have a greater ability to replace component parts. They may therefore survive much longer than individuals, who have a limited life span.

9. Symbolic communication is an emergent at the level of the group although the capacity evolved at the individual level.

10. Symbolic communication allows integration and coordination of human groups even when people are dispersed.

11. The individual cannot reproduce alone.

12. The proportion of information versus matter-energy processing increases as one goes up the hierarchy of systems. Therefore, groups and organizations process a greater proportion of information than individuals.

13. The group or organization's components may belong simultaneously to a variety of groups and organizations; the individual's components may belong only to the individual.

14. Organizations are generally less tightly coupled than individual systems.

15. The boundaries of the organization lack the clearly discernible concreteness of the boundaries of the individual.

16. Organizations have longer communication channels than individuals.

17. Cultures and some organizations, but no individuals, seem to have elaborate shared systems of meaning.

18. As one goes up the hierarchy of systems, complexity increases. Organizations are more complex than individuals.

19. Organizations are capable of a higher degree of differentiation and specialization.

While this list does not attempt to be comprehensive, it does give some substance to the differences that exist between systems at the individual and at the collective level. Some of these items will be referred to in various parts of this work to clarify differences in neurotic behavior between individuals and organizations or to explain differences in neurotic organizational behavior between kinds of organizations.

A False Representation of Reality

Neurotic organizational behavior is characterized by the organization or one of its subsystems developing a false representation of reality. The organization maps in itself a distorted image of part of its reality. Chapter 6 deals with the mechanisms that organizations use in developing these false representations of reality. These mechanisms are called neurotic mechanisms. The chapter following deals in more detail with these distortions and false representations of organizational reality. They are called organizational delusions and the chapter attempts to examine some of the forms they may take.

Throughout this work a number of terms will be used synonymously for the false representation of reality that characterizes neurotic organizational behavior. These terms are: delusion, illusion, distortion, false mapping, and fantasy. Fantasy and the intermediate zone are the terms Perls uses most often to refer to the distortion of reality associated with neurotic behavior in individuals. The intermediate zone is an unfamiliar concept to most people and will be used less often. Although fantasy can have functional creative connotations, it will sometimes be used. The terms in this work were chosen because they are commonly understood and, except for fantasy, represent a dysfunctional distortion of reality.

Organizational delusions, as used here, need to be differentiated from organizational myths. The concept "organizational myth" has become more in vogue in organizational literature in the past few years. It is used differently by different authorities and a distinction between it and organizational delusions needs to be made. Hedberg (1981) writes:

Several organization theorists have used the concept of myths to denote organizational theories of action. The term myth emphasizes the multiple origins that theories of action may have. Some are born out of observations from reality, others are sheer fantasies, but most myths have some connection with reality. (p. 12)

Hedberg and Jonsson (1977) propose that myths change clinically. They write:

A ruling myth is challenged when it no longer can produce convincing strategies; it is also challenged by the arrival of competing myths. (p. 12)

Organizational delusions developed in neurotic organizational behavior differ markedly from the description of myths given above. *Delusions are not "born out of observations from reality" and do not "have some connection with reality." Delusions have not been observed to "change cyclically," do not "produce convincing strategies," and do not seem to be challenged by the arrival of competing delusions.* Westerland and Sjostrand (1979) devote a book to organizational myths. They see myths as "mapping a number of organizational phenomena," being "handed down from one generation of organizational theorists and organizational practitioners to another," and as having been brought into being to protect people from awareness of uncertainty. They describe in detail a variety of myths. These are held by organizational theorists and practitioners and are various aspects of accepted organizational and management theory, the authors regard, as a misrepresentation of organizational reality. An example would be "the myth of organizational change as a planned, sequential, spectacular phenomena" (p. 68). They see change differently.

Organizational delusions, as used here, are not the same as the myths described above. They are not a misrepresentation of organizational theory, used by organizational theorists and practitioners, to protect from awareness of uncertainty. *Organizational delusions, as described here, are distortions of organizational reality by an organization's members to keep on living in an unbearable, seemingly unchangeable organizational situation.*

Personnel in a buggy whip factory might maintain that all that is needed is a few more oil crises and horse-and-buggy transportation will be back. This would probably be a delusion.

An example of a myth would be when the buggy-whip factory as an organization maintains that it should keep going no matter how much money is lost because the founder and his family who run the business really have the welfare of the country as their ultimate concern, and without the existence of this factory to be there "when it is needed," there could be a national disaster.

Boje and colleagues (1982) deal with the phenomenon of myth making. They write: "Myth making is an adaptive mechanism whereby groups in an organization maintain logic frameworks within which to attribute meaning to activities and events." (p. 18)

They also see myths as "social attempts to 'manage' certain problematic aspects of modern organizations through definitions of truth and rational purpose" (p. 18). As a whole myths are seen by them as beneficial and serving numerous functions.

Organizational delusions as described here are not adaptive mechanisms. They are maladaptive mechanisms that deepen organizational pathology. Organizational delusions are not definitions of truth and rational purpose. They are neither beneficial nor functional.

The description of organizational myths that is closest to organizational delusions is that of Bradford and Harvey (1970), who deal with dysfunctional organizational myths. Their definition is: "An organization myth is an ill-founded and untested belief which powerfully affects the way in which organization members behave and respond" (p. 2).

The authors see myths as dysfunctional, as used by organization members as defenses not to accept responsibility and as difficult to uproot. Bradford and Harvey describe these characteristics of myths: (1) They frequently develop from events or situations that occurred in the past. (2) They are assumed but seldom tested. (3) The individuals who believe in them have information that could disprove them. (4) They are usually held in one or more levels of the organization. (5) They permit their holders to be passive, dependent, and ultimately irresponsible in coping with organization problems.

These characteristics, except for the first, fit organization delusions. Organizational delusions are not necessarily characterized by development from events or situations in the past. They depict organizational reality as it is seen in the present. Events and situations in the past may have contributed to developing the delusion, but are not a significant aspect of it.

To summarize, the differences between organizational delusions and the different versions of organizational myths are:

1. Myths stress roots in the past history traditions or legends of the organization. Delusions are characterized by a distortion of the organization's reality in the present.
2. Myths, as seen by some, may be adaptive and functional for the organization. Delusions are always seen as maladaptive and dysfunctional for the organization.

A possible way of integrating the organizational literature on myths with the concept of organizational delusion in neurotic organizational behavior is to regard the delusion as a subset of myths, which are not necessarily grounded in the past and are maladaptive and dysfunctional. The difficulty with this is that it evades the traditional, legendary aspects that are so much a part of the concept of a myth.

It might be worthwhile to stress that the discussion in this section was not meant to deny the existence of organizational myths, nor to evaluate studies of this area. Its purpose was to clarify the difference between organizational myths and the concept of organizational delusions as it will be used in this work.

PROPOSITIONS AND DEFINITIONS

The following two characteristics are a tentative deduction from the description of the etiology of neurotic organizational behavior. They need research.

★ Neurotic organizational behavior in an organization is not necessarily the result of environmental deterioration, but with an increase in environmental deterioration, the percentage of organizations displaying neurotic organizational behavior may tend also to increase.

★ With the increasing turbulence of today's environment, neurotic organizational behavior may be on the increase.

The following are based on clinical observation and are in need of further research.

★ Neurotic organizational behavior is a repetitive reoccurring pattern of behavior and not a one-time occurrence.

★ Neurotic organizational behavior is an organizational pathology of abnormalities in internal information processing.

★ Neurotic organizational behavior does affect the unit where it is present but need not affect the total organization's effectiveness.

★ In declining organizations production is affected to a degree that endangers its survival.

★ Neurotic organizational behavior is not easily amenable to the regular approaches of organizational consulting and development.

★ Neurotic organizational behavior is a collective organizational-level phenomenon and not a characteristic of individuals in the organization.

★ A declining organization may have a higher percentage of neurotic members.

★ Organizational delusions are a distortion of the organization's present reality.

★ Organizational delusions are not the same as organizational myths, when the latter are seen as adaptive and functional and having their roots in the past.

*Reality is not depicted here in the dictionary sense as "that which exists independently of ideas concerning it." This definition would separate the observer from the observed. Nor is reality understood as a consensual view of what exists. Reality is placed in a definitional context of functions, operations, and behaviors, and is tested empirically.

CHAPTER *3*

EXCELLENCE AND DECLINE

OVERVIEW

In this chapter the differences between declining organizations and organizations displaying neurotic organizational behavior are clarified and sharpened by comparing these organizations with each other. And comparing both of them with high performing, excelling organizations further accentuates the differences.

The dynamics of organizational decline are discussed, with an emphasis on some of the conditions that facilitate an organization's movement from one stage to another.

The relationship between neurotic behavior and the different stages of an organization's life cycle are examined. It appears that, at this time, there is no evidence of a special relationship between organizational neurosis and any particular stage of an organization's life cycle.

NEUROTIC ORGANIZATIONAL BEHAVIOR, DECLINING AND EXCELLING ORGANIZATIONS

Neurotic organizational behavior is repetitive patterns of pathologic, seemingly unchangeable, organizational behavior, involving distortion of reality. A declining organization is an organization with a negative self-image in which neurotic organizational behavior has reached such a magnitude and depth that the organization is in a process of decline. A declining organization may be identified by the following seven criteria: (1) a failure self-image; (2) a low-energy climate; (3) breakdown of communication; (4) disagreement on goals, values, and norms; (5) organizational dysfunctioning; (6) deteriorating condition; and (7) difficulty in changing these patterns.

It is possible to compare the characteristics of declining organizations with those of an organization displaying neurotic organizational behavior. This might highlight similarities and differences between the two. The characteristics of declining organizations may be taken from the data in the list of 15 characteristics, which were detailed in Chapter 1. The characteristics of organizations displaying neurotic organizational behavior will be derived from the descriptions and analysis of neurotic organizational behavior in the coming chapters.

These two lists may be compared with data from research on what Peters and Waterman (1982) call "excellent companies." These are a group of some of America's best-run companies, which an informed group of observers consider innovative and excellent. All of these organizations were top performers in their industry by six criteria. "Three are measures of growth and long-term wealth creation over a twenty-year period. Three are measures of return on capital and sales" (p. 22). The list includes such companies as Boeing, Caterpillar, Digital, IBM, McDonald, and Procter and Gamble.

The comparison of the data on declining organizations with the data collected on the polarity—excellent organizations—may help to accentuate the specific characteristics of the declining organizations. Table 3-1 illustrates some of the differences found between the three kinds of organizations: (1) organizations displaying neurotic organizational behavior; (2) declining organizations; and (3) excellent organizations. These organizations will be compared on the dimensions of the short list of seven criteria of declining organizations.

Fantasy

In neurotic organizational behavior, the neurotic mechanisms help to avoid facing an unhappy reality. Delusions may take a

Table 3-1

A Comparison of Neurotic Organizational Behavior, Declining and Excellent Organizations

Criteria	Neurotic organizational Behavior	Declining Organizations	Excellent
Fantasy	Neurotic mechanisms, delusions, e.g., avoidance, false image, games.	Negative self-image; failure script of organization.	Positive, success self-image.
Climate	Members' dissatisfaction in parts of the organization.	Energy well down, organization pervaded by low motivation, frustration, unhappiness, boredom, hopelessness in organization.	High energy, high motivation and enthusiasm, innovation and experimentation; involvement and high morale.
Communication	There may be disruptions in communication, disowning of and conflicts between parts.	Communication breakdown. Interpersonal and intergroup hostility and conflict. Distrustful relations, scapegoats.	Widespread, intense, open, formal and informal communication across all levels and parts.
Goals, values, norms	May have difficulty identifying/prioritizing needs and controlling what enters boundaries.	Disagreement on goals and values throughout organization. Norm disruptment with extreme deviations. Organized life loses meaning.	Driven by a coherent value system and set of beliefs. Strong normative structure. People find in the organization

Criteria	Neurotic organizational Behavior	Declining Organization	Excellent
Functioning	Difficulties in controlling boundaries and balancing attendance to task and maintenance.	Pervasive organizational dysfunctioning, production-cycle dysfunctioning. Organization unable to cope with its problems. No planning and neglect of physical plant.	Functioning excellently. Productivity efficient and effectiveness high. High problem-solving capability. Environment closely monitored.
Trend	Steady state—inputs equaling outputs. Leadership may be rigid, neurotic, or in conflict.	State of decline—outputs greater than inputs. Eating up reserves. Breakdown of leadership. Negative selection of membership. Recurring, intensifying periods of crisis.	State of expansion—inputs greater than outputs. Building reserves. Leadership that infuses purpose and significance. Human resources growing.
Change	The organization avoids taking responsibility for itself; blocks outside help.	High magnitude of dysfunctioning, lack of reserve resources, failure self-image and fear of letting go make change extremely difficult. Rational organizational development methods give no results.	The organization is geared to change itself constantly. It monitors changes and adjusts; encourages learning and innovation.

variety of forms, such as living in the past, living for the future, creating a false image, or playing organizational games (Chapter 7).

A declining organization may use any of the neurotic mechanisms. The delusion that plays a major role in framing the organization's behavior and climate is a negative self-image and failure script. Members see their organization as unable to cope with its problems and incapable of taking responsibility for itself. The organization's failure self-image is not only a passive image held collectively by the organization's members, but it affects the organization's behavior so that organizational reality conforms to the negative image. The failure self-image constructs a social reality (Berger & Luckman, 1966), which mirrors the image. The declining organization is pervaded by fantasies, delusions, and myths, all expressing and symbolizing the organization's inadequacy and negative self-image. The organization has a failure script as if predestined to fail in all it does. The self-image of inadequacy, the failure script, and the failures in reality all feed into each other and create a closed vicious circle. The organization sees itself as a failure and proves this to itself by continually failing in all it does.

Peters and Waterman describe how excellent organizations are pervaded by rich networks of myths, legends, parables, and rituals, all symbolizing and expressing the organization's self-image and ideology of success, action, innovativeness, quality performance, and so on.

Climate

In organizations displaying neurotic organizational behavior, the inability of the organization or part of it to adapt to necessary change may lead to organizational dysfunctioning that, in certain cases, frustrates attaining organizational goals and satisfying members' needs. Some individuals in the organization may feel frustration and unhappiness (Chapter 5). All this may be contained in a subunit without affecting the organization as a whole.

In declining organizations low-energy symptoms have deeply pervaded the entire organization. The climate of the organization is one of lack of energy, low motivation, much individual frustration and unhappiness, and low morale. People cannot be aroused to action. They do not have the energy to get things moving. Leaders and members alike have lost hope that they ever will be able to change the organization's state of affairs. The organization has dissipated all its reserves of surplus energy and resources to continue maintaining itself in the face of disintegrative processes. Most of the capable, energetic, innovative people have left the organization. New members joining the organization are socialized into this low-energy, low-motivation climate. Many people are unhappy, frustrated, and dissatisfied with life in the organization. There is much bitterness about lost opportunities and wasted lives. There is boredom, lethargy, and fear of experimentation and innovation. People have lost belief in their ability as an organization to do anything about their condition.

This contrasts sharply with the excellent organizations. High-performing systems have a high-energy, highly motivated climate. People in these organizations "bubble" with enthusiasm, and thrive on action, innovation, and experimentation. They are highly autonomous and motivated and their efforts are recognized and supported. Champions are encouraged. Most of the people in these organizations are deeply involved in their organizational life. The companies all have high morale and much pride in their achievements.

Communication

Organizations displaying neurotic organizational behavior may have manifestations of some disruptions in communication within the organization. The organization may disown one of its parts such as a category of people (e.g., young or old) or a department. Groups in the organization may disown each other, become alienated, and stop all communication. There also may be conflict between parts of the organization. The neurotic mechanisms may lead to ignoring feedback and to breakdowns in the organization's ability to monitor the deviations of essential variables beyond their limits (Chapter 7).

According to the data on the list of 15 criteria, in declining organizations communication breaks down completely with disruption of feedback and monitoring. The organization is wracked with interpersonal and intergroup conflict. Communication is distrustful, limited, critical, and full of suspicion. Feedback is blocked by delusions and filtering processes. Important information is not transmitted to management and the organization is unable to monitor what is happening within it and outside it among customers, suppliers, and so on. Barriers of suspicion and hostility develop between different parts of the organization in different departments or between people with different backgrounds, ages, education, or professions. Newcomers are made scapegoats. Groups withdraw and barricade themselves against each other. There is much hostility and destructive conflict.

Peters and Waterman describe the "intense communication" existing in excellent organizations. They discuss a beehive of ongoing informal, temporary, ad hoc, and project-type meetings. These communications cut across all formal lines of departments, functions, and status levels within the organization. In these organizations "communication systems are informal" and "communication is given physical support." People meet and discuss all the issues connected with their work, and find ways to improve things. Groups compete with each other to excel, but do not engage in destructive conflict. The climate is one of support and trust for the individual. There is an effort to create synergistic conditions that exploit the creativity of people with differing views meeting with and confronting each other. Information and feedback are encouraged. The organization invests resources constantly to monitor and react to changes inside it and in its relevant environment, including its customers.

Goals, Values, and Norms

Organizations and groups displaying neurotic organizational behavior may run into difficulties when their capacity to discriminate becomes confused: A group cannot decide what is harmful and should be barred access to organizational boundaries and what is growthful and should be encouraged and assimilated (Chapter 9). A department may be unable to identify its needs and to choose priorities for its problems (Chapter 10).

In declining organizations there is disagreement throughout the organization as to its goals and the values that should serve as yardsticks to evaluate the goals. The normative structure of the organization is in disarray.

The organization's members have stopped communicating with each other and are suspicious and hostile as individuals and as groups. They cannot agree on priorities among the organization's objectives. There is no common set of values that has the same priority among different groups and sections of the organization.

The organization's members are not unified around a mission or purpose that can give meaning and significance to organizational existence. There is a disruption of the norms guiding everyday behavior in the organization. There is disagreement as to what is acceptable behavior, and the disruptions find expression in extremities of deviant behavior. Organizational life loses its meaning and significance.

Peters and Waterman found that excellent companies are driven by a coherent value system and a well-defined set of guiding beliefs. They "seem to understand that every man seeks meaning (not just the top fifty who are 'in the bonus pool')" (p. 76). The organization's work, goals, mission, and purpose have meaning and significance for its members. The excellent companies maintain a strong normative structure, so strong that people either buy into their norms or get out. In a study of high-performing systems, Peter Vaill (1982) sees a commonly held sense of purpose as the most distinctive feature of such systems.

Organizational Functioning

In organizations displaying neurotic organizational behavior, delusion has blocked feedback to part of the organization. It is unable to monitor fluctuations of variables beyond their critical limit. This has led to some dysfunctioning, which affects the control of opening and closing boundaries and imbalance in cyclical attention to task and maintenance functions. Subunits may have problems, but the organization as a whole may be functioning well (Chapter 9). While parts may be dysfunctioning, the organization is not in a state of decline.

In declining organizations there are decreasing inputs and outputs; the organization has difficulty coping with its everyday problems, it is unable to plan ahead, and its dysfunctioning has spread into the production cycles of input–throughput–output and the work cycles. Both input and output are decreasing. Outputs are exceeding inputs. The organization is eating up all its reserve resources. Productivity, efficiency, and effectiveness are down. The work cycles have been disrupted, as expressed in absenteeism and other forms. The failure self-image, low-energy climate, breakdown of communication, and disagreement on goals, values, and norms have all contributed to undermining the organization's ability to cope with its problems. The organization's decision-making structure has ceased to function effectively. It is caught in a crisis management mode of putting out fires throughout the organization.* There is no energy left to plan for the future. The organization has no strategic policy or long-term plans. It has ceased monitoring changes in the environment and does not prepare itself for dealing with changing trends. The physical facilities of the organization are neglected. Buildings, grounds, and equipment all reflect lack of care and maintenance.

The excellent companies all function well, by all accepted criteria of growth innovation, adaptiveness, and financial performance. Their production standards are the top in their particular line. Their members at all levels are highly motivated and innovative. Their productivity, efficiency, and effectiveness are high. These organizations are able to deal effectively and innovatively with their problems in an action-based, experimental, innovative mode. The excellent organizations were continually monitoring their environment (especially their customers) and adjusting themselves to external changes. Peters and Waterman write that "innovative companies are especially adroit at continually responding to change of any sort in the environment" (p. 12). Much attention is paid in these organizations to facilities that serve people's needs.

Developmental Trends

In organizations displaying neurotic organizational behavior, parts of the organization may be dysfunctioning; nevertheless the organization as a whole may be retaining a steady state or outputs may be greater than inputs. The organization may not be building up reserve resources, but also is not eating up its resources as in a process of decline (Chapter 2). In some cases leadership may be functioning effectively, and in others may be rigid and neurotic (Chapter 5). The organization is capable of returning to healthy functioning.

Declining organizations are in a trend of organizational disintegration. The organization's outputs are regularly greater than its inputs and it is eating up its remaining resources. Its declining condition is marked by a breakdown of all leadership, by a constant

---

*L. Iannaccone has suggested that when an organization does perceive its daily life as crisis, it will behave in a neurotic manner. This is because the mechanisms used for dealing with crisis become part of the daily repertoire.

negative selection of organizational membership, and by intensifying recurring periods of crisis. Many of the capable, talented,
autonomous, innovative leaders have left the organization, and
others are not joining in their stead. The organization loses its
ability to maintain, develop, and attract leadership. There is no
leadership with a vision and a mission to unite the organization
around a common meaningful purpose. There is a process of
negative selection in membership with most of the talented people
leaving the organization. Simultaneously, highly capable people
are not attracted to join the organization. Those who remain are
older, with less talent, less innovative capabilities, and less specialization; they are people with fewer options. The organization
is caught in a vicious circle of recurring intensifying periods of
crisis. Periodically, when matters come to a head, the organization
passes through a crisis. Many matters come to a critical point and
the stress level goes up. These crises keep repeating themselves;
each time the organization's condition becomes more and more
difficult.

Peters and Waterman's excellent companies belong to the state
Adams (1975) describes as expanding systems, in which input is
regularly greater than output. These organizations are neither declining nor maintaining a steady state, but expanding their economic resources. Excellent companies do not have a leadership
vacuum. They have transforming leadership in which leaders and
followers raise one another to higher levels of motivation. The
leaders infuse the organization with value. In Vaill's (1982) terms,
they imbue the organization with purpose. The excellent organizations do not lose talented people, but attract and develop them.
They encourage the development of champions; they create conditions for innovation, experimentation, and creativity. While the
declining companies descend in the vortex of deepening crises,
excellent organizations ascend to higher achievements, development, and growth.

Change

Up to now it has not been easy to change the patterns of an
organization displaying neurotic organizational behavior. This was
dealt with in Chapter 2. The organization subsystem avoids dealing
with its problems and taking responsibility for itself. It may block
efforts from outside to help it. The neurotic organizational behavior

patterns can seem to be impervious to the regular intervention approaches of organizational development and consulting.

In declining organizations the difficulty of helping the organization to change is compounded by the magnitude and depth of organizational dysfunctioning and the organization's deteriorating condition. The organization's condition is continually worsening. Energy and morale are low. There is no leadership and no common sense of purpose. Communications have broken down and conflict is rife. The organization has dissipated all of its reserve resources and energy; there are none left for training, development, and change. *The problems are not on a rational level.* The situation cannot be changed by dealing with some of these problems. These attempts will not succeed because of the organization's failure image. Achievements will be rationalized to fit the failure self-image. The delusion is not at a rational level that can be dealt with by relevant information. The organization's failure self-image is a paradigm through which it approaches the world and apprehends it. Changing the self-image, like all paradigmic shifts, is a qualitative step—one that is resisted strongly and is extremely difficult and complicated.

The excellent companies are geared to change and thrive on it. They encourage experimentation and innovation. They are learning organizations that regard failure as a learning experience. They invest more than other organizations in training and development. When they do not like something they change it. They monitor the environment for change and act accordingly. They are open to new ideas, to inner innovation and outside consultation.

Summary

The comparison of declining organizations with excellent organizations accentuates the differences between the two kinds of organization. On all of the dimensions, the two organizations are polarized. The excellent organization, as identified by Peters and Waterman, appears to typify a model of organizational health and well functioning. The declining organization, its counterpart, exhibits the other extreme of organizational pathology and malfunctioning.

The comparison of a declining organization with an organization displaying neurotic organizational behavior brings out features of a declining organization, which are worth noting.

1. *The failure self-image is dominant.* Neurotic organizational behavior may be expressed through a variety of delusions, all of which may appear in a declining organization. But the fantasy that dominates the neurotic organization and differentiates it is the failure self-image. This self-image of inadequacy plays a major role informing and framing the organization's world. The organization's malfunctioning and drift to decline has enhanced its negative self-image—which is a paradigm through which the organization views its world and in whose image it creates its dysfunctional social reality. The organization is in a self-created vicious circle.

2. *The pathology is deeper and more widespread and affects total organizational functioning.* On most of the dimensions, the declining organization is a far more dysfunctioning, pathological form of neurotic organizational behavior. The malfunctioning is more widespread, and is not contained in one or some subunits. It has engrained itself deeper in the fibers of organizational functioning. The climate is one of lower energy and lower motivation. Communication is more alienated and hostile. Mission, purpose, values, and norms are all disrupted. Production is down and leadership is gone. The pathology has affected the organization's production cycles. The difference between neurotic organizations and neurotic organizational behavior, then, is a matter of degree and pervasiveness, and qualitatively affects total organizational functioning.

3. *The declining organization is in a state of deterioration.* The organization's condition is continually worsening. It is on a downward spiral, with all of its resources diminishing and its reserves dried up. There is no leadership to reverse the trend, little ability to wrestle with everyday problems, and neglect is showing up on all sides. Recurring crises are constantly making the situation worse. Robbins (1983), in summarizing the literature on organizational decline, writes in similar terms. He describes how conflict increases because there is less slack of stored resources. There is much politicking of self-interest groups in conflict. Critical data and information are twisted. There is a decay in motivation and morale. Skilled technicians, professionals, talented managerial personnel, and other mobile individuals all leave the organization. Especially in the early stages, there is high resistance to change.

When juxtaposing the neurotic and healthy individual from a Gestalt point of view with neurotic organizational behavior, declining organizations, and excellent organizations, the protocols of Gestalt are readily applicable if one keeps in mind the distinctions made earlier between the individual and the organization. There is one possible qualification in that declining organizations' behavior borders on what would be classified as psychotic individual behavior. What accounts for this difference, however, relates to the differences between the individual and the organization. When the organization begins to self-destruct, it is dissolved through bankruptcy or some other mechanism and ceases to exist. The individual does this only in the case of catatonia or suicide.

THE DYNAMICS OF ORGANIZATIONAL DECLINE

Throughout time an organization may move through a number of states of increasingly dysfunctional neurotic behavior. The organization may move from a state of "normal" functioning to one of neurotic organizational behavior. From neurotic organizational behavior, the organization may descend to the state of a declining organization. From a declining organization, it will probably move to a state of organizational demise.

It seems reasonable to assume that the severity of the development of the neurotic organizational behavior symptoms plays a part in catalyzing an organization's move from one state to another. This proposition, like the following propositions, is suggested by clinical observation and has a rationale. But there is, as yet, no empirical research to support it. When some evidence exists from research and other studies it will be cited to give indirect support. However, within the context of this work it is impossible to deal with the subject thoroughly; therefore, the former proposition and the following ones will only be stated and explained, with no attempt made to substantiate them. This will be left for future study.

The following questions express conditions, which, all other things being equal, probably facilitate the shift of an organization from neurotic organizational behavior to a declining organization.

1. How tightly coupled is the organization?
2. How significant is the organization for its members?
3. How involuntary is membership in the organization?
4. How total is the organization?

1. *How tightly coupled is the organization?* An infection in the body may spread to other uninfected parts. The human body is tightly coupled in the sense of having a strong connection and interdependence between its parts. A disturbance in one part of the body is likely to affect the others. The same rationale holds in organizations. The more tightly coupled an organization is, the greater is the chance that a disturbance in one of its parts will affect the other parts. The less tightly coupled an organization is, the more likely it is that the neurotic behavior of one of its departments will remain contained within that department. The more tightly coupled the organization is, the more permeable are the boundaries between its parts. The more connections, interactions, and interdependencies there are between a neurotic department and other departments, the greater is the chance that its malfunctioning will spread to other departments. An illustration will make this clear.

In a large conglomerate, one company will not affect other autonomous companies with its malfunctioning. In a small company, a malfunctioning production department may affect the entire organization. All other things being equal, a loosely coupled organization displaying neurotic organizational behavior may have less chance of becoming a declining organization. A number of researchers and theoreticians (e.g., Glassman, 1973; Weick, 1976; Aldrich, 1979) argue that a loosely coupled structure contributes toward long-term organizational adaptabilities.

2. *How significant is the organization for its members?* If an organization plays an insignificant part in most of its members' lives, they will not invest much energy in it. They will not depend on it, and if they are dissatisfied with it, they will refrain from attending its activities or they will leave it. If an organization is very significant for its members, they depend on it; what happens in it is important to them and they do not leave it easily. Neurotic dysfunctioning of an organization with little significance to its members will probably lead to them abandoning it.

On the other hand, an organization that is significant to its members, even when dysfunctioning neurotically, is not easily abandoned. Such an organization can continue dysfunctioning for a considerable period and become more and more neurotic without its members leaving it. As an illustration, people will more easily change restaurants than political parties or religious affiliations. The more significant an organization is to its members, the more leeway it has for neurotic behavior without this leading to its losing all members. Coser (1956) drew attention to the intensity of conflicts in social and political movements. All other things being equal, organizations that have much significance for their members (e.g., ideological, political, religious organizations) may have greater chance to develop from neurotic organizational behavior to declining organizations.

3. *How involuntary is membership in the organization?* If a factory or a bank's climate becomes oppressive and frustrating for the people who work in it, they may have other options and, unless there is severe unemployment, can find work elsewhere. Unless the factory or the bank has some kind of hold on the people who work in it, in normal times it faces two alternatives—to change its ways or to lose its employees. The more choice, mobility, and freedom of movement people have between organizations, the less these organizations can maintain neurotic patterns of behavior for long periods. The less choice people have in their belonging to an organization, the more the organization can persist in its neurotic dysfunctioning without paying the price for this in shortage of members, workers, essential professionals, and so on. A variety of organizations consist of people whose membership is involuntary—for instance, prisons, mental institutions, or the army. All other things being equal, organizations whose membership is involuntary may have greater chances of developing from neurotic organizational behavior to a declining organization.

4. *How total is the organization?* Miller (1978) writes: "A living system which is capable of carrying out all critical subsystem processes necessary for life is toto-potential" (p. 25). Goffman (1961) calls organizations such as hospitals, monasteries, and ships, "total institutions." In such organizations members' "separation from the wider world lasts around the clock and may continue for years" (p. 14). Total institutions are by necessity tightly coupled. Having control of most aspects of the lives of their inmates, they need to coordinate these in a tight daily schedule. These organizations, whether voluntary or involuntary, cover important aspects of their members' lives, and what happens in them is significant to their members. All other things being equal, total institutions may have greater chances to develop from an organization displaying neurotic organizational behavior to a declining organization.

The conditions that contribute to an organization moving from the state of neurotic organizational behavior to the state of a declining organization are not necessarily the same as those that maintain the organization in the state of declining organization. A declining organization may continue functioning for years without necessarily disintegrating completely and passing into a state of demise. As a declining organization is defined as being in a state of disintegration, the general trend should be toward increased dysfunctioning, intensifying crisis, and finally disintegration and demise. The question, therefore, is what factors contribute to maintain an organization functioning as a declining organization, without this leading to the collapse of the organization. As with the former list of propositions, this list will be suggested without empirical or theoretical support. The list must be treated very tentatively until study and research show that it is justified. At this stage it is supported only by clinical observation and rational deduction. Three conditions may be supportive of an organization's continued functioning as a declining organization without this leading to organizational demise:

5. How measurable are the organization's outputs?
6. How monopolistic is the organization?
7. How important is the organization to its suprasystem?

5. *How measurable are an organization's outputs?*

An organization may continue dysfunctioning as long as its environment allows it to do so. The environment supplies the organization with inputs necessary for the throughput and maintenance processes. If an organization ceases supplying or decreases the supply of outputs the environment values, the environment reacts by diminishing inputs. In everyday terms, if a factory sells fewer of its products, it has less income to buy supplies.

All this holds as long as the output of the organization is in products that are measurable and whose quantity and quality may be evaluated. But many organizations produce products that are difficult to measure and evaluate—for example, schools, universities, consulting firms, and therapy institutes. When an organization of this kind is dysfunctioning as a declining organization, it may be difficult for the environment to detect this in the organization's outputs, since these are extremely difficult to measure. The environment, therefore, does not detect changes in quantity and quality of outputs and there is no reaction in the form of decreased inputs. The organization may continue dysfunctioning without paying the price for it in organizational demise. All other factors being equal, a declining organization may continue dysfunctioning longer without disintegrating if it is difficult to measure and evaluate its outputs.

6. How monopolistic is the organization?

An organization may decrease the quantity and quality of its outputs without the environment reacting. This happens when the environment has no alternative source for receiving what it needs other than from that organization. In the public sector, Rainey and colleagues (1976) call this having less market exposure. This is often the case in public services, such as government or municipal services and utilities. When a person has no alternative to getting a driving license other than from the Department of Motor Vehicles, that organization has a monopoly. Whenever an organization has complete monopoly over supplying an output, this puts it into a position where it can pay less attention to the effectiveness of its production and to the quantity and quality of its products or service. If people cannot get what they need elsewhere, they will be forced to accept the organization's outputs. For this reason government and municipal departments and public utilities can persist in the dysfunctional behavior of a declining organization for a longer period, without paying the price for this. All things being equal, a declining organization may continue functioning longer without disintegrating if it has a monopoly.

7. How important is the organization's existence to its suprasystem?

In some cases a declining organization can continue dysfunctioning for years with decreasing outputs because its continued existence is for some reason very important for its suprasystem. For example, a social movement may be extremely sensitive to the possibility of a part breaking off. It will endlessly pour in financial aid, consultation, and other resources in attempts to bolster a declining branch and save it from disintegration. A consortium may maintain one of its companies at a loss for many years for reasons of sentiment, symbolic value, or other considerations. Chrysler and Lockheed are examples in the private sector.

In referring to conditions that shield organizations from transformation, Aldrich (1979) writes: "Many organizations, primarily voluntary associations, survive because they are attached to other organizations that sponsor them" (p. 199).

Bigelow (1980) writes about how, unlike a poorly operating private enterprise, a poorly operating school system may be prevented from failing by the government system. All other factors being equal, a neurotic organization may continue to function longer without disintegrating if it is of special value to its suprasystem.

An organization's behavior is always affected by both internal and external factors. Everything happening to the organization takes place within the context of the organization/environment field. It is inconceivable that an organization's movement or lack of movement from neurotic organizational behavior to declining organization will not be effected by external conditions. An organization is an open system and external conditions will affect the movement from one state to another. Nevertheless, it is worth noting that the movement of an organization from neurotic organizational behavior to declining organization may be affected relatively more by variables expressing internal relationships. In contrast, the movement from a declining organization to organizational demise may be influenced more by variables from the organization/environment interface. In other words, an organization's development or degeneration may be influenced very much by internal factors; an organization's continued existence or demise may be influenced very much by the relationship between the organization and the environment.

The conditions that may contribute more to an organization displaying neurotic organizational behavior becoming a declining organization are expressive of the quality of the relationship and interdependence between the organization's subsystems and the total organization. The kind of relationship existing between the members of the organization and their organization may play an important role in affecting containment of dysfunctional behavior to the neurotic organizational behavior level or its deepening and the organization becoming a declining organization.

The movement to the next deeper level, from a declining organization to organizational demise, may be affected more by conditions that describe the relationship between the organization as a whole and its environment. Whether an organization continues functioning as a declining organization or deteriorates into disintegration depends less on its internal relationships than its relationship as a total system to its environment. These propositions must be treated very tentatively. These are generalizations from other propositions which are only suggested here without being substantiated by research.

ORGANIZATIONAL NEUROSIS AND THE ORGANIZATIONAL LIFE CYCLE

Is an organization more vulnerable to organizational neurosis at any particular stage of its development? As the organization becomes older and older, does it become senescent and possibly a more fertile ground for neurotic organizational behavior development?

Some studies point to one stage in the organizational life cycle as being more vulnerable than the other stages to organizational pathology and demise. This is the beginning stage of an organization, the "infant" stage. Building on statistics of the death rate of businesses, Argenti (1976) points out the high proportion of younger businesses that met their death in the early stages of their development. Whetten (1980) and De Greene (1982) summarize research showing that the failure rate of new, young organizations is much higher than that of organizations at other stages of development.

There is less agreement about the other stage of vulnerability—organizational old age. De Greene writes about the problems of aging organizations that may have obsolescent structures, senescent management practices, and old technology. Snell Putney (1972) sees ossification as a natural and inevitable process that develops in all organizations in time. Putney's definition of ossification has much similarity to neurotic organizational behavior:

Systems decay and become stupid through ossification: the process by which the decision-making centers of a system come to derive their decisions independently of the information inputs and feedback. The decisions become increasingly unrelated to what is happening within and without the system. (p. 37)

The Elgin (1977) research raises questions as to whether a combination of advanced age, with increasing interdependence and complexity, might not be fertile ground for the development of neurotic organizations. The researchers describe a stage of crisis that does have similarities to the characteristics of declining organizations. Examples are increasing system rigidity, increasing alienation, increased challenge to basic values, declining legitimacy of leadership, and declining system performance. These similarities might only be similar symptoms of organizations in crisis. They might, however, also suggest that organizational old age, together with other characteristics that often accompany old age in modern organizations, may be a fertile breeding ground for declining organizations. In contrast to the Stanford research and De Greene's work, others do not support the proposition that older organizations are more vulnerable to organizational pathology. Levine (1978) writes: "Contrary to biological reasoning, aged organizations are more flexible than younger organizations and therefore rarely die or shrink very much" (p. 319). Whetten (1980) brings bankruptcy statistics showing that in 1970 only 23 percent of the bankrupt businesses were over ten years old. He writes: "For organizations as for human beings the incidence of death is not perfectly correlated with poor health or old age" (p. 356).

Clinical observations of declining organizations, and of organizations displaying neurotic organizational behavior, give no clue as to a relationship between any particular stage of an organization's life and neurotic behavior. Among both the organizations displaying neurotic organizational behavior and the declining organizations were young, medium-age, and older organizations. In this case the clinical observation of functioning organizations is not dependable. It did not include organizations that had ceased functioning because they were declining organizations. An analysis of the relationship between stages of the organizational life cycle and neurotic behavior will have to include organizations that have stopped functioning because they were declining organizations. There is no evidence to date of a relationship between any particular stage of the organizational life cycle and the incidence of neurotic behavior. But this does not mean that such a relationship may not be found in the future. The subject is in need of thorough research, and nothing conclusive, or even propositional, can be stated at this point.

At the outset we wish to state clearly that to the best of our knowledge there are as yet no well-established, empirically tested approaches to dealing with organizational neurosis. What we are doing here is describing the connected issues, and later will present intervention approaches from Gestalt that look promising.

In the early stages of neurosis, it might be possible to return the organization to healthy functioning by using regular organizational development approaches. Probably at later stages deeper interventions will be necessary. Some of the Gestalt therapy approaches described in Chapter 11 hold promise in helping organizations at early and later stages.

In dealing with the early stages of neurosis, it is important to make some distinctions we have not dealt with as yet.

1. Is the neurosis contained in an organizational subunit (a department or team), or has it spread to other parts of the organization?
2. If the neurosis is contained in a subunit, is it displaying neurotic behavior or is it in decline?
3. Is the neurosis in the management team or in a less central subunit?

When the neurosis is contained in one subunit, it is relatively approachable and controllable. There probably will be avoidance of outside help. But organization management can attempt to override resistance. At the first stage, an attempt can be made to deal with the problems through regular organizational development interventions. Possibly, if the neurosis is deeply ingrained, rational problem-solving-oriented approaches will not help. In this case deeper, confrontative interventions of a transformative quality may be needed. Finally, if these have no effect, management may have the option of a total reshuffle—reviewing both leadership and personnel in the subunit.

If the neurosis is contained within a subunit and it is in a state of decline, with a negative balance of inputs and outputs, extreme dysfunctioning, and a negative self-image, management may decide that the only practical approach is a complete turnover of the unit's members and managers.

When the dysfunctioning unit is the management team itself, the situation changes. In this case the suprasystem to which the organization belongs may have to intervene and take an active stand in the situation. This has happened to us a number of times in our consultation practice when assessment pointed to the organization's top team as the source of its problems.

When the organization is autonomous and has no "mother body" to intervene, the situation may be more complicated. The management team displaying neurosis will probably do all it can to avoid utilizing outside assistance. It might invite consultants to assess the situation, but it will find ways not to take any remedial action. In some organizations there could be some kind of internal takeover by a new management group. In business organizations without external intervention, this generally cannot happen. If this does not happen and the management team is in a state of decline, in time the entire organization will be infected. This creates the condition of a declining organization.

A comprehensive examination of transformative approaches to change in organizations is presented in a forthcoming work, *Organizational Transformation*, by A. Levy and U. Merry.

PROPOSITIONS AND DEFINITIONS

The following are based on clinical observation.

★ The negative failure self-image is the neurotic organization's dominant delusion.
★ In declining organizations pathology and dysfunctioning are more widespread than in organizations displaying neurotic organizational behavior.
★ The declining organization is in a state of organizational decline, in the direction of organizational disintegration.

All other things being equal, the shift of an organization from a state of neurotic organizational behavior to becoming a declining organization may be facilitated by:

★ How tightly the organization is coupled.
★ How involuntary membership in the organization is.
★ How significant the organization is for its members.
★ How total the organization is.

All other things being equal, a declining organization may continue functioning longer without disintegrating when:

★ It is difficult to measure or evaluate its outputs.
★ It is monopolistic in its field.
★ It is of special value to its suprasystem.
★ The movement of an organization from neurotic organizational behavior to becoming a declining organization may be affected more by variables expressing internal relationships within the organization.
★ The movement of an organization from a state of a declining

organization to organizational demise may be affected more by variables expressing the relationship between the organization and its environment.

★ There does not appear to be any relationship between organizational neurosis and any particular stage of the organization's life cycle.

THE ANALYSIS OF ORGANIZATIONAL NEUROSIS IN TERMS OF GESTALT THERAPY WITH ILLUSTRATIVE APPLICATIONS

CHAPTER 4

METHODOLOGY AND REVIEW

OVERVIEW

The reader who is familiar with the writings in Gestalt therapy on organizations or who is unconcerned about rationale for methodology may wish to skim or even omit this chapter.

The first part of this chapter addresses the methodological issue related to developing analogies from the Gestalt therapy individual level to the organizational level.

The second part of the chapter is a short review of the literature relating Gestalt therapy to organizational theory and practice. Beginning with a survey of Perls' approach to the individual/ organizational interface, the writings of others who used Gestalt therapy theory to understand organizations and advance practice are reviewed.

DRAWING ANALOGIES

The methodological approach used in this work will be to develop analogies from Gestalt therapy to organization theory and practice. Can analogies from theories and concepts developed to understand the individual be used to explain and describe phenomena at the organizational level? The answer to this question is not without ambiguity. It might be better worded: Under what conditions or circumstances can we create analogies between phenomena on different levels?

Using analogies entails taking concepts, constructs, and propositions from a domain at the individual level and applying them to an equivalent domain at the organizational level. Using lower level concepts and theories to understand phenomena at a higher level runs into the danger of reductionism.

William James (1937) in warning us of the questionable practice of reductionism reminds us that "a Beethoven string-quartet is truly . . . a scraping of horses' tails and cats' bowels, and may be exhaustively described in such terms. . . ." Zetterberg (1965) writes that a person who even borrows a term from another science may inadvertently be also borrowing some propositions of this science. Dubin (1978) points out that there may be serious logical dangers in building theories that deal simultaneously with collective and member units; "collective" meaning a set and "members" its elements.

In this work the trap of reductionism will be circumvented by dealing with both levels only within their common theoretical framework of general systems theory, and we present our approach as tentative and exploratory. The Gestalt therapy concepts and propositions from which the analogies will be developed will be those that belong to a systems approach to the individual. These will be applied to organizations only within the framework of the same systems theory.

This can be better understood with the help of the illustration in Figure 4-1.*

Using concepts and propositions from (A), the individual level, to describe phenomena at (B), the organization level may lead to reductionistic fallacies.

Taking concepts and propositions from the individual level that belong to a general systems theoretical approach (C), and within that same approach using them as analogies to describe organizational phenomena allows us to circumvent the reductionist problem.

General systems theory attempts to build theoretical models

_____

*Suggested by Laurence Iannaccone.

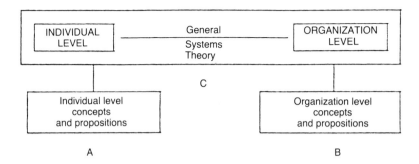

Figure 4-1.
Applying individual-level concepts and propositions to the organization level

that will be applicable to different levels of study. It provides a body of systematic theoretical constructs that will deal with the general relationships of the empirical world. General systems theory does not replace existing disciplines, but points out those similarities that exist in the theoretical constructions of different disciplines. It is an attempt to develop a level of theoretical model building that lies somewhere between the specific theories of each discipline and the generalized construction of mathematics.

Von Bertalanffy said that in one way or another we are forced to deal with complexities, with wholes or systems in all fields of knowledge. This implies a basic reorientation in scientific thinking. Van Bertalanffy (1968), Miller (1969), and Boulding (1968) see general systems theory as having the ability to unify science and help in understanding simple mechanistic systems, the biological cell, organizations, and societies. Katz and Kahn (1978) write about open system theory, which is that part of systems theory that deals with living systems.

Open system theory is . . . a framework, a meta-theory, a model in the broadest sense of that overused term. Open system theory is an approach and a conceptual language for understanding and describing many kinds and levels of phenomena. It is used to describe and explain the behavior of living organisms and combinations of organisms, but it is applicable to any dynamic, recurring process, any patterned sequence of events. (p. 752)

The use of analogies from one system level to another has been advanced by Boulding's (1968) identification of a hierarchy of systems levels. He proposes this hierarchy of system levels:

1. *Frameworks.* Systems comprised of static structures such as the arrangements of atoms in a crystal of the anatomy of an animal.

2. *Clockworks.* Simple dynamic systems with predetermined motions such as the clock and the solar system.

3. *Cybernetic systems.* Systems capable of self-regulation in terms of some externally prescribed target or criterion, such as a thermostat.

4. *Open systems.* Systems capable of self-maintenance based on a throughput of resources from its environment, such as a living cell.

5. *Blueprinted growth systems.* Systems that reproduce not by duplication but by producing seeds or eggs containing preprogrammed instructions for development, such as the acorn–oak system or the egg–chicken system.

6. *Internal image systems.* Systems capable of detailed awareness of the environment in which information is received and organized into an image or knowledge structures of the environment as a whole, a level at which animals function.

7. *Symbol processing systems.* Systems that possess self-consciousness and so are capable of using language. Humans function at this level.

8. *Social systems.* Multicephalous systems comprised of actors functioning at level 7 who share a common social order and culture. Social organizations operate at this level.

9. *Transcendental systems.* Systems comprised of the "absolutes and the inescapable unknowables."

In Boulding's typology levels 1–3 encompass the physical systems, the biological systems are in levels 4–6, the individual human system at level 7, and social systems at level 8. Boulding added level 9 so as not to close his own taxonomy.

Boulding points out that as each level incorporates those below it, much valuable information and insight can be obtained by applying low-level systems to high-level subject matter. He also notes that "most of the theoretical schemes of the social sciences are still at level 2, just rising now to 3, although the subject matter clearly involves level 8." This criticism of current theoretical models in the social sciences implies that if we can apply level

7, human systems, to describe level 8, social systems, we have the potential to advance our understanding.

This work is not an indulgence in a heuristic exercise. It is firmly based in the scientific principles of systems theory, which seeks homologous phenomena at different system levels. It is also not by chance that we have chosen to develop the subject of organizational neurosis from a systems perspective. In human systems (e.g., individuals, groups, organizations, communities, nations, etc.) we find, among others, two emergent properties that are not found in systems that belong to levels below them. One of these properties is *choice*, and the second is the ability to create mental *symbols*. These particularly human properties have opened the doors to many of the major advances of our species. Yet at the same time they have also created the conditions for the development of a specific form of human system pathology. Possibly only human systems that can create mental images and choose to project them on reality have the propensity to suffer from the peculiarly human pathology of neurosis.

To follow this up, if we can apply systems-level concepts from Gestalt therapy to the organizational level, it is possible that we can advance organization theory.

The rest of this work will try to answer that question. It will attempt to examine the possibility of adding to our understanding of some areas of organizational functioning and development by viewing these in the light of Gestalt therapy theory.

It is not by chance that Gestalt therapy was chosen and it is not surprising that Gestalt therapy constructs and theories might show promise in enriching our understanding of organizations. Our hypothesis is that at least some of these concepts and theories are in essence the application of a systems theory approach to understanding individuals and the processes involved in helping them change and develop.

In the past three decades, systems theory has developed into the major theoretical approach for understanding the complexity of organizations. Within systems theory the open-systems perspective has emerged as a unifying force among the disciplines dealing with living systems, from the cell to society. Boulding (1968) has described systems theory as the skeleton of science, in the sense that different disciplines can build themselves around the same basic structure of systemic constructs and properties. In this book *Living Systems*, Miller (1978) has proposed a general theory of living systems based on a number of common basic concepts, structures, and processes that can be found in all living systems, beginning with the cell and proceeding through the organ, the organism, the group, the organization, society, and the supranational system.

New developments in cybernetics, information theory (an offshoot of systems theory), and open systems theory applications to biology have made important contributions to our understanding of organizations. Analogies from these fields to that of organization theory have increased understanding of the dynamics of the relationship between organizations and their subsystems, control in organizations, the organization and its environment, boundary phenomena, organizational change, and so on.

A major hypothesis of this work is that Gestalt therapy is an open systems approach to the level of the individual. If this hypothesis is valid, Gestalt therapy should be particularly fruitful in providing understanding about organizations. Gestalt therapy has a history of remarkable effectiveness with clients who appear unaffected by conventional cause-and-effect or interpretive therapies. Because with organizations rational, problem-solving approaches could be described as analogical to conventional therapy, the added components in Gestalt therapy, as an open systems approach, of emotional and personal components and an emphasis on experience instead of only understanding also add to the potential of Gestalt's use in organizations. In Boulding's (1968) hierarchy of systems levels, the level of the individual is immediately below that of social organization. This means that systems concepts and theories that are applicable at the individual level should be able to enrich our insight at the organizational level, far more than those from the physical and biological levels, which are further down in Boulding's hierarchy, and are being used at present. This is an attractive hypothesis that has been somewhat validated by those who already have worked with Gestalt in organizations.

By focusing on those Gestalt therapy concepts and theories that are a systems theory approach to understanding individuals, we open the door to using these to understand phenomena belonging to levels above that of the individual. The great advantage of systems theory is that the same constructs, relationships, and processes can be applied to phenomena from different disciplines and levels of complexity. This can be done without falling into the trap of reductionism and inappropriately explaining phenomena of a higher level of complexity by qualitatively different concepts and theories applicable only to a lower level.

Burke (1980) suggests that Gestalt therapy has untapped applicability for the consulting process. He points to similarities, parallels, and overlap between Gestalt therapy, systems theory, and organizational development.

A Gestalt therapist and an organizational development consultant both emphasize (1) the here and now; (2) humanistic concerns; (3) tapping unrealized potential; (4) an organic, holistic approach; and (5) experimentation.

Burke lists five dimensions of Gestalt therapy "vis-a-vis general systems theory," which help us understand the practice of organizational development more thoroughly.

1. Open versus closed—viewing the organization as an open dynamic, changing system, as Gestalt therapy views the individual.

2. Diagnosis versus dogma—as in working with the individual in Gestalt therapy, constantly learning about the organization by helping it to change, rather than expecting immediate cure, based on one cause and dealing with one subsystem.

3. Waves versus particles, boundaries versus entities—as with individuals, viewing organizations in terms of relationships of parts and series of events, rather than focus on single parts.

4. Energy versus entropy—as in Gestalt therapy, determining how and where people in the organization use their energy and rechanneling it for productive purposes.

5. Integration versus disintegration—as the person is helped to accept and integrate unwanted parts, seeing how and if all the parts fit the total organizational effort.

Burke's study is the only one we know that attempts to go in the same direction as this work by taking those aspects of Gestalt therapy that overlap with systems theory and applying them to understanding organizations in order to advance organizational development and transformation.

It is worth noting that if parts of systems theory have already been developed in organization theory and development, there will be no particular contribution by also labeling them Gestalt therapy. Truly to advance organization theory, it will be necessary to work with those aspects of Gestalt therapy that overlap with systems theory and whose potentials for enriching organization theory and development have not yet been realized.

A REVIEW OF THE LITERATURE

A 1976 review of publications in Gestalt therapy (Kogan & Himmelstein, 1976) registered 39 books, 61 chapters in books, 68 articles in journals, and 23 unpublished papers.

A survey of these writings and more recent publications reveals that relatively little has been written on the subject of Gestalt therapy and organizational theory. Slightly more has been written on Gestalt therapy and the field of practice, especially organizational development. This seems reasonable as Gestalt therapy is an approach to changing individual behavior and as such would be examined for its relevance for changing organizational behavior.

Fritz Perls

It is only natural that a survey of Gestalt therapy literature should begin with Perls, the founder of Gestalt therapy. Perls applies Gestalt therapy concepts at both levels—the individual in the organization and the organizational. His approach is generally descriptive.* There are few instances of applying Gestalt therapy in the service of practice with the goal of changing organizations.

It would not do justice to Perls' ideas, on the individual in the organization, to encapsulate them in a few pages. From Perls' viewpoint the split between the intrapersonal and the interpersonal is an artificial one. Perls' writings are, therefore, suffused with concepts and propositions binding the individual to the social environment. Too short a review would need to sacrifice an in-depth treatment of much that is valuable. A comprehensive review will be too lengthy, and at this stage partly redundant.

To confront this dilemma, the following procedure is followed:

1. A number of paragraphs will briefly summarize the major concepts Perls uses to deal with the individual/organization inter-face.

2. This will be followed by overviews of key elements needed

---

*It is worth noting that Perls seldom mentions the most prevalent type of organization—work organizations. He sometimes speaks about bureaucracies and gives example of clubs and communities. He also, often, applies Gestalt concepts to tribes, cultures, and nations.

to understand Perls approach to the individual and the organization:

a) The relationship between the intrapersonal and the interpersonal.

b) The tension between the individual and the organization.

3. Throughout this work, when dealing with any concept and proposition, it will be defined, clarified, and placed within the context of the theory in which Perls developed it.

Major Concepts

The homeostatic process is one of reaching out into the environment to satisfy a dominant need, aroused from within or by the environment. This brings individuals into contact with the environment and the social systems to which they belong. When the need is met, the gestalt (configuration) is closed and the individual temporarily satisfied can now move on to forming and closing other gestalts, each connected with an emerging need. Unclosed gestalts, in the form of "unfinished business," are one of the major causes of tension in the individual and between the individual and the social environment, because homeostasis is not achieved and the process of living and satisfying emerging needs is interrupted.

Contact is the point where the boundaries of the individual meet other boundaries, such as those of social systems. The boundary is at the location of a relationship where the relationship both separates and connects. In contemporary terms the boundary is at the interface. Without interrelation of some kind, there can be no boundary. The individual contacts others and social systems through the senses.

Withdrawal, the polarity of contact, is a transferring of the contact from the external to internal processes. The rhythm of contact and withdrawal is part of the process of life and lasts as long as there is life; both are essential in life.

The contact point, at the boundary, is where awareness arises. With awareness the individual can mobilize energy so that the environment can be contacted to meet a need. The contact boundary is where one differentiates oneself from others. The individual's ego boundaries can be widened, by healthy identification, to include other social systems. Accompanying this identification are feelings of attraction and love. In pathological identification the person cannot differentiate self from the organization. An object or a social system may be excluded from the ego boundary, accompanied by feelings of alienation and dislike.

Neurotic behavior is typified by the dysfunctional boundary mechanisms, mediating between the individual and the social environment. *Projection*, or doing to others what one imagines they are doing to oneself; *introjection*, or doing what we imagine others would like one to do; *retroflection*, or doing to oneself what one would like to do to others; and *confluence*, or not knowing who is doing what to whom, are dysfunctional mechanisms the individual employs to perpetuate ineffective social functioning and neurosis.

Healthy, mature behavior reflects a passage from inappropriate environmental support to appropriate self-support. Self-support includes using what one needs from the environment. As a healthy individual one manifests maximum awareness, takes responsibility for oneself and one's feelings, is authentic in terms of openness to one's own experience, does not play roles to manipulate others, and accepts onself and others and one's capacity to cope with the world.

The Intrapersonal and the Interpersonal

From his holistic construction of reality, Perls took a strong stand against what he saw as totally artificial splits—the dualities of body/mind and intrapersonal/interpersonal. Perls (1950) saw the cleavage between intrapersonal and interpersonal as contrived and a hindrance to understanding. "The distinction of "intrapersonal" and "interpersonal" is a poor one, for all individual personality and organized society develop from functions of coherence that are essential for both person and society. . . ." (p. 5)

Replacing the basic dualistic view of humans and society, Perls (1980) proposes an approach that views human beings as being, at one and the same time, both individuals and members of society. "Our approach, which sees the human being as simultaneously and by nature both an individual and a member of the group, gives us a broader base of operation" (p. 52).

To deal with the split, he introduces the concept of the field, in which the person and the social environment mutually interact. Organism plus environment equals field.

The individual is inevitably, at every moment, a part of some field. His behavior is a function of the total field which includes both him and his environment. The nature of the relationship between him and his environment determines the human being's behavior. . . . The environment does not create the individual. Each is what it is, each has its own particular character, because of its relationship to the other and the whole . . . the environment and the organism stand in a relationship of mutuality to one another. (p. 16)

It is worth noting that following Kurt Lewin, Perls' thinking precedes developments in systems theory which, later, focused on disturbances in the system/environment field. In an article with Paul Goodman (Perls & Goodman, 1950) he writes: "Contact-and-boundary is prior to intra and inter, or to inner and outer. And disturbances that could be called neurotic occur also in the organism-natural-environment field" (p. 5).

The disturbances developing in the field between the system and its environment became a major issue in organizational research and theory in the late 1960s (Terreberry, 1968; Emery & Trist, 1965; Lawrence & Lorsch, 1967).

The Tension Between the Individual and the Organization

The relationship between the individual and the social systems he belongs to, is a theme Perls returns to many times throughout his writings. His descriptions of this relationship differ somewhat in different periods of his life.

In the earlier work, *Ego, Hunger and Aggression*, both society and the majority of individuals are neurotic. Society is responsible for the widespread prevalence of neurosis. In speaking about society's need to control individuals, Perls (1969) makes the following statement.

Often enough, however, the socially required self-control can only be achieved at the cost of devitalizing and of impairing the functions of large parts of the human personality—at the cost of creating collective and individual neurosis. (p. 61)

The individual is either infected with the mass neurosis or comes into conflict with the social environment and becomes isolated from it. The community becomes aggressive to the individual who is not as neurotic as it is. Unable to hit back, withdrawing and unable to satisfy gratifications, the individual becomes neurotic. This seems like a double-bind situation with no way to escape (Perls, 1969).

In order to avoid conflicts—to remain within the bounds of society or
other units—the individual alienates those parts of his personality which
lead to conflicts with the environment. *The avoidance of external conflicts*, however, *results in the* creation of internal ones. (p. 149)

In one of the few passages where Perls (1969) does mention
work organizations, he describes their adverse effects on human
beings.

The age of industrialism brought about a new difficulty; today the soul
of the workman is of no interest to the manufacturer. He needs the
function of the "body" only, and especially of those parts of the organism
that are required for the work (factory *hands*—Charlie Chaplin in *Modern
Times*). This devitalization progresses further; individuality is being killed.
The process affects highly specialized workers as well, upsetting the
harmony of their personality. (p. 121)

In a later work, however, Perls holds that, through awareness
of the self in the situation, the individual achieves the possibility
of making choices and acting on them, even sometimes beating the
system. He sees the relationship of the individual and the organization as one of mutuality. For this relationship to function
effectively, the individual has to identify with organizational needs
and the organization has to take care of the needs of its members.
On the latter Perls (1969) writes: "A sound holism requires mutual
identification. The club which does not identify with its members—protecting their interests and compensating them for their
devotion—will disintegrate" (p. 144).

Even at later stages of his life, he continued seeing neurosis as
a clash between individual needs and group and organization
needs. This is stated clearly in the following passage (Perls, 1980):
"A neurosis is a state of imbalance in the individual that arises
when simultaneously he and the group of which he is a member
experience differing needs and the individual cannot tell which
is dominant" (p. 52).

In his later works the clash between the individual and his
social systems is not inherent in his belonging to organizations
and he also has responsibility (Perls, 1980).

When an individual is frozen to an outmoded way of acting, he is less
capable of meeting any of his survival needs, including his social needs . . . If
we look at man in his environment, as both an individual and a social
creature, as part of the organism/environment field, we cannot lay the
blame either at the door of the individual or the environment . . . neither
of them can be held responsible for the ills of the other. (p. 26)

It looks as if Perls' viewpoint of the relationship between the individual and organizations evolved over time. Possibly, under the influence of the war, the earlier picture is tragic, and almost fatalistic. It depicts an "insane" world and a neurotic society inevitably creating neurotic individuals.

The descriptions at later stages of Perls' life, perhaps further from the trauma of war, are not as pessimistic as the earlier ones. Furthermore, it might even be possible to create an ideal community that could minimize these clashes:

A community in which, as its needs are determined, each member participates for the benefit of all. Such a society is in concernful contact with its members. In such a society, the boundary between the individual and the group is clearly drawn and clearly felt. The individual is not subservient to the group nor is the group at the mercy of any individual. (p. 36)

Whether in its earlier tragic version or in the moderate later forms, Perls draws our attention to one of the most basic and enduring dilemmas of organizational life—*the tension between organizational needs and individual needs.* This tension between the system and its parts can be found at all systems levels (Bowler, 1981). What we are facing is a translation of this proposition to the level of the organization and its parts. How this proposition can also be applied at the level of the individual and "the individual's parts" will be left for later treatment.

One characteristic of Gestalt therapy that seems to make it appropriate for use with dysfunctioning organizations is that it focuses on what is happening *now* by attending to the immediate process. Gestalt therapy provides ways to examine the dimensions and qualities of the processes of organizations and to construct both immediate and long-range activity to deal with what is needed. This action is continually subject to modification as conditions change, with an important part of the process learning how to discriminate and delineate what these changing conditions are, perceiving *what is* in contrast to what should be or what would be desirable. Second, because of the emphasis on process, goals are not placed in ordinary perspective. They are important in that they provide direction and help determine the means whereby to achieve them, but they are subsumed under an emphasis on process. As external and internal conditions change, this allows for an easier appropriate modification of goals as well as a change in the organization itself, and helps maintain an operational, functional focus when working internally on the organization, as well as from the outside.

Herman, Herman and Korenich

In two articles in *The Handbook of Gestalt Therapy* (Herman, 1976) and one book (Herman & Korenich, 1977), the authors attempt to develop a "Gestalt orientation to organizations and their development."

Perls' writings are rich in ideas about healthy authentic and unhealthy inauthentic interpersonal behavior and relations. *Authentic Management* collects these ideas and transcribes them into the field of organizations and managerial behavior. Managers are helped to distinguish among three ways of communicating—about-ism, should-ism, and is-ism. They are alerted to the costs of introjection and the value of full awareness, including sensory and emotional awareness. Contact and withdrawal and confluence are examined in terms of healthy relationships and conflict is examined from a Gestalt perspective.

Both Herman's articles and the book are one of the first major attempts to approach organizations and their development through a Gestalt therapy perspective. A major effort, with numerous unpublished but widely circulated papers, has been under way at the Gestalt Institute of Cleveland since it established a postgraduate training program in this area ten years ago. These all break new ground and translate Gestalt therapy concepts and theories into the realities of communication and relationships in organizations, and consulting with organizations.

It still remains an empirical question, as to which of the Gestalt therapy approaches contributes to the effectiveness and development of organizations and under what conditions. Herman and Korenich substantiate their approach by drawing on the results of its application in a number of organizations, among them an aerospace firm and a large government agency.

Some research support can be found in a study by Ennis and Mitchell (1971). They describe the effect of using a Gestalt-oriented approach to break down communication barriers between the staff members in a day-care center. After initiating the activities, they report that the approach had facilitated the staff's growth, improved relationships between staff members, and made them more openly affectionate with the children.

It is necessary to make clear that in many organizational development projects there is no need to improve team communication and relationships or to help the managers to be more effective. On the other hand, there are many instances where the organization's dominant need is for a completely different approach. Such approaches might include clarifying organizational mission and goals in terms of the individual member's needs, organizational tasks, and environmental demands; developing a different organizational structure or new managerial control systems; initiating a change in approach to rewards and motivation or a refinement of the selection and socialization process; or changing values and norms or realigning relations with the work environment.

Karp

Karp (1976) deals with a Gestalt approach to collaboration in organizations. He suggests that collaboration will produce the greatest payoff in terms of satisfaction and productivity when the individuals participating in the collaborative effort view themselves as individuals at all times. This means that the individual maintains good contact not only with others but also with self, and is clear about what he or she wants not only for the organization, but also for himself or herself. Karp suggests that successful collaboration can only be based on recognition of the power that resides in individuals and their right to be themselves.

Drawing from Gestalt therapy, Karp suggests a number of norms to enhance the collaborative process. These include "dealing with" rather than "talking about"; "is" rather than "should"; "I won't" instead of "I can't"; and making a statement instead of a question. Karp believes that an effective collaborative group is based on four underlying assumptions: utilizing an explicit norm that says "wanting what you want is O.K."; focusing first on differentiation by heightening differences that make each individual unique; using a contract approach to deal with differences; and including in the collaborative effort only individuals who wish to collaborate, are competent to contribute to the outcomes, and will be responsible for them.

In essence what Karp has done is to take Perls' theories on the relationship between the individual and the organization and detail and operationalize them into guidelines for effective collaboration in organizations.

Alevras and Wepman

Alevras and Wepman (1980) compare Gestalt therapy with organizational consulting. They focus mainly on the consulting process itself. It is worthwhile, however, to point out some instances of translating the Gestalt concepts to the organizational level. The following passage exemplifies this.

Dysfunctional behavior in organizations has many parallels to neurotic behavior in individuals. As an example of "projection" one department sees others as destructively competitive in order to justify its rejecting or sabotaging proposals that come to it from outside. "Introjections" emerge as rigid procedures and standards. These standards are "swallowed" by individuals rather than being evaluated in light of their results. "Confluence" emerges as a corporate image: a prescription that imposes a firm, narrow range of behavior on employees. Thus, one is evaluated on willingness to conform. . . . (p. 235)

Both Alevras and Wepman (1980) and Nevis (1980) compare the consultation process of Gestalt therapy and organizational consulting. The former stress the similarities between the two approaches; the latter points out and elaborates their differences.

Alevras and Wepman draw a list of the major parallels between Gestalt therapy with individuals and a Gestalt approach to organizational consultation. Table 4-2 shows some examples from a longer list.

Other categories with similarities are data-collection methods and dysfunctional behavior.

Table 4-1
The Gestalt Approach

	Individual	*Organization*
Realm of concern	Communication problems Individual's patterns no longer serving him/her, etc.	Communication problems Organization's structure, methods, no longer serving company goals, etc.
View of client	Organism with systems	Organization with subsystems
Client's expectations	Support, justification, and being cured	Support, justification, and being cured
Therapist/consultant's concept of needs and tasks	To integrate intrapersonal polarities with environmental realities To expand awareness of own functioning, etc.	To integrate interpersonal departmental needs, goals with environmental realities To expand awareness of group's functioning, etc.

There are indeed many parallels between the two approaches. Both lists could be extended even more by adding categories or by adding items to categories. There could be a parallel category for "client/consultant relationship" or "consultation stages," for example. To "realm of concern," one might add such items as "lack of integration between subsystems" and "inacceptance of parts."

The different conclusions of this study and that of Nevis can be explained by what is being compared. Alevras and Wepman compare Gestalt therapy with individuals with a Gestalt approach to organizational consultation. Nevis compares the process of Gestalt therapy with individuals with more structured schools of consultation in organizational development.

Nevis

Nevis (1980) stresses the differences between a Gestalt therapy approach and an organizational development approach to organizational consulting. He suggests using an approach to organizational diagnosis, based on Gestalt therapy, to supplement the active, directed, rational, and analytical approach he sees being used in organizational development. Nevis views the Gestalt therapy approach as more open to observations and more contactful, and as placing more weight on the consultant attending to personal sensations, emotions, and other awareness. Data are seen as a basis for hypothesis rather than for conclusions. Assessment is seen as taking place continuously during the consultant/client relationship, rather than being a one-shot affair at the beginning. The consultant's style is highly involving and oriented to mobilizing the client's energy.

In the initial stages, the consultant is more concerned with making contact and testing for awareness and energy potentials in the system than in making a correct diagnosis. The consultant is more open and receptive, and less biased by preconceived change models.

Nevis has articulated clearly what many organizational development consultants would claim that they already do. Some organizational development approaches, however, do consult in the directed, rational, analytical mode Nevis describes. The survey feedback approach, developed at the Institute for Social Research, University of Michigan, is sometimes used here. The diagnostic stage of this mode often demands much time and energy and may not be owned by the client. The result is that sometimes the results are not acted upon. In contrast to this, the whole point of Nevis' assessment approach is that the clients give up data during a highly interdependent relationship and that diagnosis in the traditional sense is immaterial to the enterprise.

One of the authors and his associates have developed a model called "self-done" diagnosis (Merry, 1981). This mode places most of the responsibility on the client. The consultant's role is to help clients develop the skills to collect the data and do the diagnosis on their own. Less value is attached to the consultant being open and receptive, and to one interdependent relationship with the organization. What is stressed is not the consultant's ability to absorb data, but the ability of the organization to do this. This approach places the emphasis on the client's own learning. Four self-done diagnostic projects have been carried out in different communities. As these were pilot projects, there is no research evaluation, only a very positive impression in terms of client acceptance and action following the diagnosis. Both Nevis' approach and self-done diagnosis are new alternative approaches to traditional rational assessment.

The different approaches can be put on a continuum of low to high client action and responsibility for the data gathering and diagnosis.

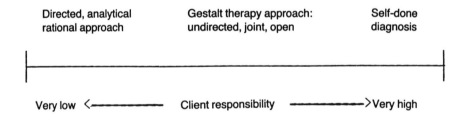

A contingency approach would initiate research to clarify the variables that should affect the consultant's decisions as to which diagnostic approach to use in different organizations, in different stages of an organization's life cycle, and under different environmental conditions.

The study by Burke (1980), reviewed at the beginning of this chapter, was the first attempt to relate Gestalt therapy, systems theory, and organizational theory and practice. To a certain extent, it can be said to have anticipated this present work.

CHAPTER **5**

THE CONTEXT OF ORGANIZATIONAL NEUROSIS DEVELOPMENT

OVERVIEW

This chapter deals with the context in which organizational neurosis develops. As with individuals, so it is with groups and organizations—the constantly changing organization/environment field necessitates that the group or organization also constantly change if it is to survive. Organizational neurosis develops when a group or an organization blocks necessary changes. Among the conditions that reinforce the inability to change are frozen or neurotic leadership, paralyzing conflict, and fear of a needed paradigmic shift.

The inability to change leads to frustration of both personal and organizational needs, which in turn can lead to substituting fantasy for reality as a basis for behavior in important areas of organizational functioning. When leaving the group or organization is not seen as a viable solution, neurotic fantasy is a collective response to unchangeable organizational conditions that do not meet needs. The term "organizational neurosis" will refer both to neurotic organizational behavior and to its more severe manifestation in declining organizations.

THE CONTEXT OF NEUROTIC BEHAVIOR DEVELOPMENT IN GESTALT THERAPY

Perls (1980) traces the development of neurotic behavior in the following passage:

The older psychologies described human life as a constant conflict between the individual and his environment. We see it, on the other hand, as an interaction between the two, within the framework of a constantly changing field. And since the field is constantly changing, out of its own nature and out of what we do to it, the forms and techniques of interaction must necessarily be fluid and changeable themselves.

What concerns us as psychologists and psychotherapists, in this ever-changing field, are the ever-changing constellations of the ever-changing individual. For he must change constantly if he is to survive. It is when the individual becomes incapable of altering his techniques of manipulation and interaction that neurosis arises. When the individual is frozen to an outmoded way of acting, he is less capable of meeting any of his survival needs including his social needs. (pp. 25–26)

In this passage Perls identifies the context in which neurotic behavior arises. The propositions he is suggesting are these:

1. The individual's life is one of constant interaction with the environment.

2. The interaction takes place within the context of a constantly changing field.

3. As the field is constantly changing, the forms and techniques of the interactions must change.

4. If the forms and techniques of interaction must change, the individual must change to survive.

5. When the individual becomes incapable of changing his or her ways of interaction, the conditions for neurotic behavior develop.

6. The individual who cannot change is incapable of satisfying personal survival and social needs.

THE CONDITIONS IN WHICH ORGANIZATIONAL NEUROSIS DEVELOPS

In developing an analogy of the propositions from Gestalt therapy to the organizational level, we obtain the following propositions. (In each of the propositions, "organization" refers either to an organization or to one of its subsystems.)

1. The organization is in constant interaction with its environment.

2. The interaction takes place within the context of a constantly changing field.

3. As the field is constantly changing, the forms and techniques of the interactions must change.

4. If the forms and techniques of interaction must change, the organization itself must change to survive.

5. When the organization becomes incapable of changing the conditions for organizational interaction, neurosis may develop.

6. The organization that cannot change may be unable to satisfy its members' needs and organizational goals.

The first four propositions have substantial support in organizational theory and research. The fifth and sixth propositions are the major ones for the purpose of this work. They have less support and need more research to be substantiated. A short survey of theory and research relevant to these propositions is given in the following.

When the organization becomes incapable of changing, the conditions for organizational neurosis may develop.

One of the initial conditions of organizational neurosis development is identified in this proposition. In effect it is proposed that the interaction of three sets of conditions is the context in which neurotic behavior may develop. These three sets of conditions are as follows:

1. The organization or a subunit blocks changes needed to adapt itself to external and internal conditions; for example, an organization resists the need to alter work conditions although changes in the composition of its workforce necessitate this.

2. A set of conditions makes it difficult to loosen this rigidity; for example, top management frozen into outmoded management approaches does not allow the introduction of necessary changes. This will be dealt with in this section.

3. The needs that members expect the organization to satisfy are frustrated and organizational goals are not attained; for example, people are frustrated in their work roles and this affects production. This will be dealt with in the next section.

It is proposed that in the context of the interaction of these three conditions organizational neurosis may develop.

There are a variety of conditions that make it difficult to loosen organizational rigidity and increase resistance to necessary change. Clinical observation points to a number of conditions as appearing singly or in combination in the background of organizations displaying neurotic organizational behavior. Three of these conditions are more common and deserve special attention:

1. Frozen or neurotic leadership.
2. Paralyzing conflict.
3. Fear of a needed paradigmic shift.

The proposition is that these conditions, singly or in combination, contribute to making it difficult to loosen the rigidity of an organization that is in need of change in order to survive. These conditions will be described in short.

Frozen or neurotic leadership. At the level of the individual, Perls (1969) identified the rigid ego function as one of the major conditions for frozen, unchanging, unadaptive behavior: "The Ego becomes pathological if its identifications are permanent ones instead of functioning according to the requirements of different situations and disappearing with the restoration of the organismic balance" (p. 141).

He writes about how the ego becomes rigid when it identifies itself exclusively with environmental demands or accepts an ideology whole hog. As the executor of a conglomeration of principles and fixed behaviors, the ego loses its elasticity and ceases to fulfill its executive function.

An analogy to the organizational level suggests the following propositions.

—Leadership becomes pathological if its identifications are permanent ones instead of functioning according to the requirements of different situations.
—Leadership becomes rigid when it identifies itself exclusively with environmental demands or accepts an ideology whole hog. As the executor of a conglomeration of principles and fixed behaviors, leadership loses its elasticity and ceases to fulfill its executive function.

Some of the forms frozen leadership takes are:

—A department manager is rigid and unable to accept new ways of doing things.

—Organizational leadership cannot relinquish an outmoded ideology and is not replaced.
—Bureaupathologic leadership resists change, seeking "safety" in maintaining the rules and regulations.
—Neurotic managers create a neurotic organizational climate.
—Overconformity of upwardly mobile managers has developed a stagnant, frozen, rigid organizational climate.
—Rigid organizational leadership is replaced, but retains sufficient informal power to sabotage new policies.
—The "opposition" leadership partly identifies with a rigid dominant leadership and supports its resistance to needed change and innovation.

De Greene (1982) writes that top managers must fit their organizations and "must maintain fit to rapidly changing organization-environment conditions." They must fit the type of organization, the stage of organizational growth and evolution, and the overall organizational climate. Miller (1978) writes:

In some organizations, preservation of structure and process without significant change becomes a purpose that is sometimes disastrous for the system. In such organizations, bureaucratic survival is often put ahead of the major goals of the system, and the top executives lose their flexibility.

Miller proposes a cross-level hypothesis: "The longer a decider exists, the more likely it is to resist change."

Thompson (1964) writes about bureaupathic behavior that is rigid, unchanging, and resistant to change. He points out: "In an organizational context dominated by the need to control, innovation is dangerous because, by definition, it is not controlled behavior." He sees the modern organization as a "prolific-generator of anxiety and insecurity," thus creating conditions for bureaupathic rigidity. Merton (1968) wrote about how structure and rules, developed to ensure performance and reliability, become ends in themselves and create a rigid bureaucratic climate. Levinson (1972) sees excessive rigidity of routine as a clearly maladaptive and disruptive activity. In diagnosing organizations, he checks the measure of the organization and its management's flexibility and openness to new kinds of knowledge. De Greene (1982) points out how management by maintaining an aged technology "can severely constrain the performance of an otherwise healthy organization . . ." or "an archaic vertical management may impede the influx of independently minded but creative young persons needed for innovation." He suggests that maintaining congruence among the subsystems and between system and the environment requires constant monitoring of even subtle changes. Maintaining the congruence "is one of the single most important aspects of both organization design and management."

In one of the few (if not only) studies of neurotic organizational behavior, Kets de Vries and Miller (1982) examine the relationship between the neurotic style of organization managers and organizational pathology. Working on material from 81 case studies of organizations, they write:

Our experience with top executives and organizations revealed that parallels could be drawn between individual pathology—the excessive use of one neurotic style—and organizational pathology, the latter resulting in poorly functioning organizations. (p. 2)

The authors identify five neurotic styles of executives and claim that each particular style infects the organization and "gives rise to shared fantasies which permeate all levels of functioning, color organizational climate and make for a dominant organizational adaptive style." The implication is that:

Organizational problems are often deeply ingrained, having as their etiology the deep seated neurotic styles and intrapsychic fantasies of top executives. They are manifested by a broad array of structural, strategic and "mythical" (shared fantasy) aspects. These are mutually reinforcing and pervasive and therefore resistant to change. (p. 40)

This study implies that organizational neurosis arises from the neurotic style of top executives. In this work it is identified as one of a number of conditions which, singly or in combination, might contribute to maintaining organizational rigidity in the face of a need to change.

The general manager asked us to consult with the transport department, which he felt was in deep trouble. We began our interviews with the department's manager, Robb. In the interview Robb was closed, suspicious, hostile, and uncooperative as much as the situation allowed him to be. He could not kick us out, as he knew we had been sent by the general manager, but he made us feel unwelcome. He blamed the situation in the department on Martin, his deputy, whom he believed wanted to take over his job. He said that Martin was inciting others against him, and he wanted to get rid of Martin.

Martin and most of the others in the department, including Al, an influential old-timer, were all working to cooperate in improving things, but felt unable to do so. They described Robb as authoritarian, rigid, closed to all suggestions of innovation, suspicious of anything new, and stuck in his old ways of doing things that were no longer relevant to the new advances in transport technology.

The tensions in the department were affecting efficiency. People did not want to leave the place in which they had worked for years. They saw Robb, who had been brought in as manager a year ago, as the source of their troubles. The climate was one of hostility, mistrust, and low morale.

We began with two confrontation meetings between the major figures in the department. In a very short time, it became clear to us how paranoid Robb was and how much he was projecting on others his own mistrust and hostility toward them. Every initiative was seen by him as a plot to undermine his authority. Every suggestion was intended to harm him. He had infected the department with his neurotic behavior.

One of the authors has consulted with organizations displaying neurotic organizational behavior, in which no signs of neurotic behavior were detectable in top management. Some of these organizations rotated their top executives every few years. This rotation decreased the possibility of retaining neurotic managers in top roles, but also increased the possibility of losing good people through a rigid rotation. Some of these organizations were decentralized, thus decreasing the influence of the top executives' style, whether healthy or neurotic. Kets de Vries and Miller suggest that neurotic executives will tend to recruit, as their support and their successors, people with the same neurotic style. The neurotic organizational climate will also support this tendency. The authors propose that there is uniformity, or at least complementarity, in neurotic styles among organizational participants in many decentralized organizations.

Further research will be necessary to clarify the role of neurotic top executive behavior in the development of organizational neurosis. In the Kets de Vries and Miller study, it is identified as the central variable in neurotic development. In this work it is proposed that it is one of a number of conditions that might support the inability of an organization to change. This inability to change is seen as one of the central conditions for the development of organizational neurosis.

Perls (1980) was aware of the relationship between neurotic individuals and a neurotic society. He wrote:

A society containing a large number of neurotic individuals must be a neurotic society; of the individuals living in a neurotic society, a large number must be neurotic. And since individuals and environment are merely elements of a single whole, the field, neither of them can be held responsible for the ills of the other. (p. 26)

The author's observations support Perls' propositions. At later stages of neurotic development in an organization, a higher proportion of neurotics will be found. This seems to be the result of two processes that belong to the "vicious circle" quality of organizational neurosis in declining organizations: (1) healthier elements among the organization's membership and management succeed in leaving the organization and finding an alternative organization and (2) the tensions and frustrations of life in a declining organization are of such intensity that people who would function well elsewhere begin to display neurotic behavior. These two processes probably support the greater possibility of neurotic executives taking over at later stages of neurotic development.

There are differences between the Kets de Vries and Miller study and this work. The former suggests that the neurotic behavior of top executives is the major factor in the development of organizational neurosis. This work sees it as one of a number of possible conditions; and the spread of neurotic behavior of individuals is seen as taking place at later stages of neurotic development. This might also account for finding more neurotic managers in declining organizations at that stage. The differences between the two approaches will need to be clarified by further research and study.

Paralyzing conflict. At the individual level, Perls (1980) saw one of the sources of neurotic behavior in insoluble internal conflict between two irreconcilable parts of the personality: "If there are two inconsistent situations requiring our attention we speak of conflict. If these are permanent and apparently insoluble, we regard them as neurotic conflict" (p. 33).

These parts developed in the process of the person accepting, in toto, without examination, two conflicting outlooks: "If you may swallow whole two incompatible concepts, you may find yourself torn to bits in the process of trying to reconcile them" (p. 34).

The two irreconcilable parts neutralize each other and paralyze the growth of the personality: "And the neurotic's internal conflict is fought to a stalemate, where neither side wins, where the personality is immobilized for any further growth and development" (p. 34).

At the organizational level, two conflicting factions may immobilize each other and paralyze the organization as a whole or one of its parts. Like rigid leadership, this situation may contribute to the development of organizational neurosis. Examples of this are:

—Two conflicting factions in the management of a department are caught in bitter conflict and rivalry. They cannot settle their differences, and neither is strong enough to overcome or dislodge the other. They can only sabotage each other.

—Conflict at the top has spread throughout the organization, splitting it into two warring camps that cannot settle their differences.

—Management is caught in the bind of two major departments demanding conflicting policy on a major issue. Neither is willing to compromise, and resolution approaches are not accepted. Each side stalemates any attempt to find a solution.

—Two top executives are caught in a dysfunctional, hostile, personal conflict. The two sides are locked in the conflict, paralyzing organizational decision making.

—A rigid leadership has been replaced but remains in the organization with sufficient informal power to sabotage new initiatives and directions.

—Top management's policy is opposed by middle management and others. The opposition has sufficient power and resources to ensure that the policy is not enforced and opposition members are not ousted.

In healthy organizations conflict is a normal aspect of organizational functioning. Studies differentiate between functional and dysfunctional conflict (Hamner & Organ, 1978). Much has been written and researched on the functional aspects of conflict (Coser, 1956; Kornhauser et al., 1959). These scholars have clarified how conflict makes differences explicit and brings differences into the open to public control and resolution. It also, they point out how it clarifies the identities of the groups involved, makes norms explicit and revitalizes them, and allows maintenance under stress without dissolution.

This conceptualization of conflict complements the Gestalt therapy proposition that healthy contact is an appreciation of differences (Perls, 1980). Functional conflict entails contact between the sides to the conflict. This makes differences between them more explicit, and helps them appreciate their differences. This is the converse of dysfunctional conflict, which involves a breaking of contact, and therefore a restriction of the ability of both sides to recognize and appreciate the differences between them. On the basis of recognizing differences and appreciating them, resolution of a conflict may take place. Evading the issues by not recognizing differences does not lead to healthy confrontation and conflict resolution, but to polarization and breaking of contact because "as a conflict emerges and develops, the adversaries tend to become increasingly isolated from each other" (Kriesberg, 1973, p. 161). Coser has detailed the safety valves organizations develop to channel the hostile aggressive aspects of conflict. He suggests that multiple group affiliations allow people to participate in various group conflicts without their total personality being involved, and without the conflict becoming destructive.

Studies and human history point to the existence of dysfunctional conflict. Some conflicts become intense, emotional, and aggressive, and paralyze organizational action and functioning. A number of the factors intensifying conflict have been identified by Coser. Among these are the totality (versus segmentality) of the relationships among organizational participants, the rigidity of the social structure, and the degree to which the issues are ideological and over core values.

Conflicts that contribute to creating conditions for neurotic development appear to be intense conflicts in which the sides cannot resolve their differences by the usual conflict-resolution methods, and neither is strong enough to win or dislodge the other. The situation cannot be changed and paralyzes organizational activity. In healthy functioning differences are settled by problem solving, decisions by higher bodies, confrontations, bargaining, and so on, but generally by some form of negotiation. Paralyzing conflict seems to develop when the differences are not resolved and conflicting forces keep the organization in a status quo of immobility. Miller (1978) sees unresolved conflicts as producing enduring pathologic relationships. He writes about destructive conflicts that can destroy a group in its entirety. Kriesberg (1973) describes it thus:

If the parties are equal they may deter each other so that coercion is not exercised but in order to maintain the equality they may engage in a power race which evokes fear and hostility in each until coercion is used preemptively by one side. (p. 12)

Wars of attrition, which continue for years without resolution, seem to have this same quality of conflicting forces paralyzing each other for long periods.

In these situations deep frustrations are felt by organization members because of lack of organizational goal attainment and frustration of individual needs. The situation seems frozen and unchangeable. The neurotic behavior pattern may be encouraged to develop in this situation and is a way of functioning in a hopeless unhappy situation from which there seems to be no escape. A few individuals may escape the situation by leaving the organization. For the majority dysfunctional fantasy-based forms of behavior are the ways people develop to function in a situation in which they can neither live nor which they can change.

At the organizational level, Carroll and Tosi (1977) describe how conflicting groups distort to the worse their perceptions of each other. Interactional communication decreases making it easier to maintain negative stereotypes and distort perception. Miller (1978) describes how, in segregated systems, separate components of the organization "may be in competition with each other and their goals may be mutually antagonistic." Levinson (1972) includes in his list of maladaptive and disruptive organizational activities "repetitive interpersonal or intergroup conflict." Coser (1956) writes that while a flexible society benefits from conflict, it can be harmful in rigid systems because "by suppressing conflict, the latter smothers a useful warning signal thereby maximizing the danger of catastrophic breakdown." De Greene (1982), writing about organizational pathology, describes it thus:

Like organisms, organizations can get sick. Many organizations show symptoms of pathology . . . conflicting parties locked in a spastic paralysis similar to that produced by the opposing muscles in tetanus, and total energies dissipated in simple maintenance. (p. 9)

Kets de Vries and Miller (1982) include among their five types of organizational neurotic styles the schizoid organization. In this kind of organization: "The initiatives of one group of managers are often neutralized or severely mitigated by those of a politically opposing group." This paralyzes effective action: "This divided nature of the organization thwarts effective cross-functional (and, where relevant, interdivisional) coordination and communication" (p. 32).

Therefore, one of the conditions in which organizational neurosis develops may be when two parts of an organization are locked in a conflict they cannot resolve and which is paralyzing decision making and activity. There is, at present, some evidence to support this statement, but further study and research are needed.

A particular department within a corporation is headed by an individual who tends to do things in his own manner regardless of the established norms, accepted procedures, and regulations, and with no concern for the impacts and implications of his behavior and what it does for business relations on an internal as well as external basis. His neurotic organizational behavior leads his department and personnel into a "we versus they" position regarding both other departments and colleagues in the corporation. That department, based upon its leadership, refuses to work with the other units and auxillary departments as a team, but rather strictly as a competitor—one to be defeated or outfoxed. As a result of this behavior, the cross-functional coordinating communication between departments and personnel is thwarted.

The situation is exacerbated by the fact that corporate personnel has employed an individual to assist in both the development and monitoring of the research as well as personnel functions. Within a short time, the relationship between the corporate consultant and the department head evolves into a frozen, paralyzing conflict. Communication between the two entities has become extremely unprofessional and personally insulting. Complaints of potential harrassment are pending. Rather than the unit representatives being able to augment and facilitate the mutual goals of the units, they have engaged in an all-out war that disables both from any possibility of successfully meeting their goals. As the internal relationship has escalated into a no-win, low-self-esteem, difficult situation, so has the external one.

Coordination with the corporation's service units is at a minimum. The harder the department head tries to maneuver the service units, the more difficult and inflexible the behavior of those service units becomes. Despite the fact that the department needs the auxillary services more than they need it, the neurotic behavior increases to the point that each is trying harder and harder to sabotage the other. The conflict is in fact paralyzing in that bottom-line issues do evolve so that the department can attain research monies, for example, but cannot get these funds set up through the accounting system without assistance from one of the auxillary departments. Behavior has had an isolating effect on most of the departments that had been designed to assist the program. The conflict is in a position of stalemate.

The final episode of the paralyzing conflict with the corporate consultant is such that he resigns from the organization, one to which he had contributed successfully for almost a decade. The only way for him to resolve his part in the paralyzing activity was to save himself both physically and psychologically by withdrawing his participation in the organization.

Fear of a needed paradigmic shift. Perls (1980) writes about the patient who comes for help because he is in an existential crisis. "He feels that the psychological needs with which he had identified himself, and which are as vital to him as breath itself, are not being met by his present mode of life" (p. 44).

Yet while the patient may not continue as he is, he is unable to take the steps needed to change his ways of functioning. The person may be caught in what Perls calls "the impasse." The person is hurting, but is stuck. He cannot bring himself to face the suffering of letting the old familiar ways go and experiencing the new and unknown. Perls (1976) describes it thus:

The impasse is marked by a phobic attitude—avoidance. We are phobic, we avoid suffering, especially the suffering of frustration. We are spoiled, and we don't want to go through the hellgates of suffering: we stay immature, we go on manipulating the world rather than suffer the pains of growing up. (p. 60)

Organizations may also get themselves into impasses. Changing external or internal circumstances may necessitate a major change. But the organization is unable to make this basic shift in its way of functioning. The existing situation is causing much difficulty and dissatisfaction, but the alternative of striking out in a new direction provokes so much anxiety that the organization is incapable of making that change. Examples of this are:

—Changes in consumer taste demand a complete change of an industry's line of products. Management is afraid of taking the step with all it involves in investment, change of production line, and so on. Nothing is done, thus creating a dysfunctioning organization and no change option.

—An organization's accepted ways of dealing with some of its major issues has broken down. No one can suggest an alternate viable policy within the framework of the organization's existing paradigm (world view). New conditions press for change. But abandoning the existing paradigm demands a reframing of reality and restructuring of the organization that seems more threatening than continuing with the existing situation.

—A political party or a social movement or a religious institution finds parts of its basic ideology conflicting with current reality and people's needs. Yet the organization is afraid to abandon the security of an approach that has guided it for years and replace it with a new one.

—After many years and much effort, an organization that set out to achieve certain goals (for example, to control a disease) succeeds in attaining its objectives. The organization needs now either to dissolve itself or to adopt a new set of goals. The organization seems to be incapable of doing either.

—A total reorganization, including a new computer technology, is an absolute must in the accounting department. The department is afraid of the new technology and resists introducing it. Tension with other departments increases and morale goes down.

All of these situations contained these elements:

1. Environmental and/or internal occurrences brought about the need for a major change in the organization and its basic outlook on reality (paradigm).

2. The change appeared so threatening to the organization that it did not make it.

3. Alternatively, continuing functioning as before caused much dissatisfaction and dysfunctioning and was not viable.

In Perls' terms the organization is at an impasse and is incapable of breaking out of its "catatonic paralysis" into the new possibilities of "the fertile void."

In the past ten years, attention has been drawn to two kinds of change that take place in organizations. The two kinds, or types, or levels of change have been given different names by various scholars. However, most have in common the differentiation between (1) regular, everyday adjustment changes and (2) a basic major change that restructures an organization and its view of reality. Hegel and Marx wrote about small quantitive changes that accumulated, leading to a major qualitative jump. Arygris and Schon (1978), building on Bateson's ideas, distinguish between single-loop and double-loop learning. In single-loop learning, "members of the organization respond to changes in the internal and external environments of the organization by detecting errors which they then correct so as to maintain the central features of organizational theory-in-use." "Double-loop learning" describes "those sorts of organizational inquiry which resolves incompatible organizational norms by setting new priorities and weightings of norms, or by restructuring the norms themselves together with associated strategies and assumptions." Watzlawick and colleagues (1974) differentiate between first-level change and second-level change. First-level change takes place within the system without any basic change in the system itself. In second-level change, the system itself changes. The authors illustrate this with an example of a nightmare. None of the things one does in the dream changes one's state. When one wakens from the dream, a second-level change has taken place.

There are differences between the different descriptions and definitions of the two levels of change. But most of them do have in common these features:

—The first level of change is adjustive, quantitative, and a change of variables within the system.
—The second level of change is a qualitative change of the state of the system itself, necessitating a paradigmatic shift and a restructuring of the organization.

Feeling threatened by the new and unknown, and fearing to leave the familiar, organizations may resist the need to make a second-level change. This condition of, on the one hand, being unable to exist within the existing paradigm and, on the other hand, being unable to accept a new paradigm may create conditions amenable to neurotic organizational behavior development. People unable to satisfy their needs and achieve organizational goals, and with no way to change the situation, may find solace in a flight to fantasy instead of facing an unacceptable reality without hope.

The order was in a dilemma. For centuries the rules, codes of behavior, and norms had served them well. They were always assured of a steady, inward flow of pious, young women willing to serve with devotion both the church and the hospital, named for the order. But times were changing and on all sides unrest and dissent were rife. Sisters were raising objections to almost all of the accepted ways of doing things. There was a demand to wear regular clothes and do away with the "nun's uniform." Many were pressing to widen work activities into other fields. A group had decided on its own to devote themselves to the down-and-outs in the local poverty pocket. There was clamor for major changes in all aspects of life. Even the virtue of abstinence was being called into question.

The demands for change were met by a determined stand of the heads of the order not to budge an inch. This fueled the fire of rebellious spirits and increased the demands for a major change. Dissatisfaction and frustration grew; morale went down. Fewer and fewer young women were joining the order, and more and more were breaking their vows and leaving. It was becoming impossible to supply the workforce needed to service the hospital. Each house that could supply lodging for 20 nuns had three to five inhabitants.

The conditions continued to worsen. The order could not continue as before, but also could not face the option of a major change that would break the tradition of centuries.

Tannenbaum (1979) writes about the need of organizations to hold on to the familiar accepted ways of doing things. A major change is a move into the unknown, "a little death" with all its fear and uncertainty. Better then is "the certainty of misery than the misery of uncertainty." Hedberg (1981) describes how the total restructuring of the organization that may be needed after profound changes is often strongly resisted. Hedberg and colleagues (1976) describe the difficulty of accepting the uncertainty involved in change, especially when the organization and its members have been immersed in stress and change for some time. Delays in making the necessary changes lead to dysfunctioning.

If an organization avoids changes, its effectiveness degrades, its capacity to accept changes weakens and needs for change build up. By the time changes can no longer be held off, needs may have accumulated to revolutionary proportions, and the organization may have lost most of its ability to take changes in stride. (p. 60)

Kets de Vries and Miller (1982) describe five neurotic styles of organizations. One of these styles is that of the "compulsive" organization, which is unable to make major necessary changes demanded by environmental conditions. In the compulsive organizations:

Change is difficult. The *fixation* on a specific line of thought makes a new strategic orientation hard to push through. Usually, a changeover is preceded by a protracted period of doubt and ambivalence due to the difficulty of relaxing existing decision rules. (p. 18)

The proposition suggested here is that *when conditions demand a paradigmic shift to make a second-order change and the organization is incapable of making that shift, this will be a context that encourages organizational neurosis development.* The organization continues to function as it did before when conditions are unsuitable for this. It cannot make the necessary changes. In Gestalt terms the organization is in an impasse, marked by avoidance and phobia. It cannot go on as before and is afraid to change.

To summarize this section: An organization's ability to change may be rigidified by various circumstances. Three of these conditions (and there probably are others) were identified. Three conditions enhance rigidity, and therefore the conditions for organizational neurosis development. These conditions are (1) rigid and sometimes neurotic leadership; (2) paralyzing conflict between two parts of an organization; (3) fear on the part of the organization to make a necessary paradigmic change.

FRUSTRATION OF NEEDS AND INABILITY TO CHANGE OR LEAVE THE ORGANIZATION

Perls (1980) wrote "when an individual is frozen to an outmoded way of acting, he is less capable of meeting any of his survival needs including his social needs."

An organization that has frozen to an outmoded way of acting, and cannot change it, may have difficulty satisfying its own needs and those of its members.

Frustration of peoples' needs in combination with their belief that they cannot change the organization or leave it is probably the major source of organizational neurosis development. Stated in a different way, when people are in an unhappy situation and feel that they cannot change the situation, they may resort to neurotic mechanisms as a way of living with their condition.

The proposition is that creating a neurotic mechanism is a response that still retains a measure of loyalty or commitment to the organization. That is, *when the organization frustrates needs that are important to people and they see the organization as unchangeable and they have some loyalty to the organization, their response will probably be to create a fantasy-based interpretation of the organizational condition.* If people are less identified with the organization, they probably react with any of the other responses. This proposition complements theories that the probability that a person will leave an organization can be explained by an inducement–contribution balance (March & Simon, 1958). March and Simon's theory examines how the decision to remain in or leave an organization is affected by the balance between attracting and deterring factors in each alternative. The model of responses described here is not intended to replace that theory, only to add to it. What the model does is make explicit different ways in which people behave when they are dissatisfied in an organization, believe that change is impossible, and do not see leaving as a viable alternative.

Possibly three factors need to combine to create a breeding ground for organizational neurosis development:

1. Members of an organization feel that important needs they expected to have satisfied by the organization are not being satisfied.
2. The members believe that they cannot bring about change in the organization that will remedy this situation.
3. The members have difficulty leaving the organization.

In all three, organization refers also to a subunit in the organization.

When these three factors combine, members of the organization may collectively resort to neurotic mechanism as a way to live with their unhappy condition. The way in which the individuals' fantasies reinforce each other and become a collective fantasy, an organizational-level phenomenon, will be discussed in the coming chapters.

To summarize up to this point: The first section of this chapter dealt with the need for an organization to change if it is to survive. The organization, or part of it, which is in constant interaction with a changing environment needs to change itself (and the environment) as their field of interaction changes. When the organization does not make necessary changes, it begins dysfunctioning, thus creating adaptive and survival problems. The organization's dysfunctioning and survival problems will affect its ability to attain its goals. They may also, possibly, frustrate the satisfaction of needs that are central to the organization's members.

The frustrated members attempt to initiate changes in the organization, in order to create conditions in which their needs will not be frustrated. If they succeed, and if the change comes about, all is well. But if the organization is perceived as unchangeable because of rigidities such as neurotic leadership, paralyzing conflict, or the fear of a major paradigmic shift, attempts to bring about change will be blocked. When this occurs, and if the organization's members find it difficult to leave the organization, they are caught in a bind that may bring them collectively to develop neurotic mechanisms, that is, to substitute fantasy for reality to enable them to keep living with their untenable situation.

These propositions supplement the work of Hirschman, Birch, and Aldrich on responses of people to deteriorating organizational conditions. Birch (1975) suggested that people had four options. If they believe in the possibility of improvement, they would stay in the organization, and either remain silent or voice their discontent. If people did not believe in the possibility of improvement, they would leave the organization, again either silently or voicing discontent. Hirschman (1972) stressed only two major options: (1) staying and voicing discontent or (2) leaving silently. He suggested that the higher the person's loyalty to the organization, the longer the person would wait before leaving. Hirschman saw loyalty as a commitment to the original goals of the organization. Aldrich (1979) wrote that exit is most readily chosen when better-quality alternatives are available. He mentions other options of people who chose to remain in the organization. They may express their discontent or they may appeal to outside authority or they may remain and do nothing. Expressing discontent while remaining in an organization can make a person vulnerable to retaliation from leaders or managers.

When fustration of peoples' needs combines with their belief that the situation cannot be changed, this may lead in organizations to developing mechanisms that are a collective flight into neurotic fantasy. This statement is probably the very core of neurotic development. What is said here is that when people in an organization feel unhappy and frustrated, and they also see their condition as unchangeable and inescapable, they may, to continue functioning, collude in creating a make-believe world. They may collectively collaborate in developing mechanisms for substituting a mythical, unrealistic, fantasy-based interpretation of organizational life instead of a factual, reality based one. The fantasy-based interpretation of organizational life is what Perls calls "the intermediate zone."

Teachers and administrators, from a combination of a professional socialization that emphasizes "don't rock the boat" and experiences with highly vocal minorities where most of the community is not involved in what happens in the school district, retreat into the collective fantasy symptomized by such cliches as "pursuit of excellence," "emphasis on the basics," "we give homework in this school," along with "teachers are never appreciated" and "most parents don't care." One of the authors, early in his career as an elementary school teacher, visited every home of his students by Christmas. Parents did care and did appreciate that teacher. It was simply a matter of moving out of the fantasy, the intermediate zone, into contact with real parents.

This illusionary interpretation of organizational life is one of a number of ways in which people can live with an unbearable situation in which they are happy and frustrated and which they see no way of changing. The escape to delusion, fabrication, and fiction serves to bridge the dissonance between feeling extremely frustrated and at the same time seeing no way out of the frustration. This is not a healthy survival mechanism. While understandable, it is not going to improve conditions and deal with the frustrations. The frustrations may be eliminated from awareness but will affect behavior and increase organizational dysfunctioning. The ineffective department will be projecting its anger on management and not taking responsibility for its own malfunctioning. People in organizations may collectively act like the cat in the experiment that after some time, when it could not get its food pellets without receiving an electric shock, began to display all the outward signs of neurotic behavior. But the use of a mechanism to create a neurotic fantasy is not the only way people respond to an unbearable situation that seems also to be unchangeable. Members of an organization may react by leaving the organization or "working the organization" or "sitting on a fence" or becoming pathological grumblers, and so on.

John Le Carré's novel, *The Looking Glass War*, provides an excellent example of organization members colluding in their creation of a make-believe world. In this novel, two British government departments, The Department and The Circus, see themselves as being in competition with one another. The Department's status and budget have deteriorated badly since the war. In an attempt to re-create the golden illusion of their past, the members collude with one another in creating a crisis that will require their intervention, mobilize their collective energy, and restore their status and credibility. The crisis is necessary to counteract the internal demise of the organization and to renew vitality. The characters, all civil servants, overidentify with and reify the organization. Lacking a sense of personal integrity, inner vision, or a clearly defined value system, their collective need to belong, to be a part of something bigger than themselves, overwhelms them. These men live in Perls' "intermediate zone," out of touch with reality and themselves, suppressing their own life force in order to accommodate their constructs of organizational life. No one dares to ask "What am I doing?" or "What is going on here?" Apparently it is nobody's job to ask questions. In their blind acceptance and compulsive homage to the organization, they have become servo-men, possessing no thoughts independent of their organizational conditioning. They function as if in a trance, fixated on unquestioning conformity.—*D. McKinnon*

Here are a few of the most common ways of reacting to an organization that frustrates and seems unchangeable.

1. *Leaving the organization.* A person feels that what he or she has invested in the organization is not worth the suffering, especially when there is an option of joining an alternative organization.

2. *Working the system* (Goffman, 1961). The person stays in the organization and exploits it as best as possible for his or her own self-interest. For example, if in the army, one might try to find a comfortable job, abstain from volunteering, evade unpleasant duties, and so on. In companies, one might illegally use the company car for personal use, participate in featherbedding, and the like.

3. *Sitting on the fence.* The person exploits the organization by threatening to leave it. This can be used when the person is needed and the organization is losing members it needs.

4. *Persistent grumbling.* The person always complains and grumbles about conditions and how things are in the organization.

5. *Finding a niche.* The person tries to create a private safe enclave in the organization, decreasing interdependence with others and creating a barricade. This is less brazenly selfish than working the system.

6. *Withdraw inward.* Almost catatonically facing inward, the person lives in an inner world and stops almost all communication with others.

It might be possible to see these various responses as expressing different measures of commitment to the organization's goals. Also involved could be differentiating between stated and actual goals. Leaving the organization would be at the low-commitment end of the continuum and creating a distortion or illusion might be at the higher commitment end. Figure 5-1 illustrates this possibility. It should be understood in terms of the combination of persons and situation. Neither the organizational conditions alone nor characteristics of categories of people can explain their choice of actions. The actions chosen are a combination of both. In Gestalt terms it is impossible to separate the figure from the ground. Figure 5-1 illustrates that when people have varying degrees of commit-

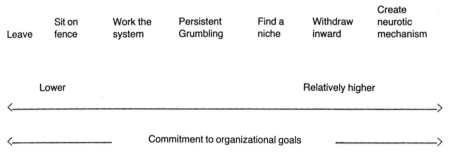

Figure 5.1
Possible responses to frustrating unchangeable organizational situations

ment to the organizational goals, they will choose different behaviors (such as leaving the organization or creating a neurotic mechanism). All this holds within the context of an organization that is blocking necessary change, dysfunctioning in the sense of not attaining organizational goals, and frustrating member's needs, and is seen as being unchangeable.

The Continuing Education Department of a large school system prided itself on its creative, innovative, dynamic approach to adult education. The department had expanded from its meager beginnings to become one of the largest such programs attached to a school board and had become a model for other continuing education departments across the country.

Creating a Collective Fantasy

Initially new staff members were reminded daily of how fortunate they were to have been hired to work in such a department. Their experiences were contrasted regularly with the department's view of how things were in the larger system. The mythology was so pervasive that program coordinators were strongly motivated to see their experiences in terms of the department's rhetoric. Those who were not experiencing personal success and fulfillment blamed themselves and tried harder. Those who articulated the discrepancies between the fantasy and reality were publicly criticized or ridiculed by the director. For instance, when one of the coordinators questioned the program-evaluation procedures, she was lectured on the department's long history and well-established procedures and reminded of her own inexperience. Expressions of frustration and exhaustion were responded to with sarcasm, the implication being that the individual, not the department, was somehow lacking.

For several months the new coordinators attempted to deny their own experiences, perceptions, and frustrations in order to feel accepted and competent. They talked to one another about the "challenges," "flexible hours," "creative colleagues," and "opportunities for growth, learning, and recognition." No one mentioned the low salaries, lack of benefits, endless meetings, long hours, crowded working conditions, unending paperwork, rigid procedure, or shortage of support staff. Because most of the co-ordinators were hired on a part-time basis, and because no staff lounge existed, there were, in fact, very few opportunities for people to compare their experiences in confidential one-to-one encounters.

And so the delusion continued, each member feeling a personal deficiency in being unable to experience the promise of fulfillment. As the frustration level of each coordinator increased, and the director's stance became more controlling and rigid and less supportive of individual initiative, a number of responses to frustration became visible within the department.

Leaving the Organization

One coordinator, who had taken a leave of absence to try out the promises of the department, announced, at the end of the year, her intention to return to the larger system. Although this disclosure was initially met with scorn, ridicule, and a questioning of her ability to "take the heat," it became apparent that having this member announce her intensions to "return to the system," and making her reasons explicit, would not only leave the department short an experienced and competent coordinator (the third in this particular position in a two-year period), but would undermine the department's image. She was encouraged to remain in the position and was rewarded with a private office, secretarial help, a new title, and a full-time, tenured contract, complete with the benefit package.

Working the System

Another coordinator, seeing no real future for himself under the current leadership, began to fantasize his place in the organization once the director had retired. His fantasy allowed him to endure the situation and, in the meantime, he began to "work the system." He secured all the benefits that were available to him, avoided all possible committee work and other duties for which volunteers were required, spent as much time out of the office as possible, and began looking for other jobs on company time and serving on as many interagency committees as possible to "make contacts" who might later assist him in finding a more satisfying position.

Finding a Niche

One talented and upwardly mobile administrator began to look at her own needs both for survival and achievement. On a day-to-day basis, she "found a niche" by delegating most of the work that required her presence in the office to her assistant, and spending her time in the schools with her teaching staff. In this way she remained relatively unaffected by the office politics, and began building networks with other supervisory personnel, while, at the same time, meeting her own needs for professional integrity and service. In addition she began applying for promotions that would take her out of this department and give her more visibility in the larger school system. This was not seen as threatening to the director, who identified with her subordinate's high achievement needs and imagined that the subordinate would carry the department's banner and vision to the rest of the system. Because there appeared to be very little chance of promotion, this farsighted administrator began making a careful case for having her own office relocated in another building and for reporting to another director. Her proposal made good sense, and as it helped solve a space problem in the department, it was accepted. She was able to wait the year required to make such a move, but her assistant was not. The assistant took a leave of absence and came back to work with the administrator in another capacity, once the reporting structure had been altered and the move completed.

Persistent Grumbling

The group of part-time coordinators responsible for women's programs was located in another building. Although able to avoid the disenchantment in the main office, they felt alienated from, and somewhat hostile to, the rest of the department. As a group they grumbled incessantly about low salaries, poor access to services, unreliable secretarial services, long hours, and impossible demands. Their sense of alienation, powerlessness, and misery seemed to bind them together. At the end of two years, all had left to try new ventures. One wrote and published a cookbook, another went back to school, and another, who decided that the income she was receiving did not justify the price she was paying in terms of stress, returned to home-making.

Developing a Splinter Group

Two more members, who had been working as part of a team to develop and implement a successful family-life program, left the department, taking with them the fruits of their labors, and joined another agency.

A different way of viewing the distortion of reality, which symptomizes organizational neurosis, is to see it as a *collective* response, in contrast to most of the other responses, which are *individual* responses. Leaving the organization, working the organization, finding a niche, withdrawing inward, and so forth, are all individual responses and can be done by people without others collaborating. But an individual cannot create an organizational fantasy alone. People collude, collaborate, and reinforce each other in doing so. The emperor's new clothes needed the collaboration of many people to be maintained as a common perception of reality. The neurotic mechanism is an organizational phenomenon, a collective phenomenon, that can only come into existence out of the interdependent behavior of people. It is not a category of a kind of individual behavior. The neurotic mechanism in organizations is a collective phenomenon that could not be developed and maintained without mutual support in fabricating the delusion. Creating a 2 × 2 table might further illustrate this point; see Figure 5.2.

The organization, or department, or team is seen as frustrating important needs and unchangeable. The four boxes in Figure 5-2

Possibility of leaving the organization

	A viable option	Not an option
Level of response Individual	(1) Leave the organization	(2) "Work the system," "find a niche" and other individual responses.
Collective	(3) Develop a splinter group and leave	(4) Develop a neurotic mechanism

Figure 5.2
Individual and collective responses to unchangeable frustration in the organization

are behavioral responses of people when important needs of theirs are frustrated and they cannot see a possibility of changing the organization. The four options are arrived at by crossing the level of the response (individual, collective) with the degree to which people can leave the organization, or department, or team (possible, impossible).

1. *Leave the organization* (individual level; leaving possible). When leaving is a viable option, the individual may opt for a personal solution and leave the organization. If many people choose this, it generally worsens the organization's condition as the younger, most capable, energetic, skilled, and sought-after people are the ones who have the option of leaving and finding an alternative. This leads to a process of negative selection in the organization, leaving it with more of the less capable and adaptive of its members. This also increases the frustrations in the organization and creates conditions where more and more people will display neurotic behavior.

2. *"Work the system,"* etc. (individual level; leaving impossible). Leaving may not be a viable possibility for some people. Alternative organizations (e.g., jobs) may be hard to find or the person's liabilities (age, tenure, disabilities) may make leaving almost impossible. People might choose any of the individual responses. This aggravates the organization's dysfunctioning by people exploiting the organization, sitting on the sidelines, avoiding responsibilities, and so forth.

3. *Develop a splinter group and leave* (collective level; leaving possible). People may band together to leave the organization collectively. Some try to convince others to leave with them (Aldrich, 1979). Leaving is a viable option, and by taking the step collaboratively with others, they can bargain for better terms—even, in some cases, for part ownership of organizational property or resources. This may be a split that demands a part of the existing organization or a move to another organization or individual solutions.

4. *Develop a neurotic mechanism* (collective level, leaving impossible). Members may not see moving as a viable possibility. They may collaborate with others who feel the same as they do, rationalizing their internal dissonance and creating a fantasy-based deceptive image of organizational reality. The collective quality of this delusion will be discussed in the next chapter.

Examples of Individual and Collective Responses to Unchageable
Frustration in the Organization

1. Work the System

I can use myself as an example of someone working the system. In
a company I worked for, the bookkeeper and I created our own fringe
benefits to compensate (we told ourselves) for our low pay and general
frustration. Our fringe benefits included paying ourselves for working from
8 a.m. until 5 p.m. when our day actually began at 8:30. Whenever we
worked through our lunch hour, we included the time it took to walk down
to the local deli and back as part of working through our lunch hour.
Another benefit was going out to lunch with the money we collected
when people bought "personal" stamps from the company. (The money
was, of course, supposed to be saved to buy more stamps.)

2. Develop a Splinter Group and Leave

Two of the top designers of the aforementioned company attempted
to become part owners of the company and were rejected by the owner.
The two decided to break off and form their own company (taking the
top designers with them). When this announcement was made, the owner
decided he would, in fact, take them on as partners. (In this particular
case, the two designers refused and formed their own company anyway.)

3. Create a Collective Fantasy

With reference to example of working the system, the bookkeeper and
I reiterated over and over again, almost daily, the fact that we had our
special fringe benefits. We reminded each other of our appreciation for
being able to dress casually and have occasional flexibility in our hours.
We would convince each other that our situation really wasn't that bad,
taking turns at being the convincer and the convincee (depending on
which of us was upset that day). We actually had a way of bitching that
we enjoyed, and there was a certain amount of pleasure in knowing that
the time we spent complaining was wasting the company's money.—*M.
Lobnitz*

All of these responses, individual and collective, have their
etiology in the same set of organizational conditions. They develop
in conditions of people frustration and organizational rigidity. All

four types of response may be found in organizations displaying neurosis. Organizational members will collude in maintaining a deceptive organizational delusion. Individuals will have a tendency to leave the organization and seek their personal solutions elsewhere. Groups of members will create internal schisms and organize to leave collectively, hoping to get as much as they can out of the organization. Individuals who cannot leave will try to exploit the organization, or find their niche. All these responses work together to aggravate the organization's condition and increase its dysfunctioning.

To summarize: Colluding in developing a neurotic mechanism that is a fantasied misrepresentation of organizational reality is a collective response of frustrated members who have difficulty leaving the organization or one of its subunits.

A summary of the factors involved in the context of neurotic development is presented in Figure 5-3.

ALTERNATIVE THEORIES AS TO THE CONDITIONS OF ORGANIZATIONAL NEUROSIS DEVELOPMENT

Two other studies have suggested explanations about the conditions under which organizational neurosis develops. An earlier study by Harvey and Albertson (1971) is called "Neurotic Organizations: Symptoms, Causes and Treatment." The authors ask: What are the causes of neurotic organizational behavior? Their answer is that there are two causes:

1. Organization members are unaware of their behavior and the consequences it has for them as individuals and for the organization.
2. Members have rich and varied fantasies about what will happen if they do confront the problems.

Harvey and Albertson refer to these causes as the symptoms of a neurotic organization that can be used for a diagnostic checklist.

In this work behaviors of the kind described are called symptoms. The conditions, or context, for the development of such behaviors are not given or described by Harvey and Albertson.

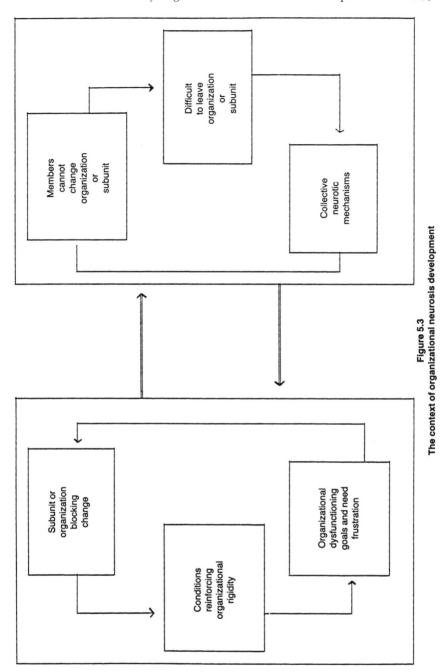

Figure 5.3
The context of organizational neurosis development

The second study is by Kets de Vries and Miller (1982) and it is called *Neurotic Style and Organizational Pathology*. The authors describe five common pathological types of organizations that are "caused by the neurotic behavior of their top executives." As discussed earlier, the neurotic behavior of executives is here seen as one of a number of factors that may enhance organizational rigidity and inability to change. This inability to change is one of a number of conditions that jointly contribute to the development of organizational behavior neurosis. Whether neurotic executives are the major cause or one of a number of conditions for neurotic development will need to be clarified by research.

PROPOSITIONS AND DEFINITIONS

The following four propositions have strong theoretical and empirical support.

★ The organization is in constant interaction with the environment.
★ The interaction takes place within the context of a constantly changing field.
★ As the field is constantly changing, the forms and techniques of interaction must change.
★ If the forms and techniques of interaction must change, the organization itself must change to survive.

The following descriptions of the conditions of organizational neurosis development have not been proposed before and are in need of research and study.

★ When an organization becomes incapable of changing, the conditions for organizational neurosis may develop.
★ Organizational neurosis develops out of the interaction of three conditions:
    1. The organization blocks changes needed to adapt itself to external and internal conditions.
    2. A set of conditions makes it difficult to loosen the organizational rigidity.

   3. The needs that members expect the organization to satisfy
   are frustrated.
★ Three conditions, among others singly or in combination, contribute to making it difficult to loosen the rigidity of an organization. The three are:
   1. Frozen or neurotic leadership.
   2. Paralyzing conflict.
   3. Fear of a needed paradigmatic shift.

   The following deal with the development of neurotic mechanisms. They are in need of empirical validation.

★ An organization that is not adapting to necessary change begins
dysfunctioning.
★ In certain cases the organization's dysfunctioning frustrates organizational goals and the central needs of its members.
★ When the frustration of people's needs combines with their
belief that the situation cannot be changed, this may lead to
developing mechanisms that serve as a collective flight into neurotic fantasy.
★ Organization members may respond to a frustrating unchangeable organization condition with a variety of responses, such as
leaving, "finding a niche," or neurotic fantasy.
★ Creating a neurotic mechanism versus leaving and other responses is generally chosen when there is a relatively higher
loyalty to the organization.
★ Neurotic delusion is a collective (versus individual) response
to a frustrating, unchangeable situation when leaving the organization is not seen as a viable option.

CHAPTER 6

THE NEUROTIC MECHANISMS

OVERVIEW

The preceding chapters dealt with neurotic organizational behavior and other forms of organizational dysfunctioning and with the conditions under which neurosis develops. It was suggested that when organizational members find that (1) important needs they expect the organization to satisfy are frustrated and (2) they cannot change their situation, they will collude in creating a neurotic mechanism. These collective delusions are a way to live with an unbearable situation people think they cannot change. This and the following chapter will deal with organizational delusions. This chapter will address itself to the mechanisms an organization uses to create the delusions: projection, introjection, confluence, retroflection, and disowning. Each mechanism will be examined, first as described in Gestalt therapy on the individual level, and then in more detail as it manifests itself at the organizational level. At the organizational level, some dimensions of each mechanism will be singled out and different forms of the mechanism, resulting from variations in the dimensions, will be detailed.

The chapter begins with a discussion of the functions of the neurotic mechanisms. These are seen as outlets for frustrated feelings, ways to relieve the organization of the responsibility of dealing with its problems, and support for the organization's delusions.

THE FUNCTIONS OF THE NEUROTIC MECHANISMS

Polster and Polster (1974) explain that a person who is behaving dysfunctionally will be unable to satisfy personal wants and needs. This will result in a collection of frustrated, negative feelings that seek an outlet. The neurotic mechanisms of projection, introjection, and so forth, serve as the channels of outlet for these feelings. They are not reality based on genuine contact with the environment.

Perls suggests that the neurotic mechanisms block the process of growth, self-support, and maturity. They preserve handicaps rather than get rid of them. They relieve a person of the responsibility of dealing with problems. When caught in the neurotic process, the person does not, and in fact cannot, deal with reality.

The neurotic mechanisms may be filling similar functions at the organizational level.

1. They may serve as an outlet for pent-up frustrated feelings.
2. They may create and maintain the organization's delusion.
3. They may relieve the organization of the responsibility of confronting and then dealing with its problems.

Dysfunctional organizational behavior leads to frustration and pent-up feelings because organizational goals are not being met along with people's needs not being satisfied. People can see no way to change the situation, and frustration leads to feelings of distress, aggression, hostility, blame, anger, and so on. The feelings need an outlet for expression and the neurotic mechanisms may serve as channels through which the feelings can flow and be expressed without the organization taking responsibility for dealing with its problems.

The organization attempts to deal with its dysfunctioning, frustration, and inability to change by developing a mechanism. It does this by distorting reality and replacing the reality with a "fantasy." It is in need of some way to maintain, support and bolster its illusion in the face of feedback it is receiving. The mechanisms the organization may use to do this are the neurotic mechanisms. Perls wrote that the neurotic's manipulations are directed toward preserving the handicap rather than getting rid of it. The same phenomenon appears to take place with organizational neurosis. The organization utilizes the neurotic mechanisms to maintain its delusion. The function of the mechanisms is to bolster and maintain the organization's delusion. The organization's delusion is a way to live with a painful situation that seems unchangeable. The neurotic mechanism creates and supports the delusion and blocks the way to awareness of reality. Thus the neurotic mechanism relieves the organization of the responsibility of confronting and dealing with its problems—problems the organization (1) imagines it has no power or capacity to deal with and (2) to which it can perceive no alternative response.

Problem solving depends on recognizing a problem (the gap between what "is" and what "is wanted"), creating alternatives to close the gap, and taking action to do so. Denying the existence of the gap, or of the possibility of closing it, or of the organization's ability to do this closing, blocks the possibilities of effective problem solving.

In introjection the organization may be saying, "Things *should be* as they are." In projection it might say, "*Others* are responsible." In confluence the organization might say, "Everybody has these problems." In retroflection the expression might be, "I'm to blame but I'm helpless." The disowning organization might ask, "What problem?" or "Who has such a problem?"

In each of these cases, the organization may be avoiding responsibility for dealing with its problems. It may do so by thinking that things should be as they are; or by placing the responsibility on others; or by not seeing any problems; or by denying its ability to deal with the problems. Each of these approaches is a way to block action and allow the organization to continue maintaining its delusion, substituting this for real action.

The organization is caught in a vicious circle, which enables it to avoid confronting its problems:

1. Dysfunctioning, frustration, and disbelief in change have led to substituting a delusion for reality.

2. The delusion is being supported and maintained by neurotic mechanisms that deny the existence of problems or the possibility of dealing with them.

Some examples will make this clear:

1. *Context.* The organization is rigid, and has difficulty adapting. Dysfunctioning, frustration, and disbelief in the possibility of changing conditions have developed. "We will continue making and stockpiling our buggy whips even though our company gets no appreciation or reward from the world because some day buggies will be coming back. All we need are more OPEC blockades."

2. *Delusions.* Everything was fine in the past. We need to return to how things were then and all we need is more of the same. "Life was simpler and sweeter when we drove buggies. Even though it took more time to get from place to place, there was less stress and high blood pressure. Everyone was happier. Even the horses loved it."

3. *Neurotic mechanisms.* "They" are to blame for everything that has gone wrong (projection). The way we ran things then is the only way to manage an organization (introjection). All the other organizations have these problems. There is no difference (confluence). We are too weak to face such immense problems (retroflection). What problems? We don't see any problems (disowning).

THE NEUROTIC MECHANISMS IN GESTALT THERAPY

Perls (1980) sees the source of all neurotic behavior in the relationship between the individual and the environment.

All neurotic disturbances arise from the individual's inability to find and maintain the proper balance between himself and the rest of the world, and all of them have in common the fact that in neurosis the social and environmental boundary is felt as extending too far over into the individual. The neurotic is the man on whom society impinges too heavily. His neurosis is a defensive maneuver to protect himself against the threat of being crowded out by an overwhelming world. (p. 31)

The neurotic mechanisms a person uses to deal with this situation leads to confusion at the boundary between the individual and others. They allow the person not to take responsibility for him/herself and his/her problems. They "relieve" the person of self-support and allow him/her to evade confronting the hard data of his/her reality.

They are nagging, chronic, daily interferences with the processes of growth and self-recognition through which we reach self-support and maturity. And whatever form these interferences and interruptions of growth may take, they result in the development of continuing confusion between the self and the other. (p. 32)

The Polsters (1974), also Gestalt therapists, see the neurotic mechanisms as arising in a situation in which one cannot get what one needs from the environment. When this happens one collects deep feelings of frustration. "If his efforts don't get him what he wants, he is stuck with a whole laundry list of troublesome feelings: anger, confusion, futility, resentment, impotence, disappointment and so on" (pp. 70–71).

In this situation the person develops ways to evade genuine sensory, reality-based interaction with the environment. "He must divert his energy in a number of ways, all of which reduce possibilities for contactful interaction with the environment" (p. 71).

The neurotic mechanism a person chooses assists the person in circumventing facing problems and creates a specific style of behavior. "The specific directions of this diverted interaction will color the person's style of living as he establishes favorites among the channels open to him" (p. 71).

Perls deals with four neurotic mechanisms: projection, introjection, confluence, and retroflection. Other Gestalt therapists, the Polsters for example, have suggested other mechanisms, for example, deflection. Enright (1980) adds "disowning" to Perls' list of four mechanisms. It is not clear why Perls singled out the four he dealt with at great length. Two possibilities are: (1) Perls regarded these as the only boundary mechanisms; or (2) he postulated that they were used more than other mechanisms. This work will address itself to Perls's four boundary mechanisms: introjection, projection, confluence, and retroflection, and to Enright's "disowning." These five mechanisms appear to be widely used in neurotic organizational behavior. This does not preclude the possibility of, later, finding other widely used mechanisms.

INTROJECTION

Introjection in Gestalt Therapy

> "An introject . . . consists of material—a way of acting, feeling, evaluating—which you have taken into your system of behavior, but which you have not assimilated in such fashion as to make it a genuine part of your organism . . . even though you will resist its dislodgment as if it were something precious, it is actually a foreign body" (Perls et al., 1951, p. 189).

Perls describes introjection as a dysfunctional boundary mechanism in which a person moves the boundary of the environment into the self. In other words one sees oneself as part of the environment that one has taken in but not assimilated. In order to grow and develop, people need to destructure, digest, and assimilate whatever they ingest from the environment. By being destructured and broken up, the foreign material becomes part of the person and can serve as a source of maintenance and growth. Like the introject, food needs to be digested in order to nourish and be a source of energy and growth.

Not only do matter and energy need assimilation to be a source of nourishment, but ideas need it as well. As Perls puts it (Perls et al., 1951):

When it is not physical food but concepts, "facts," or standards of behavior, the situation is the same. A theory which you have mastered—digested in detail so that you have made it yours—can be used flexibly and efficiently because it has become "second nature" to you. But some "lesson" which you have swallowed whole without comprehension—for example, "on authority"—and which you now use "as if" it were your own, is an introject. (pp. 189–190)

A person needs to grapple "aggressively" with new ideas and information. For example, the information has to be compared and integrated with other information the person has. Without an active process of digestion, assimilation, and reality testing, new information remains a foreign body, whole and unattached within a person's system. Introjection has dysfunctional effects on a person in a number of different ways. One who swallows many introjects whole is not one's own person. Such a person is being guided by sets of belief systems that have not assimilated. Not having assimilated the beliefs, the person has little choice in accepting and rejecting them according to changing circumstances. In fact people who introject may have problems of adapting to change. They do not develop in creative continuous adjustment with the environment. An introjective type of person may therefore wish that changes would not take place and that life would continue, as it is, unchanged. The introjective type also may not be able to learn from experience. To learn from experience, it is necessary to be able to extract the nourishment from the experience, by contacting it fully. The introjective type may have a tendency not to do this, but to swallow whole, to be spoonfed, to be attracted to gimmicks and simplifications, and to be too impatient, lazy, or greedy to deal with experience in the necessary depth. The introjective type may also swallow conflicting concepts whole and become immobilized by conflicting tendencies.

Introjection in Organizations

Perls' theory about the similarity between digesting food and digesting ideas may seem strange when first met. In terms of living systems theory (Miller, 1978), the two processes are not dissimilar. Matter-energy (food) brought into a system passes through similar boundary and transformation processes as information (ideas) brought into that system.

By the input, processing, and output of matter-energy and information, living systems maintain themselves for different periods of time in steady states. An equilibrium that is preserved in the face of dynamic flux is a steady state (Miller & Miller, 1983). The fact that living systems are more complex than nonliving systems permits them to fight for different lengths of time the inevitable increase in entropy that leads to matter-energy dissolution of all sorts. In contrast, according to the second law of thermodynamics, nonliving systems disintegrate with increasing entropy. Living systems ingest matter-energy of lower entropy, use part of it in their process, and then output matter-energy of higher entropy. To carry out these processes, which are basic to life itself, every living system needs a subsystem that will change matter-energy, coming from outside the system, into forms more suitable for the special processes of that system. This subsystem is called the converter. Similarly a subsystem is needed to alter outside information into a code that can be used internally by the system. This is the decoder.

Introjecting food (matter-energy) without digesting it is a breakdown or dysfunctioning in the convertor, whereas swallowing ideas (information) whole, without assimilation, is a breakdown or dysfunctioning of the decoder subsystem. These same processes and their dysfunctioning have been shown to be basic processes occurring in all living systems, beginning with cells, through individuals and organizations, and ending with supranational societies (Miller, 1978).

A number of organizational researchers and theoreticians have touched on the phenomenon of introjection in organizations. Some examples of this are: De Board (1978), who writes about introjection in groups, teams, and organizations as creating rigid procedures; Herman and Korenich (1977), who have noted the introjection of management theories; and Coser (1956), who dealt with the relationship between introjection and organizational identification. Perls believed that introjection, when used temporarily and in particular circumstances, could be healthy. In this it was no different than the other mechanisms. He regarded introjection as neurotic only when used excessively, inappropriately and chronically. Perls et al. (1951) wrote: "The 'I' which is composed of introjects does not function spontaneously, for it is made up of concepts about the self-duties, standards and views of 'human nature' imposed from the outside" (p. 190).

The same probably may be said of an organization that is functioning according to duties, standards, and views of human nature, imposed from outside.

Perls noted the effects of social force in creating introjection. He wrote: "Forced feeding, forced education, forced morality, result in literally thousands of unassimilated odd introjects" (Perls et al., 1951, p. 202).

Also the members of teams and organizations can have experienced, collectively as individuals, forced education, forced morality, and forced identification. The result is "thousands of unassimilated odds and ends" lodged in the organization as introjects. Therefore, "social" often loses its true meaning. Perls wrote (Perls et al., 1951):

As commonly used, "social" often means being willing to introject norms, codes and institutions which are foreign to man's healthy interests and needs and in the process to lose genuine community and the ability to experience joy. (p. 190)

Introjections are belief systems, ideologies, norms of behavior, ways of evaluation and feeling an organization has accepted in their entirety, without putting them through a thorough process of review, examination, and assimilation. The mechanism by which undigested attitudes, beliefs, and ways of behaving, feeling, and evaluating are accepted by an organization is called introjection. The introjection is not the sum of individual beliefs; it is the product of collusion in which people interact with each other and through this accept a commonly held belief. People speak to each other, express opinions, make statements to each other, and so on. When this results in an agreed belief that has not been examined, evaluated, and reality tested in the organization, it is an introject.

An organization, as do all other living systems, grows and develops by ingesting from the environment matter-energy and information. These are then destructured into new forms in a transformation process. In their new form, which is assimilable to the organization, the inputs are then a source of energy to power its activities and for material to renew itself (Miller, 1978).

Organizations may grow and develop through ingesting new ideas, standards, concepts, values, and behavior patterns imported from the environment. This growth, however, is dependent upon the new inputs being destructured and transformed into a form the organization is able to assimilate and integrate with existing components and structures. If this process does not take place, or is faulty, the inputs are not destructured, taken apart, analyzed, and then selectively put together again in an integrated form that is assimilable and valuable to the organization. If the inputs are not in a form that is assimilable to, and can be integrated into, the organization, they cannot serve it as a source of energy and growth. Introjected ideas, values, theories, and norms can generally be recognized by the taboo on subjecting them to any process of reevaluation, review, or examination.

Miller has demonstrated how all living systems, beginning with the cell and ending with the supranational system, must, and do, have subsystems such as the converter and the decoder in order to change inputs into forms assimilable by the living system. Introjection can be understood as a process in which the organization (as the individual) has not used its decoder to transform information inputs into its private code that it can use internally. The information is in the system but has not been assimilated by the system.

A pathological process can occur with the introjection of matter-energy. An example of this is an organization accepting as members a new group of people who are very different in some way from its present members. If the organization does not "convert" the new group by a thorough process of absorption and assimilation, it may discover that it is facing a problem of housing a foreign body in its midst. Although outwardly the new group may look as if it is part of the organization, it may, in a sense, be more part of the environment. If the new "alien" group has not been absorbed and assimilated thoroughly by the organization, difficulties may develop between it and other parts of the organization, or with the organization as a whole. For example, Swedish and Swiss industries accepted groups of foreign workers from Mediterranean countries. The workers were part of each industry's work force, but were not thoroughly absorbed and assimilated in each factory. After some years the factories discovered that they had in their midst a "foreign body," with all the attendant problems and tensions.

Kinds of Introjection

Two dimensions are useful in differentiating between kinds or types of introjection. One dimension is what is introjected, that is, the content of introjection. The second dimension is who does the introjection—the organization or a specific part of it.

The Content of Introjection

The following contents of introjection are worth noting.
1. Organizational procedures and standards.
2. Management theories.
3. Belief systems about how the organization works.
4. Ideologies and total belief systems.

Organizational procedures and standards. Some organizations introject procedures and standards. For example, the organization accepts in toto an outside procedure for hiring, firing, and controlling its work force. The procedure is swallowed whole without confronting it with the organization's own experience in these matters. Alevras and Wepman (1980) suggest that organization introjections emerge as rigid procedures and standards, and these standards are accepted by individuals rather than being evaluated in the light of their results. An organization that has introjected a standard or procedure is not going to do any reality testing, and might rigidly retain the procedure even in the light of continual negative feedback.

Management theories. Some organizations introject outside theories as to how they should be managed. An outside theory is accepted as it is and is not assimilated and changed to suit the particular contingencies of the organization. An example of this would be a U.S. industry accepting a Japanese form of management that was successful in Japan, without examining its suitability to the particular circumstances of the U.S. firm. Swallowing whole a Japanese form of "quality circles" would exemplify this. Herman and Korenich (1977) drew attention to a typical introject accepted in many organizations as to what constitutes a good manager. An accepted introject is that a manager "makes quick decisions and must appear decisive and self-assured at all times," and so on.

Belief systems about how the organization works. Some organizations swallow whole belief systems and theories about how their organization works. Westerlund and Sjostrand (1979) describe many cases of organizations that accept whole what they call "myths." These are belief systems about the organization and how it works and are accepted by the organization members from organization theorists and experts. The authors point out that "these myths seem to be obviously true, and thus are hardly ever questioned or discussed by those who believe in them." This description sounds very similar to the process of accepting an introject, although the authors do not use the latter term and prefer the concept of "myth." An example of such a myth is "the myth of single causation." According to this myth, which is commonly accepted in some organizations, the cause of an organizational phenomenon is described as just one factor, thus ignoring both multiple and two-way causation. Another myth is "the myth of the true description," according to which there is only one true description of the organization, and often this coincides with the description given by management. Myths may be seen as introjects, the content of which is how the organization functions, and how it should be managed.

Ideologies and total belief systems. In moving from business and industrial organizations to social, political, religious, and military organizations, it is possible to discern introjection of total encompassing belief systems and ideologies. In these cases the object of introjection may be a total world view, an orientation to life, reality, creation, society, the human race, the world, and so forth. Here the introjected ideology may become the central focus of organizational life, and around it all aspects of organizational functioning will evolve. Questioning this kind of belief system may be treated in the organization as heresy and reacted to accordingly. It is this kind of introjected ideology, its questioning, forsaking, and undermining, that serves as the subject matter of many serious dramatic novels such as Arthur Koestler's *Darkness at Noon*. Political and religious sects, especially those that we see themselves in conflict with the outside world, are prone to introjecting ideologies. Coser (1955) describes how such groups react violently, not only against the heretic, but also against every form of dissent, which is perceived as an attack upon the very basis of the group's existence. The Jim Jones group in Guyana and the Palestinian terrorists are typical examples of this type of behavior.

> The youngsters who had joined the sect appeared to be inhabiting a different world. Not only had they changed their hair style and clothes, but also their view of life and relationships seemed, outwardly, to have changed. They walked as if they were floating on thin air. They held hands and continually embraced each other, speaking about the flow of eternal energy between them and extolling THE WAY, which would bring happiness and salvation to all humankind.
>
> It was impossible to reason with them or question anything they believed in. They reacted with a knowing smile of understanding, condescendingly brushing aside any reaction that could, in any way, produce a crack in their world view. They had been brainwashed. They had accepted in its entirety a total system of beliefs, an entire "religion." They had taken it all in whole, in toto, without confronting it with their common sense, experience, knowledge, and intuition. They had not examined it, compared it, tried it out; they had swallowed.
>
> They lived together and strengthened each other in their beliefs by maintaining their daily rituals and special way of life. They lived in a strange, unreal world, not allowing anything that might possibly undermine their belief system break through into their consciousness.

Who Does the Introjecting

The second dimension that useful for differentiating kinds of introjection is that of who is doing the introjection. Worth noting are the following three introjectors.

1. *The total organization.* All or most of the organization's

members collude in having a common introjection. This may have far-reaching effects on organizational adaptability.

2. *Leadership.* The organization's leadership (management, dominant coalition, etc.) has introjected a theory, approach, or belief system and may be attempting to impose it on the organization.

3. *Polarized groups.* Two groups in the organization have introjected conflicting approaches, beliefs, and so forth. Their polarization may be immobilizing the organization.

These forms of introjection may be the first stage of neurotic organizational behavior, and so were addressed in more detail in Chapter 5. In one sense introjection appears to be different from the other neurotic mechanisms. All four are mechanisms a person may use to create delusions. Introjection, however, often occurs also in the initial stage of neurotic organizational behavior development and helps to create the conditions of rigidity and frustrated needs. With rigidity, frustration, and the feeling that conditions cannot be changed, the organization's members may begin colluding to create and maintain delusions. The neurotic mechanisms, including introjection, are the means by which they do this. Introjection is therefore a factor contributing to the development of neurotic organizational behavior, and also a mechanism used to maintain it.

The Introjective Type of Organization

Both Perls and the Polsters point out the special case of a kind of introjective type of individual. Polster and Polster (1973) write: "He is duck soup for the symbol, the oversimplification, the gimmick, the lesson which is easy to reiterate obsessively" (p. 77).

Perls (1969) writes:

Nothing is ever assimilated, nothing reaches the personality.... These intellectuals can swallow anything, but they do not develop a proper taste, an opinion of their own; they are ever ready to hang on to this or that "ism" as their specific dummy.... When they switch over from one intellectual dummy to another, it is not that they have assimilated the content of one "ism" and are ready for new mental food. The old dummy has become distasteful to them mostly as a result of disappointment, and they get hold of another "ism," with the deceptive hope that the new dummy will be more satisfactory. (p. 126)

These descriptions by the Polsters and Perls may be applied to an introjective type of organization. It has a tendency to embrace (introject) "isms."

An introjective type of organization looks as if it feels safe only when it is guided by a total belief system. It may be possible that the encompassing ideology is felt as a necessity to give meaning, sense, and significance to a reality of turbulent change and complexity in the environment and in the organization. The belief system is introjected piecemeal and accepted uncritically, without passing through a thorough process of critical examination and translation into terms meaningful to the organization's reality. When the ideology is accepted, it becomes the organization's philosophy, affecting activities, attitudes, and feelings in all spheres of organizational life.

This continues for a time until "the old dummy becomes distasteful" and is replaced by a new "ism." After a period of time, this new "ism" also loses its attractiveness, and is replaced with another new "ism."

An introjective type of organization has the tendency to move from one fad or fashion to another. Each fad reigns for a time and may seem, to the organization's members, to be the answer to many problems facing the organization. It then fades away to be replaced by a new introjected belief system.

These aspects of introjective types of organization are postulated as worth noting.

1. The organization appears to have a strong need to have an encompassing belief system. This might grow from a desire to create a meaningful significant order in the complexity of environmental and organizational turbulence.

2. The organization has a tendency to oversimplify reality. It attempts to replace life's complexity with simplistic models and gimmicks.

3. The organization seems to be able to get rid of and replace a "used" ideology as easily as it was able to accept it, when it was novel. The process of paradigmatic change in this kind of organization is not an earth-shaking event.

4. The organization tends to swallow whole total ideologies without examining and comparing them and integrating them with the organization's experience.

The introjective type of organization is one specific form of organizational introjection. Other examples of organizations in an introjective mode are:

—A traditional family-owned business has been built according to a set of management practices that no longer are relevant to its present reality. The organization is dysfunctioning and many members of management and long-time employees are unhappy and frustrated, but have too much invested to leave the organization. Top management, which has introjected the set of management practices, entrenches itself in and enforces even further the outdated, irrelevant management system.

—A revolutionary antiestablishment social movement has introjected a total ideology. All members are expected to embrace the belief system in its totality. Expression of reservations and doubts is regarded as betrayal, treason, and renegadism.

—A hospital that trains new doctors is caught in the polarized conflict of two introjected views of the hospital's mission. Those professionally socialized, with an emphasis on the importance of basic research in medicine and a Nobel prize as the ultimate aim, see the hospital as a place of study. Those who have been encouraged to see themselves as helpers of the sick and enemies of pain see the hospital's mission in the community. The introjected polarized views penalize the hospital's development.

PROJECTION

Projection in Gestalt Therapy

"A projection is a trait, attitude, feeling, or a bit of behavior which actually belongs to your own personality but is not experienced as such; instead, it is attributed to objects and persons in the environment and then experienced as directed toward you by them instead of the other way around" (Perls et al., 1951, p. 211)

Perls and colleagues write that projection is the tendency to make the environment responsible for what is in the self. People develop assumptions based on their fantasies, and do not recognize that they themselves have created these assumptions. People throw on the environment parts of themselves that they cannot accept. They project outside their boundary aspects of their personality with which they refuse to identify.

The projections often are the result of introjects. As the Polsters (1973) write: "The projector is an individual who cannot accept his feelings and actions because he 'shouldn't' feel or act that way. The 'shouldn't,' of course, is the basic introject which labels his feeling or action unpalatable" (pp. 78–79).

When one becomes aware one has feelings, needs, and beliefs that one "should not" have, one resolves the dilemma by disowning them and projecting them on others.

Not all projection is neurotic. Planning is a healthy form of projection into the future. Planners who are aware of what they are doing put themselves into the future situation, project themselves into another environment, and analyze what all this entails. Projection, like the other boundary mechanisms, "constitutes neurosis only when inappropriate and chronic" (Perls et al., 1951, p. 212). Projecting oneself into another person, in the sense of empathy, understanding, and feeling, can be healthy and functional when there is awareness of boundaries and appreciation of differences. It can be pathologic and dysfunctional if overdone or incessant.

Healthy mental metabolism requires expression, not projection. The gestalt (configuration) needs to be closed by satisfying the need or feeling in appropriate action on the environment. The projector does not do this but instead attributes the feeling or need to others. Aggression is not expressed but others are seen as being aggressive toward the projector—the gestalt remains unclosed.

Paranoids rationalize their projections. Not accepting their own aggression toward others, they project these feelings on individuals or groups in the environment. They see others as being aggressive towards them, persecuting them, attempting to cause them harm, and even wishing to destroy them. Paranoids rationalize this situation by fantasizing various kinds of explanations for this mythical situation created by their own imagination. Others may envy them, or wish to have their possessions, or with to replace them, and so on.

Projection is a boundary disturbance. In Perls' (1969) words:

The projecting person cannot satisfactorily distinguish between the inside and outside world. He visualizes in the outside world those parts of his personality with which he refuses to identify himself. The organism experiences them as being outside the Ego boundaries and reacts accordingly with aggression. (p. 157)

It is as if the projector has moved his/her boundary out into the environment. The boundaries are unclear to the projector, who sees as being beyond these boundaries parts of the self that belong inside them. Most projection is outward on someone in the environment. Nevertheless, it may take various forms. Projection may take place within the person by projecting on parts of the self. The person can project his/her aggression on the conscience. Not wishing to take responsibility for a feeling, a person can attribute that feeling to a part of the self.

Another form of projection may take the projection onto the past. Perls (1969) writes: "A person can also project into the past by invoking memory" (p. 158). Instead of expressing an emotion, the person produces a memory.

Projection in Organizations

Perls recognizes that projection is not a mechanism which is confined only to the level of the individual. Perls wrote about groups of people projecting in the form of racial and class prejudice. In an inventory of scientific findings, Berelson and Steiner (1964) bring findings from a variety of studies that support Perls' propositions. Projection of unacceptable and unrecognized aspects of the personality play a major role in racial and class prejudice. Projection in the form of prejudice and scapegoating is not confined to the level of the individual. Parsons, as cited by Coser (1965), writes:

Prejudice is not only directed by individuals against scapegoat groups, but can readily become a phenomenon of group attitude, that is, become partly institutionalized. Then instead of being disapproved by member's of one's own group for being prejudiced one is punished for not being prejudiced. (p. 108)

Perls also writes about projection beyond the organizational level. He refers to nations projecting aggression on other nations. "The frightfulness of the aggressive nation is increased by the same amount of aggression which the victim projects into them" (Perls, 1969, p. 158). Various scholars (Coser, 1956; Herman & Korenich, 1977; Alevras & Wepman, 1980; De Board, 1978; Kets de Vries &

Miller, 1982) deal with different manifestations of projection on the organizational level.

A special case is illustrated by Poland's hierarchy blaming Solidarity's 16 months of influence for the deteriorating economy, ignoring the past and present party control.

Dimensions of Projection

Different types of projection, in organizations, may be differentiated. The dimensions that may be used to differentiate the types of projection are:

1. The projector—who does the projecting.
2. The projectee—who is being projected on.

The projector may be the total organization or part of it, such as a department or departments or management. The projectee may be the total organization, part of it, or part of the environment. Another dimension that contributes to classification is what is being projected, such as, guilt, aggression, or omnipotence.

In using the first two dimensions, the following types of projection can be discerned.

1. The organization projecting on part of the environment.
2. The organization projecting on part of itself.
3. An organizational subsystem projecting on another subsystem.
4. An organizational subsystem projecting on the organization as a whole.

The organization projecting on part of the environment. An organization may project its frustration or aggression on other organizations in its environment or on its suprasystem, that is, the organization or society of which it is a subsystem. An organization displaying neurotic organizational behavior may feel angry and aggressive because of constant failures in goal attainment and members' need satisfaction. Instead of taking responsibility for itself and its condition and working to change them, the organization shifts the responsibility to others. It sees other organizations or its suprasystem as responsible for its condition by discriminating against it. It sees the suprasystem as being aggressive toward it.

The furniture plant produced a number of good products and had a steady market. Some years before it had moved to a new modern building that was not large enough to accommodate all the production departments. The department that produced TV tables was left behind in part of the dilapidated old building that was about half a mile from the air-conditioned, modern, comfortable new building.

We were called in to do an assessment to initiate a sociotechnical development project in the plant. One of our first steps was to interview people from management and the various departments.

As a whole work morale in the production departments was not high, but the TV table department was something special. In this department people grumbled about everything. They disliked their work, they were dissatisfied with how the department was managed, and they envied all the other departments for their superior working conditions. There was a lot of in-fighting and intrigue going on, and whoever could wangle it managed to leave the department and move to another. Those who remained projected all their frustration and anger on plant management. Plant management was seen as the cause of all their troubles: "It was not by chance they left us here—they are settling an old debt with us." "They want to close us down but are afraid to do so." "They have singled us out to make life difficult for us." "Those bastards with the air-conditioning want to screw us up."

A 40-year-old industry was in the throes of a severe crisis after years of failure after failure. Instead of assuming responsibility for its condition, the organization blamed everything on the corporation of which it was a subsidiary. It projected its own aggression on the corporation. Common expressions used in the organization were: "They have not helped us." "They have discriminated against us." "They would be glad if we ceased functioning." "They want to get rid of us."

The projectee need not be a social system; it may also be a human artifact, or a natural system, or even a supranatural being. Perls (1969) writes about how "more and more activities are projected on to, and invested in, the machine which thus assumes a power and life of its own" (p. 121).

The term "anthropomorphic" means ascribing human form to beings or things not human. The projectee can be part of nature. A failing agricultural community, disrupted for years by internal schisms, blames its fractionated lands for all its woes. Ignoring the economic success of neighboring communities, who, with the same kind of land, have thrived and prospered, the community projects all its frustration, despair and anger on those "broken up, fractionated plots of land or poor quality."

The projectee may be a supranatural being. Perls (1969) writes about religious groups projecting omnipotence on their deity. Anthropology and the comparative study of religion bear witness to the numerous cultures, tribes, and religions that have projected their own particular cultural qualities onto their deities.

Kets de Vries and Miller (1982) describe the paranoid style of neurotic organizations. Some of their descriptions seem close to that of organizations that are projecting. They write about "distortions of reality due to a preoccupation with confirmation of suspicions" (p. 8a). In this organization's characteristics, they include "readiness to counter perceived threats; over concern with hidden motives and special meanings" (p. 8).

The organization projecting on part of itself. A common form of the organization projecting on part of itself is scapegoating.

Scapegoating can take two forms. The first form has been noted in that of an outside enemy or an outside organization or group. The second form is toward an internal group: Coser (1956) sees the "evocation of an outer enemy or the invention of such an enemy" as a mechanism that "strengthens social cohesion that is threatened from within." He continues, "Similarly, search for or invention of a dissenter within may serve to maintain a structure which is threatened from the outside" (p. 110). The dissenter (or dissenter group) is treated with hostility and aggression. The same hostility and aggression the organization feels toward the outside threat are projected onto the internal scapegoat, which is seen as hostile and aggressive to the organization.

The projectee in organizations seems often to belong to one of two kinds of groups: The underpowerful and the powerful. Organizational hostility and aggressiveness are often projected either on management (the powerful) or on a deviant marginal subgroup of different race, age, or sex (the underpowerful).

Coser points out that often organizations that have suffered defeat search for internal scapegoats who "through their sacrifice, cleanse the group of its own failings." Coser also notes that this tendency to search for internal objects for projecting aggression seems to occur mainly in societies where the rigidity of structure inhibits realistic conflict.

Coser's descriptions are worded on the social level. Translating them to the individual level gives the basic propositions about projection developed by Perls. An individual who feels aggression, hostility, or other emotions that he cannot accept may deal with them by projecting them on others. Likewise an individual who feels frustrated and blaming may not take responsibility for these feelings but instead project them on part of the self.

The ultimate current projection in an organization is to blame what goes wrong on "computer error."

An organizational subsystem projecting on another subsystem. Ogre building is the name Herman and Korenich (1977) give to a form of projection commonly found in organizations. The "ogre" generally is management, of which some of the organization members may build fearsome, scary images. "They are compounded of some degree of organizational reality, plus our own projections and predictions of dire consequences" (Herman & Korenich, 1977).

Scapegoating can be the result of one organizational subsystem projecting its fears, frustration, and aggression on another group. When their cars were not selling, the sales force of a large automobile agency blamed the service department for having developed an antagonistic reputation among the customers. Actually the new cars were overpriced and had a poor safety record. Newcomers to organizations are prone to being the projectees of frustrated groups of organizational members. The marginal, unprotected position of the newcomer makes the person easy prey to the frustration and aggression of others. It is legend, now, how every new wave of immigrants to the United States became the object of old-timer aggression by being seen as aggressive, pushy, or whatever trait the projecting group disliked in itself. A similar phenomenon is found in organizations; when the organization is going through difficult times, the group of latest newcomers becomes the receptor of organizational anger and dissatisfaction and is accorded characteristics the organization wants to disown.

An organizational subsystem projecting on the organization as a whole. Perls and colleagues (1951) have drawn attention to the power members and groups in organizations project on the organization: "Institutions that take over our functions, that are to 'blame' because they 'control' us, and that wreak on us the hostility which we carefully refrain from wielding ourselves—as if men did not themselves lend to institutions whatever force they have."

This point is worth noting as it clarifies an important aspect of organizational life. Organizations draw power, control, and force from the power, control, and force projected on them by their members. Were the members not to project these on the organization, it is questionable how much power the organization would, indeed, possess. In ogre building the scary qualities of power are projected on management only. In this case power, control, and force are projected by parts of the organization on the organization as a whole. Coser (1956) describes the extremes this can reach in revolutionary political organizations.

Alevras and Wepman (1980) describe projection in terms of part of an organization projecting on the rest of the organization. They give as an example of projection a department in an organization, which sees others as destructively competitive, in order to justify its rejecting or sabotaging proposals that come to it from outside.

CONFLUENCE

Confluence in Gestalt Therapy

> "When the individual feels no boundary at all between himself and his environment, when he feels that he and it are one, he is in confluence with it. Parts and whole are indistinguishable from one another. . . . The person in whom confluence is a pathological state cannot tell what he is and he cannot tell what other people are. He does not know where he leaves off and others begin" (Perls, 1980, p. 38).

Perls sees confluence as a dysfunctional boundary mechanism by which the individual loses the ability to differentiate between the self and what is not the self. Ritual may produce a feeling of exaltation when the self–other boundary may be temporarily dissolved, as the individual identifies closely with the group or the organization. However, when "this sense of utter identification is chronic and the individual is unable to see the difference between himself and the rest of the world, he is psychologically sick" (Perls, 1980, p. 38).

A person in confluence does not distinguish between him/herself and the group or organization. The person is in a state of confusion, unable to differentiate between what he/she really needs and wants in contrast to the needs and demands of the groups and organizations to which the person belongs.

Perls and colleagues (1951) and Polster and Polster (1973) stress the unhealthiness of relations between people that are based on confluence. Healthy relationships demand self-differentiation. Polster and Polster suggest as antidotes to confluence "contact, differ-entiation and articulation." Herman and Korenich (1977), Perls and colleagues (1951), and Polster and Polster (1973) describe social systems, such as families and organizations, as unhealthy when they are based on confluence without self-differentiation.

Perls (1980) writes about confluence with another meaning—confluence between an individual's parts.

The man who is in pathological confluence ties up his needs, his emotions, and his activities in one bundle of utter confusion until he is no longer aware of what he wants to do and how he prevents himself from doing it. (p. 39)
If our component parts . . . are brought together and kept together in pathological confluence, neither will be able to perform its own job properly. (pp. 38–39)

In its first form, confluence was described as lack of differen-tiation between the individual and the environment. In this second form, confluence is the lack of differentiation between the parts of an individual. In system terms the first form of confluence was between a system and its suprasystem; in the second case, the confluence is between subsystems within a system.

This second, intrasystem form of confluence is conceptualized as demanding likeness and conformity and refusing to tolerate any difference between parts within a system. As Perls points out, "as long as differences are not appreciated, they are likely to be per-secuted." Perls gives as an example children—who are not con-fluent and do not identify with their parents' demands—meeting with rejection and alienation.

There can also exist a more pervasive confluence, an intrasys-tem confluence combined with a confluence between an individual and the environment.

Polster and Polster (1973) note that frequent feelings of guilt or resentment are clues to disturbed confluent relations. A party to a confluent relationship who senses that he/she has violated the confluence may try to make up for this and will experience feelings of guilt. The other person in the relationship will probably feel resentment for being transgressed against.

Confluence at the Organizational Level

At the organizational level, Perls (1980), Herman and Korenich (1977), and Alevras and Wepman (1980) have dealt with the phenomenon of confluence, using the concept "confluence" itself. Other organizational theoreticians have dealt with confluence in organizations, but they have done this under the guise of other names. Alderfer (1981) uses the term "underboundedness," Coser (1956) uses the term "identification," and so forth.

Using the dimensions of who is confluent with whom, it is possible to differentiate a number of distinct types of confluence in organizations. These types of confluence are symptomatic of neurotic organizational behavior:

1. Confluence between the organization and its environment.
2. An organization treating its parts in a confluence mode.
3. Part of an organization being confluent with the organization.

Confluence between the organization and its environment. This will refer to the situation where an organization's boundaries are open to a degree that creates difficulties in differentiating between the organization and between the environment. This openness refers to a variety of forms of matter, energy, and information such as members, ideas, customs, behavior patterns, norms, and rates of interaction. The rates of interaction between members in an organization are generally higher than their rates of interaction with people who do not belong to the organization (Berelson & Steiner, 1964; Miller, 1978). In an organization in confluence with its environment, this rule may not hold true; members may be interacting with outsiders no less than they interact with other organization members.

Boundaries differentiate a system from other entities. Bowler (1981) writes that if an entity is recognizable as such, it must be describable in such a way as to differentiate it from other entities and from the system in which it participates. If there were no boundaries, there would be no differentiation, only random homogeneity. From a general systems viewpoint, Bowler (1981) points out that:

Every system has a set of boundaries that indicate some degree of differentiation between what is included and what is excluded from the system. Every system is selective among possible relations and with reference to transmission across its boundaries. (p. 220)

In confluence these functions of the boundaries of the organization are not being filled.

Alderfer (1981) uses the term "underboundedness" instead of confluence. He points out that there is a curvilinear relationship between permeability in an organization's boundaries and the organization's vitality, that is, its tendency toward survival and growth. An overbounded boundary closes the organization to essential inputs from its environment. An underbounded (confluent) boundary endangers the organization with inputs that are unfiltered and may cause harm. The optimal state of an organization's boundary lies somewhere midway between the underbounded confluence and overbounded closeness. Selective boundaries are necessary for the survival of the organization.

Confluence is more predominant in the later stages of neurotic organizational behavior. In the earlier stages of crisis, the organization generally tends to tighten its boundaries and not to open them. Members close their ranks and tend to barricade themselves and the organization's boundaries against what they generally see as outside dangers. At a certain stage declining organizations pass this point and move over to the other extreme of confluent, underbounded boundaries. When this occurs organizational membership and identity may lose their meaning. Norms of behavior from the environment may flow freely into the organization without passing through any boundary filtering process. Members leave the organization without feeling they have done anything special or lost anything. The boundaries between the organization and its environment become fuzzy and difficult to locate and define. The case study of Whitestone exemplifies the process of passage from introjection to confluence.

Whitestone was a cooperative community that had existed for about 50 years passing from one crisis to another. During its earlier years, the community had charismatic leadership that identified itself completely with the organization and its mission. As time went by, the original leadership was replaced by a management-minded authoritarian type of leadership. Members developed new needs in tune with the more consumer type of society developing around them. Tension began to develop between the more production-oriented leadership and the consumer-type orientation of many of the members. The leadership reacted to the situation by becoming more and more rigid, and trying to close the community's boundaries both to new ideas and to new members. In Alderfer's terms the organization became overbounded. The frustration of people's needs led to some leaving and others becoming more frustrated. The community began to display more and more symptoms of neurotic organizational behavior.

On the one hand, there was a strong introjective tendency. Most of the old-timers clung to the basic ideology they had swallowed whole, not willing to budge an inch and to change and adapt to all that was taking place. Some of the younger generation began to give the community an introjective character. They developed a tendency to flit from one "ism" to another. The young people of Whitestone became forerunners of every new "ism," whether in its encounter group manifestation or its folk music cult.

Leadership reacted by becoming more and more rigid, closing the organization to everything from outside, including new professional know-how and technology. This resulted in economic and technical backwardness and increasing economic and financial difficulties. Crisis followed crisis; finally leadership resigned and new people took over as the dominant coalition. The community, as if in reaction to its former way, began to move into a confluent mode of behavior. Boundaries were completely broken open; it began to be difficult to distinguish where the organization ended and where the environment began. People joined and were accepted as members without any filtering process. Norms from the surrounding society and even deviant subcultures infiltrated the community's boundary with no attempt to resist or filter out what might be harmful.

Everything now was possible; everything was accepted. The organization became confluent with its surrounding culture, without the ability to differentiate itself and maintain its boundaries.

This condition continued for some time, resulting in assimilative and disintegrative processes, in social, cultural, and economic disruption. Finally organizational development consultants from outside the community were requested to come in and help it deal with its problems.

An organization treating its parts in a confluent mode. In this form of confluence, internal boundaries are broken and dissolved and all parts, with different functions, are treated as if they were the same. Rigid rules and procedures are enforced with complete disregard of individual differences; conformity and internal confluence are demanded. This type of confluence is similar to the second mode of confluence that Perls described in which people bring together their component parts in pathological confluence.

The manager who treats all subordinates the same regardless of their different skills, tasks, working styles, and so on, makes a confluent mass out of all personnel, and thus denies the possibility of knowing what they can do individually. Contact opportunities from which this could be found out are minimized. The CEO who views the organization as a confluent whole in terms of certain categories, such as internal resource support, and rationalizes this as being "fair," will not appreciate differences and similarities among subsystems—data that are essential for efficient management.

Alevras and Wepman (1980) see confluence emerging as a corporate image; a prescription that imposes a firm, narrow range of behavior to which employees are expected to conform.

In the fall of 1973 I dropped out of high school and answered an ad in the newspaper by a bed factory. I had previously worked at some summer jobs, but this was my first fling at a "career-type" job. I was prepared to work 9–5 all winter if need be to finance weekend escapades and summer motorcycle junkets.

I drove to work that first day full of anticipation and apprehension. I was surprised to see dozens of people outside the business establishment carrying placards and signs. A welcoming committee? Unfortunately not. My car was soon being pelted by rocks and kicked by steel-toed work-boots—decidedly unpleasant. I had been hired as a scab, a union breaker, although I was too naive to make sense of it.

My job consisted of nailing spring assemblies into previously assembled wooden frames, and stapling covering cloth and edging around the perimeter. Exciting work. I worked with a fellow named Romeo, a family man who had worked there for eight months and was earning 20 cents over the minimum wage. Lots of potential for advancement.

Romeo had told me that the average output for our section was 55 box springs a day. As a competitive and reasonably creative person, I was sure that with a little redesigning of our system of work, we could do much better. Sure enough, by the end of the day, we had done over 75 box springs, and we could have done even better if we had not exhausted our supply of frames 20 minutes before shift's end. Tired but content, I sat down on a forklift to savor a cigarette and a job well done, while Romeo puttered around restacking our finished product.

It turned out Romeo had the right idea—the shift foreman walked by and gave me royal hell for sitting on the job. My explanation fell on deaf ears, while Romeo gave me the glance of the wise old pro. I know now how he had survived all of eight months. While leaving at the end of the shift, I was met by sour glances from the frame makers—I had probably been complicating their lives as well. As I drove away through another hail of abuse from the placard wavers, I realized that I had learned a great lesson—I was not a bed maker. I phoned in my resignation the next day.

This example illustrates an aspect of confluence, specifically, an organization treating its parts in a confluent mode. Rigid rules and procedures were enforced with complete disregard of internal differences; conformity to a firm, narrow range of behavior and inner confluence were demanded. Strict adherence to regulations induced timidity, conservatism, and technicism, where keeping to the rules, which developed as a means, became an end in itself.—*R. Kroeker*

A number of systems theorists have stressed this problem as a basic system issue. Bowler (1981) generalizes the problem and sees it as *an inevitable stress found in all systems between system dominance and subsystem autonomy.* As each subsystem is also a system that attempts to maintain its own integrity, it is inevitable that there will be stress between it and its suprasystem, which is attempting to maintain its own integrity. Bowler sees the internal stresses between system dominance and subsystem autonomy as a universal polarity.

Specialization is a development of uniqueness among subsystems that makes possible levels of complex systems that would not otherwise be reached. Bowler (1981) summarizes it this way:

The larger and more complex a system becomes, the greater the degree of system ordered behavior required of the lower levels of the hierarchy. In other words, the larger and more complex the system, the less deviation in behavior can be tolerated in those functions that are vital to the survival of the system. (p. 43)

March and Simon (1958) point out that a source of mounting tension in organizations lies in the conflict between the organization's tendency to constrain variety by rules, regulations, and procedures and the ever-increasing variety of the organization's components that have difficulty fitting into the slots of these rules and procedures. The components increase both because complexity leads to specialization of subsystems such as departments and teams, and because of the increasing individualization and variety among people in modern society. A simple peasant society needs fewer rules and has less functional and human variety than a modern society. March and Simon suggest that this conflict is inherent in modern organizations. When the organization presses for more and more conformity among people who are increasingly different, problems begin to arise.

Summarizing these theories leads to the proposition that, within our present paradigm, some measure of organizational neurosis seems inevitable in complex modern organizations. Increasing internal variety seems to clash with an organizational tendency to constrain variety by rationalization, in the form of norms, regulations, rules, and procedures. In other words, as organizations grow, modernize, and develop, they become more complex and differentiated, which creates greater variety in the organization's components. This same process leads to increasing interdependence between these parts, pushing the organization into demanding more internal confluence in order to ensure system dominance. One author of this work became aware of this problem while giving training courses for top executives of some organizations.

The executives were continually complaining about ever-increasing pressures that resulted in personal stress. The source of the stress was a dilemma they did not know how to handle. They felt caught between two possibilities of action, both of which they regarded as negative and dysfunctional. They either had to try to enforce more and more new regulations and procedures on organization members who were less and less willing to abide by them, or to make more and more decisions for which they had no criteria, and which were overburdening them.

This situation had grown out of a number of trends:

1. Modernization, growth, and complexity were leading to ever-increasing functional and individual differentiation among organization members.

2. With increasing differentiation and greater affluence came a growing variety of individual needs, wants, and requests of the organization.

3. Initial attempts to deal with this were to create codes of norms, rules, and regulations, thus pressing for rationalization.

4. These rationalization attempts were foundering on the difficulty to attempt to codify the increasing variety and differences.

5. Members were becoming less and less willing to accept and abide by decisions they felt did not recognize their particular individual circumstances, and were demanding individual hearings not guided by generalized codes.

6. The result was a strain on the decision makers. They were having to treat each case as an individual case, without clear-cut criteria by which to make their decisions. They were also aware that their decision could open the door to a flow of requests of a similar nature, because of increasing interdependence among members.

7. Feeling stress from growing pressure and sensing that "matters were getting out of hand," the executives were again demanding more rules, regulations, and codes to cut down their backload in decision making and to attempt to ensure system dominance out of a belief that they alone could make all decisions.

They exacerbated, in a feedback loop, increased uniformity of norms, rules, and regularities, and thus increased confluence between themselves and other personnel and among all personnel.

Part of the organization being confluent with the organization. A form of confluence in which part of the organization is in confluence with the organization has been dealt with both by Parsons and by Coser. Parsons (1951) uses the term "representative" role. A representative role is one in which an individual acts in the name of a collectivity to which that individual belongs. Parsons restricts his use of the term to leadership roles. Coser (1956) extends the term to the role of any member "who has outside the group relations in which he acts and is expected to act as its representative" (p. 113). Those who fill this role see themselves as the embodiment of the organization's purposes. They make the group part of themselves and make themselves more a part of the group by giving up personal needs for the group's sake (Coser, 1956).

The member who for the sake of the group relinquishes some of his immediate interest feels that he has invested in it; he has projected upon it part or all of his personality. Through introjection of the group's purpose and power through projection of his own self into the group, the group has become but an extension of his own personality. Under these conditions, threats to the group touch the very core of his personality. (p. 119)

Although Coser describes processes of introjection and projection, the state finally depicted is one of confluence, with no border between the individual and the group or organization.

Coser points out that individuals who fill representational roles will be all the more ready to respond to impersonal appeals. When they are fighting, not for themselves, but for the ideals of the group they represent, they are likely to be more radical and merciless than were they to have fought for personal reasons.

Coser's insights (developed from Simmel) can be extended to the general case of a group or a team identifying itself completely with the organization to which it belongs. When this identification becomes symbiotic in the sense of having no boundaries, it is possible to see this as a confluent relationship.

This form of confluent relationship can often be detected between an organization's leadership and the organization. The boundaries are dissolved and the leadership sees itself and the organization as one. The executives believe that putting in overtime makes them important, and that to take work home makes them even more important, regardless of whether there is a real need to do either, but under the fantasy that they and the organization are one and that more is always better. There can be confluence between an individual and the organization to the point where the organization can do no wrong, and the capacity for judgment, skepticism, and criticism can be lost. Leaders of subsystems can become so confluent with the organization that (1) they do not take care of their subsystems when appropriate, or (2) they think they are protecting the organization by keeping all information and data to themselves leaving others in the dark and unable to act except through the leaders. In this situation it is possible to detect various manifestations that resemble Coser's descriptions. Leadership is able to be more radical and merciless toward organization members and groups than if it were interacting with them on a personal basis. This occurs especially in political, religious, and ideological organizations.

A woman runs a nursing credential program within a large university. She is not the head of the program itself on an official level, but is the staff administrator of one basic credential program and three nursing specialist credential programs. In her position she is responsible for implementing the credential requirements for the state credentialing agency. She attends meetings two or three times a year, receives information updates by mail, and interprets and applies the information for and to students, faculty, and the programs. She is the liaison between the university and the state nursing professional credential commission.

In her role as the staff supervisor for the basic credential program, she leads and directs the staff in assisting students entering the program and in applying to the state for their nursing credentials. This position is an important one, and touches the personal and professional lives of many individuals—students, staff, and faculty. She takes her job very seriously, and is extremely committed to it. She is so committed and caring, in fact, that she has lost her personal and professional boundary and has entered into a state of confluence. She works not only a normal 40-hour work week, but weekends and evenings as well. Her overcaring and confusion between herself and her environment have led her into using questionable judgment at times. She sees herself as "The University" and is very concerned about representing it in a complimentary manner. She has lost sight of her own humanness and individualization. She has lost touch with receiving feedback and seeing reality. For example, rather than state that she has too much work to do, she does not ask for help and continues to wear herself out working evenings and weekends. As one with "The University," she wants to represent it as a strong, sensitive, and virile organization. What she actually does is represent it as an overworked, confused, and out-of-touch entity. Her effectiveness is lost in her lack of boundaries.

But not only does she see herself as "The University," she also sees herself as "The Nursing Professional Credential Program." She is the one who makes decisions and implements policy, not the actual head of the program. This seems to work well for the leader on the surface level as he is certainly getting his money's worth, experiences less stress, and is able to work a shorter week knowing that she will take care of whatever arises. Unfortunately her overextension into becoming the programs themselves adds to the leader's feelings of impotence while it increases her power and responsibility. What neither of them is aware of are the image and reputation of the program. Her overextended boundary displays itself in questionable communication and frustration by many of the students as well as concern by the teaching hospitals. Her confluence has removed the reality filtering of input and feedback and displays a rather neurotic image of the program rather than a strong and effective one.

In addition to being "The University" and "The Nursing Program," she also sees herself as "The State Professional Nursing Credential Commission." As she is the only one on campus to receive information from the commission, and is responsible for conveying its messages, she has lost touch with reality and the environment. While her intentions are excellent, her neurotic organizational behavior illustrates confluence and a lack of boundary definition. This in turn severely alters her effectiveness and the image she exemplifies of her subsystem and the organization. The organization's lack of awareness of this confluence has weakened that part of the system.

It seems probable that some measure of identification between leadership and the organization is necessary for leadership to devote its energies to serving the organization. Problems arise, however, when this identification becomes confluent. Confluence between leadership and organization can lead to leadership disregarding information, reactions, and feedback from groups of members who see things differently. Another example of confluence can occur in a symbiotic relationship within the organization where individuals cannot separate themselves from one another. The symbiotic relationship could originally have occurred as a response to stress—"circling the wagons." However, symbiotic relationships themselves can create stress because they are antithetical to individuality and autonomy. There are individuals who would feel stress from having to sacrifice their uniqueness to the larger symbiotic entity. Confluence may also allow leadership to hurt parts of the organization more easily, as this is seen as being done for the good of the total organization. Clinical observation of many organizations results in to the proposition that confluence between leadership and the organization leads to organizational dysfunctioning. This proposition, however, will need to be substantiated by methodological scientific evidence.

RETROFLECTION

> "The retroflector does to himself what he would like to do to others. . . . He stops directing his energies outward in attempts to manipulate and bring about changes in the environment that will satisfy his needs; instead he redirects his activity inwards and substitutes himself in place of the environment as the target for behavior" (Perls, 1980, p. 40).
>
> "Retroflection means that some function which originally is directed from the individual towards the world, changes its direction and is bent back toward the originator" (Perls, 1969, pp. 119–120).

Perls describes retroflection as one of the four dysfunctional boundary mechanisms commonly found in neurotic behavior.

A frustrated person feeling aggression toward others redirects the aggression inward, deriding and blaming him/herself. One who wishes to discount others discounts oneself. One who is unable to express love and nurturance to others expresses them toward the self. Energy that should have been channeled outward to affect or change the environment is redirected inward towards the self.

Retroflection in the form of blaming oneself needs to be distinguished from taking responsibility for oneself. People who take responsibility for themselves initiate action in the environment on the basis of their responsibility. Because they feel responsible, they are not passive. Retroflective persons may seem to be assuming responsibility as they blame themselves for their sorry plight. In effect they are evading responsibility and substituting the retroflective act of self-blame instead of effective action to bring about change. It is also possible to retroflect by insisting on doing something for yourself, no matter how badly, what someone else might do much better for you. One can become so defended or closed off that appropriate outside resources are ignored.

Retroflection on the Organizational Level

Perls himself raises the phenomenon of retroflection from the individual to the social level. He illustrates retroflection by a religion that channels inward aggression that should have been expressed outward (Perls, 1969).

The religious Jew does not blame Jehovah for any failure or misfortune. He does not tear out *His* hair, does not belabor *His* chest—he retroflects his annoyance, blames himself for every mishap, tears out his own hair, beats his own chest. (p. 120)

In this example Perls is not referring to a single individual, but to an entire collectivity of religious Jews.

What struck me most about the community was its inability to receive help. It has always been a loner. It had never been able to make demands or work on receiving the public funds that were coming to it. It suffered its problems and misfortunes in silence, never looking for outside assistance. When the electricity supply was causing problems, the bus service was bad, and roads were not being taken care of, the community never lifted a finger to deal with these. It seemed to be unable to make demands on outside bodies.

When problems worsened it rolled up like a hedgehog and closed itself to outside offers of help. A district commission assigned a number of social workers to help deal with the growing list of hard-core social cases multiplying in the community. But while there was much suffering and people in deep trouble were not receiving aid, the social workers sat idly without work. There seemed to be no one guiding or connecting those in need to those who wished to give.

Difficult times brought in their wake an intensification of problems. There was a rise in unemployment, crime, and the number of people leaving the area. But proposals for bringing in an outside expert community consultant were always rejected. The community seemed determined not to allow outsiders into the system. When I was finally consulted, I had the constant feeling they did not want to let me in.

The research and theoretical literature on organizations do not mention retroflection. It might be possible that retroflection is more common on the individual level than on the organizational level.

When an organization imagines that it alone can help itself, it can shut off external resources. The system becomes closed to consultation or other expertise at a time when it especially might need that fresh perspective or new information.

In another case a manager might blame him/herself for what is happening when actually the root of the trouble could be in some other part of the organization. The same might happen with a subsystem when the problem could have its genesis somewhere else inside or outside the organization.

Retroflection appears to be very close to the depressive style, in Kets de Vries and Miller's (1982) categorization of neurotic organizational styles. Some characteristics used by the researchers are:

Feelings of guilt, worthlessness, self-reproach, inadequacy, sense of help-lessness and hopelessness, of being at the mercy of events; diminished ability to think clearly, loss of interest and motivation; inability to ex-perience pleasure. (p. 8)

Retroflection may possibly be more predominant in the final stages of neurotic organizational behavior development. After phases of introjection, projection, and confluence, the organization may move into a retroflective, self-blaming, hopeless mode. This may possibly occur when neurotic organizational behavior has devel-oped into a declining organization. Retroflection may be more common when disintegrative processes are spreading.

DISOWNING

Disowning in Gestalt Therapy

Perls wrote a lot about disowning, but did not include it in his list of mechanisms. This was probably because he dealt with boundary mechanisms, whereas disowning is generally an intra-systemic mechanism. Enright (1980) adds disowning as an impor-tant fifth neurotic mechanism. Perls (1976) wrote: "If some of our thoughts, feelings are unacceptable to us we want to disown them. . . . There are many of these kinds of ways to remain intact, but always only at the cost of disowning many valuable parts of ourself" (p. 11).

Disowning may be another way of describing what happens in projection, retroflection, and introjection, but it can provide one more way in which to examine pathological organizational behavior. It could be a first step before other mechanisms centered around scotoma, blind spots, not putting out into the world, and other internal mechanisms.

Disowning is creating a fantasy that something that exists does not exist. If one finds parts of oneself, one's thoughts, or one's feelings objectionable, one may attempt to disown them.

The unwanted parts are ignored; they are pushed out of awareness and become blind spots, "holes," the person is unaware of and does not sense. Although out of awareness, these disowned parts continue expressing themselves through the person's feelings, behavior, and body. Many of the neurotic's difficulties are related to this unawareness, these blind spots. The missing parts are always there. They come out in projections, dreams, muscular tensions, facial and body movements, postures, and other expressions of the person beyond the range of conscious awareness. The disowned, unwanted disassociated parts of a person's personality continue to have an effect, although he/she attempts, in every possible way, to block their expression.

The person is unaware of the ways in which the expression of the alienated parts is being blocked. Postures, gestures, breathing patterns, voice, muscular tensions, and other ways of deadening expression of the unwanted parts are below the level of conscious awareness. The person cannot see how he/she is creating the difficulties by blocking and interrupting parts of the self.

The disowned part either is not recognized as existing, or it is alienated. When the part is not recognized, it is pushed below awareness and becomes a blind spot. Perls (1976) describes this as "creating a role."

Everyone of us has roles. Where something should be there is nothing. Many people have no soul. Others have no genitals. Some have no heart . . . others have no legs to stand on. Many people have no eyes. . . . Most of us have no ears. (p. 39)

When a disowned part is alienated, it is recognized as existing and it is within the person's awareness, but it is seen by the person as not being part of him/herself. The disowned part is seen as being beyond the person's boundaries, as not belonging to the person and not being his/her responsibility. The person can do this by projecting the unwanted part or feeling on others. If one cannot accept one's own aggression, one relieves oneself of responsibility for it by projecting it on others and seeing them as being aggressive. The person remains intact by alienating valuable parts of the self.

> A senior cost analyst is asked to train a new, junior analyst in the fundamentals of cost estimating. The senior analyst herself does not really understand many of the fundamentals but is generally able to do the work anyway. Years ago she learned by rote procedures, not theory.
>
> When the junior analyst has difficulty grasping the ideas because of the senior analyst's inability to communicate them clearly, the senior analyst believes that the junior analyst (a) isn't paying attention to what she has said, (b) is too new to really understand, and (c) has some sort of learning difficulty.
>
> To avoid acknowledging that she doesn't really understand that which she is trying to teach, she disowns her lack of understanding and ridicules the junior analyst whenever she brings up a question about something they have already covered, or patronizes her for being young and full of questions. To avoid being ridiculed and patronized, the junior analyst stops asking questions and pretends to understand, hoping that she will be able to pick up the concepts on her own.—*M. Lobnitz*

By disowning more and more parts of the self, the neurotic's boundaries shrink more and more. According to Perls (1976):

You do not allow yourself—or you are not allowed—to be totally yourself. So your ego boundary shrinks more and more. Your power, your energy becomes smaller and smaller. Your abilities to cope with the world become less and less. (p. 12)

Disowning in Organizations

In systems theory terms, disowning may be conceptualized as the control subsystem not perceiving, or not recognizing, or misinterpreting, or distorting information about subsystems, problem states, or stresses. Bowler (1951) observes that:

There may be stress on systems that are not perceived, not recognized, as stresses, and perhaps not perceived at all by the control subsystems of a system. The energy-matter information may be beyond the range of the system's receptors. It may be received as meaningless noise or distorted for assimilation into existing maps which interpret it as routine stress or as insignificant. (p. 194)

In his list of maladaptive destructive organizational activities, Levinson (1972) includes such items as "cutting of parts of the organization" and "cutting of established departments" (p. 542). He suggests that those things that an organization does not heed—if they are relevant to its survival—will be the source of its downfall. He notes that if an organization cannot recognize relevant stimuli, this suggests impairment or pathology in organizational functioning.

Organizations may fantasize that parts of themselves do not exist. An organization may disown, alienate, or disassociate itself from and repress parts of itself. The organization may see the part as a foreign body lodged in its midst, and decline taking any responsibility for it. The disowned target may be a category of members (e.g., women, older people, foreign workers), a department (e.g., research and development, auditing) or thoughts, feelings, and desires (e.g., people's need for meaning and significance in their work). In most history books, almost all written by men, it is as if women never existed. Until 20 years ago, the Laps in Norway were almost invisible. Top management believes only a small percentage of women need to help the family financially and thus disown the need for providing child care facilities. Statistics indicate that actually 60 percent of women need help.

The disowned part can be struck out of awareness in the sense of not being recognized as existing. For example, an organization can refuse to recognize that it has a group of people who are handicapped in some way and need special treatment and consideration. Kanter (1977) writes about how organizations disown women managers. Alternatively, the organization can be aware of the part but treat it as if it did not belong to the organization. It can be alienated as if it is a foreign body that has taken residence within and should be dispossessed. An organization can treat a foreign minority group in this way, as exemplified by the reaction of the Texas fishermen to the Vietnamese immigrant fishermen who settled in their midst. A demand made by members of the organization that the organization management does not want to recognize can receive a similar response. For example, those who demand better working conditions can be treated as a foreign body from outside, working within. The alienated disowned part can be treated with suspicion, dislike, and hostility, as the early unions were in this country.

When an organization disowns parts of itself, the boundaries of the organization shrink. The organization remains intact by disowning parts of itself, but shrinks in the process of doing so. The disowned parts are either nonexistent or are seen as foreign bodies not belonging to the organization, beyond its boundaries and not its responsibility.

The unwanted parts are ignored or alienated. If the disowned part is a category of people or a group or a team, its members may leave the organization. If they do not leave, they drift out of organizational consciousness and become blind spots of which the organization is unaware. Nevertheless, the disowned parts do continue to express themselves in various ways. Though they may be beyond the organization's awareness, they can be detected in the organization's emotional climate, level of energy, behavior, and structure.

An organization's difficulties may be related to its disowned parts, its blind spots. These missing parts are always there. They come out in organizational tension, projections, and the organizational climate. The disassociated, unwanted parts of the organization continue to affect the organization although it may attempt, in every possible way, to block their expression.

The organization is often unaware of the ways in which it blocks the expression of its alienated parts. The organization's delusions, neurotic mechanisms, and other ways of deadening emotional expression are often executed below the level of conscious awareness. The organization does not see how it creates its own difficulties by blocking expression of parts of itself. It is unaware of how it "interrupts" itself.

PROPOSITIONS AND DEFINITIONS

Systems theory, a variety of organizational theorists, and clinical observations lend a measure of support to the following statements.

★ The dysfunctional mechanisms of introjection, projection, confluence, and disowning can be discerned at the organizational level.
★ Within the pattern of organizational neurosis, the neurotic mechanisms serve dysfunctionally in being an outlet for pent-up

feelings, in relieving the organization of the responsibility of dealing with its problems, and in creating and maintaining the organization's delusions.

★ An organization introjects when it totally accepts information from the environment without the information going through a process of assimilation.

★ The contents of organizational introjection often are organizational procedures and standards, management theories, belief systems about how the organization works, ideologies, and total belief systems.

★ Forms of organizational introjection may be classified by who does the introjection: the total organization, leadership, or polarized groups.

★ An introjective type of organization has a tendency continually to accept and reject, one after another, encompassing belief systems.

★ An organization projects by attributing to others feelings and attitudes the organization wishes to disown.

★ Organizational projections may be classified by who is projecting on whom.

★ The following forms of projection may be discerned: the organization projecting on part of the environment; the organization projecting on part of itself; an organizational subsystem projecting on another subsystem; an organization subsystem projecting on the organization.

★ Confluence is the dissolving of boundaries between an organization and its environment or between the internal components of the organization.

★ The following forms of confluence can be found in organizations: confluence between the organization and its environment; an organization treating its parts in a confluent mode; part of the organization being confluent with the organization.

★ Within the present organizational paradigm in complex modern organizations, there seems to be an inevitable tension between increasing internal variety of components and the organization's tendency to constrain this variety by rationalization (confluence), in order to ensure system dominance. An imbalance in the favor of confluence may be one source of organizational neurosis.

The following proposition and definition have, at present, very little empirical, theoretical, or clinical support. These, however, may be found in the future.

★ An organization retroflecting is doing to itself what it would have wanted to but does not express to others.
★ Retroflection is a dysfunctional boundary mechanism found at the organizational level.

There is clinical support for the following.

★ An organization disowning part of itself is deluding itself that the part does not exist or does not belong to the organization.
★ An organization's disowning may take two forms:
    1. Not recognizing the existence of a part of the organization that does exist.
    2. Seeing the part as a foreign body the organization must get rid of.

CHAPTER 7

ORGANIZATIONAL DELUSIONS

OVERVIEW

The former chapter dealt with the neurotic mechanisms and their function in organizational neurosis.

This chapter deals with some of the effects and the forms the neurotic mechanisms take in organizational delusions. The organizations' delusions are seen to block it from taking action on feedback it is receiving. The organization appears to be getting more and more enmeshed in a vicious circle from which it will have difficulty freeing itself. In this situation the organization is dissipating much of its energy on its own delusions.

The organization delusions may take a variety of forms, of which a common one is an escape from or avoidance of present-day reality by living in the past or living for the future. Another common delusion is to replace a reality-based organizational self-image by a false image built on fantasy. Organizational "games" are also a commonly used way of replacing reality with a delusion.

FANTASY IN GESTALT THERAPY

Introjection, projection, confluence, retroflection, and disowning are specific mechanisms that may manifest themselves in various combinations and in different forms in neurotic behavior. Perls (1976) called these forms "the intermediate zone of fantasy." He wrote:

Awareness covers, so to speak, three layers or three zones: awareness of the self, awareness of the world and awareness of what's between—the intermediate zone of fantasy that prevents a person from being in touch with either himself or the world. (p. 53)

Living in a world of fantasy blocks awareness of self and of the environment, and consequently healthy functioning in the environment. As so much energy is spent living in the fantasy world, little is left to be in touch with inner and outer reality.

This loss of contact with our authentic self, and loss of contact with the world, is due to the intermediate zone ... there is a big area of fantasy activity that takes up so much of our excitement, of our life force that there is very little energy left to be in touch with reality. (p. 53)

Perls saw the aim of therapy as the emptying out of this intermediate zone of fantasy so that one could be more in touch with oneself and the world. The person who mistook fantasies for reality was a neurotic, or even a psychotic. If fantasy were integrated with the reality, it could be creative; it could be art. But confusing *maya* and reality, taking fantasy for reality, is neurotic.

Perls describes the person who is in the intermediate zone as being stuck. The person is phobic, is afraid to leave the fantasy to face the responsibility of dealing with problems. Facing up to reality is more frightening than the false security of the fantasy. The person does not realize that he/she has created a fantasy. To acknowledge this might necessitate functioning without it and dealing with reality as it is. The neurotic is afraid to do this, is afraid to take responsibility for him/herself.

THE ORGANIZATION'S DELUSIONS

Developing an analogy from the individual to the organizational level leads to the following propositions.

1. Organizational neurosis involves the organization or part of it living with a delusion that is a false mapping of reality.

2. The organizational delusion blocks taking effective action on incoming feedback.

3. The organization may get caught in a vicious circle and find it difficult to break out of it.

4. The organization expends so much energy on its delusion that little is left to be in touch with inner and outer reality and effective functioning.

1. *In organizational neurosis the organization lives with a delusion.*

Neurotic mechanisms may take various forms in the way they distort organizational reality. *An organizational delusion is the manifestation of various combinations of neurotic mechanisms in a particular organization.* One organization may be living in its past, another may be seeing itself as saving the world, a third may see itself as completely impotent. These are the delusions. A delusion is a distorted mapping of reality that is maintained despite continual disconfirmation.

Writing about organizational neurosis, Harvey and Albertson (1971) suggest that even when members are cognizant of the way they maintain dysfunctional norms, they are unable to take effective problem-solving action because of the "*rich and varied fantasies*" organization members may have about the consequences. Bradford and Harvey (1970) suggest that these fantasies have a mythlike quality that frequently is unrelated to reality. These authors also suggest that underlying the fantasies is a great deal of emotionality and concern that must be dealt with if organization members are clearly to differentiate fantasy and reality. Hedberg (1980) points out that several organization theorists use the term "myth" to denote organizational theories of action, most of which have some connection with reality although others are sheer fantasy.

From a general systems viewpoint, Berrien (1968) views the various fantasy-like uses of dysfunctional boundary mechanisms such as projection as defense mechanisms that permit the system to maintain its self concept; that is, they "permit the system of self-perceptions, beliefs, and evaluations to survive."

Organizational neurosis entails some form of fantasy life, and this means creating a false map of reality. Kets de Vries and Miller (1983) write:

The intrapsychic fantasies of key organization members are major determinants of their prevailing neurotic style. These in turn give rise to shared fantasies which permeate all levels of functioning, color organizational climate, and make for a dominant organizational adaptive style. (p. 4)

In a certain union, members must complete an arduous apprenticeship program—one in which it is extremely difficult to enroll. Candidates must be recommended by present members and be voted in as participants in the apprenticeship program. Once in the program itself, they must pass a variety of barriers, and may eventually, after four or five years, be admitted to the international brotherhood and the local organization as journeymen.

From the primary initiation ritual (apprenticeship school) to the monthly meetings and the selection process for acquiring jobs and being given the opportunity to become temporarily employed, the process and related experiences are not easy ones. The atmosphere and procedures are filled with an air of competition, unappreciation, and fantasy.

Neurotic organizational behavior is demonstrated through the "macho," "red-neck" communication patterns, the lack of trust and appreciation that underlies most interactions, and the low morale of some of the participants. While the opportunity to earn high wages surely exists, so does the opportunity to gain a jaundiced perspective of the self, the community, and the environment.

With the increase in the number of semiskilled laborers available, as well as of those willing to work for substantially lower wages, the chapter has faced a critical dilemma. As the amount of construction has decreased over the past few years, the competition, as well as the neurotic organizational behavior, has greatly increased.

Over the past few years, the organization has met its frustrations and inflexibilities with a collective flight into neurotic fantasy. Rather than observe, evaluate, and discuss the situation, it has continued its "more of the same" behavior. In a labor market with decreased building opportunities and high wages, it has not reacted to the diminished need by making itself more appealing, but rather has *increased* its hourly wage and decreased its work schedule (black Fridays, first and third Fridays off) and become more and more critical of competitive workers as well as its own. The behavior between both co-workers and management has been extremely cruel, hurtful, and juvenile.

Union members over the past few years have seen the "writing on the wall" in regard to increased competition, but have colluded in creating a make-believe world with expectations that concern for quality would prevail and that there was no need to rethink its position in the marketplace. The harder they pushed against the competitors, the harder they pushed against themselves with the delusion that with the increase of local oil development in this city and the expansion of a local military project, the situation would be saved and their methods and rationale vindicated.

As it finally (three–five years) became more and more obvious that the oil companies and the military base—the two last hopes—were planning to give most of their work to nonunion laborers, the union at last withdrew from its delusion and began to face reality. It held a crisis meeting to vote on a revised wage and policy plan. The result of the meeting was to lower wages so as to be more realistically competitive, to return the "black Fridays," and to lower its benefit package. Here is an example of an organization that, on both an international and local level, was demonstrating neurotic organizational behavior with collective flight into neurotic fantasy and was about to lose its elasticity and to increase and facilitate its decline.

Delusions are manifestations of neurotic mechanisms and develop out of them. As described in the preceding chapter, people in a team or organization, as a result of their interaction in particular circumstances, collude in developing neurotic mechanisms. The particular forms in which the mechanisms express themselves are the delusions. For example, a work team may project its anger on another department and develop a delusion that the department is harassing it because it envies and covets the special attention the team is getting from management. That is a delusion.

The company or department develops an imaginary edifice that replaces a picture of reality that could be agreed upon and testified to by independent witnesses from outside. The members of the organization seem to collude in maintaining their delusion, somewhat in the way the public in the famous fairy tale colluded in seeing the emperor's new clothes.

In the past few years, people have become very cognizant of the extreme forms organizational delusions can take. The case of the Jones sect in Guyana, which, inspired by an irrational fantasy, committed collective suicide, touched the imagination of many people and brought home in tragic form the power of organizational delusion.

On a completely different plane, though probably as well known, is the case of the American auto industry. This case shows that not only a single organization, but also a number of organizations, may share a common delusion. Without the delusion concept it is difficult to explain how Detroit continued for years to produce cars that belonged to a different era and were unsaleable in times of soaring gas prices. Argyris and Schon (1978) describe a large chemical company they call the Mercury Corporation. They detail how untested myths were widely diffused throughout the organization. Numerous case reports written by other organization theorists bring similar evidence as to organizations or their subunits creating delusions and their members colluding in maintaining them. These delusions may take a variety of forms, and further study and research will be needed to clarify why an enterprise or team develops its own particular delusion and not another. We have not studied or clarified this issue, and it remains to be dealt with by others.

2. *Ignoring feedback.*

False mappings of reality are generally first corrected by feedback mechanisms and later by breakdowns. If an organization continually takes action misguided by a false picture of what is happening inside it and around it, it will clash with the facts of life. Reality, so to speak, turns around and raps it on the knuckles. For example, an organization may see its environment as needing and wanting its product while this is not the case. The organization cannot keep on holding to this belief indefinitely. At some point feedback on the facts of life in the form of reduced sales or lower incomes forces itself on the organization. It is extremely rare for an organization to take action repeatedly on the basis of a false map of reality without, at some point, getting feedback that something is wrong. If the organization is insensitive to the feedback, is unaware of it, or ignores it, a crucial point is always reached where reality makes itself felt in the form of a crisis, a breakdown, a severe disruption of activity, and so forth. The organization that ignored signals that portended a decrease in sales at some point has a glut of warehoused products, trouble in obtaining credit, or some other disruption that cannot be ignored. This may occur more swiftly with organizations than with individuals who are less single purposed and can "get away" with neurotic behavior longer.

Steeltin was a small, family-owned company in the metal industry that had specialized in one particular product. Since the early 1920s, it had been functioning in its area of specialty with little competition and relative success. Expertise in the special patented production processes the plant had developed was transferred from one generation to another through a kind of mentor system.

With changing times and the development of new technologies and foreign competition, the plant began to face difficulties. The changing work force was also a source of troubles. The new generation was not as willing as its elders to persist for years in repetitive, tedious, uninspiring jobs. The more capable, innovative, and better educated members of the work force tended to leave the plant and seek their fortune in more inspiring careers that led to greater personal development. The company had no internal training program and did not send people to advance their technical or professional abilities in outside courses.

People who remained were dissatisfied and low in energy. Management seemed to feel threatened and on the defensive. Instead of bringing in outside expertise or sending its own people to learn the new technologies, the people at Steeltin developed a delusion that was phrased approximately like this: "There is nothing to learn from outside. We have nothing we can learn from others. People who go to learn outside just don't want to work." When one of the younger brothers in the family that owned the plant wanted to go away for a number of years to study the new advancements in the field, the family did all it could to forestall his efforts and pressure him not to go. When he did go—despite the pressure put on him—he was treated almost like a traitor.

Steeltin persisted for a number of years with its delusion until a financial crisis brought matters to a head.

Organizational neurosis unfortunately involves ignoring feedback and disruptions because the organization is living in a fantasy world. The organization does receive signals that something is wrong but persists in maintaining its delusion. The organization's members and management do know that something is wrong, that matters are not as they should be. The members do feel frustration and pain. Harvey and Albertson (1972) summarize their observations of organizations displaying neurotic behavior by noting that members of these organizations do feel frustration, pain, and loss of self-esteem. But knowing that something is wrong and feeling pain do not affect the organization in a way that will terminate the dysfunctional behavior. "Knowing" may not involve fully experiencing, and does not necessarily lead to taking appropriate action to remedy the situation.

But not only do the organization's members experience pain and frustration. In a declining organization, a false mapping of reality has to affect the organization's functioning, effectiveness, efficiency, and development in some form or another. Disruptions in organizational functioning and difficulty in organizational problem solving will be felt at some stage by both members and management. In describing experience with organizational neurosis in the training wing of Northfield Hospital, De Board (1978) writes:

He perceived this common enemy to be "the existence of neurosis as a disability of the community," and concluded that this neurosis should be displayed as a problem of the organization (a problem that was hindering the training wing from working effectively). (p. 36)

The declining organization is dysfunctioning but this will not necessarily lead to actions that will eradicate the source of the dysfunctions. In healthy organizational functioning, feedback, and at the worst breakdowns, will lead to the organization taking corrective action to eliminate the source of the disruptions. The declining organization will feel pain, will be aware of disruptions in its functioning, and seemingly may take action purported to deal with these. But the action taken will not change the situation because it is governed by the delusion and is usually more of the same neurotic behavior intensified. Harvey and Albertson (1972) write:

In analogous terms, it would be as if an outside observer viewed the following vignette involving twenty people from a neurotic organization:
    Observer (approaching a group sitting around a camp fire): How are things going?
    Organization members (who are holding their hands over an open fire): Awful. It's too hot. We are burning up. The pain is excruciating. Our hands are too close to the coals.
    Observer: What do you intend to do about it?
    Organization members: Move our hands closer to the fire, what else? (pp. 696–697)

The department's members persist in doing more of what they already do, as with neurotic individuals who, if they do anything at all, do more of what they are already doing to maintain their neuroses. The department knows that "something is out of order." Yet knowing this can have no effect in changing the delusion, removing it, or substituting for it a more factual picture of reality. It is precisely this *continual maintaining of a self-defeating behavior pattern based on delusion* that differentiates organizational neurosis from healthy organizational functioning. The organization does know that things are not as they should be, but is unable to change its own behavior in a way that will return it to healthy effective functioning.

    3. *The organization may get caught in a vicious circle.*

    Living in a world of fantasy partially blocks the organization's awareness of what is happening in the environment and what is happening in the organization internally. The delusion fantasy, image, myth, or face in which the organization enfolds itself comes between it and a reality-based picture of what is taking place.

    Information about what is happening is filtered out, distorted, ignored, given a different meaning, or in some other way blocked from organizational awareness. *Information is manipulated to conform with the organization's delusion.* If incoming information contradicts the organization's fantasy, a way must be found to reduce the dissonance. Under threat the perceptual field is narrowed. Alternatives actually available in reality are not differentiated. Berelson and Steiner (1964) summarize experiments that demonstrate how threatening or otherwise damaging materials may be less apt to reach consciousness than neutral materials. The information may be ignored, or it can be distorted to fit the fantasy, or its meaning and significance can be altered to fall in line with the organizational fantasy.

In a declining organization, it appears as if the organization is caught in a vicious circle. The organization has used the neurotic mechanisms to create a delusion that comes between it and its inner and outer reality. Living out of touch with reality has led to organizational dysfunctioning. The organization's feedback mechanisms are relaying messages reporting the dysfunctioning. The organization avoids taking effective action on these messages by ignoring them, or distorting them, or taking inappropriate action based on the delusion. This leads to further aggravation of the organization's dysfunctioning and increases the organization's fear of facing the facts of its deteriorating reality. The delusion, with all the pain and frustration it involves, is preferred by the organization to coming face to face with reality and taking responsibility for itself and its problems.

Detailing the cases of various corporations and companies and describing how they were out of touch with reality in the organization and reality outside the organization, Levinson and colleagues (1972) advise consultants that if they find an organization that has difficulties in perception both internally and externally, this should raise serious questions about the kinds and quality of assets available to the organization for its rejuvenation.

The vicious circle of organizational neurosis has many similarities to the state described by Perls as the *impasse*. Perls (1976) describes this state in terms of the person "being stuck and lost." The impasse is "marked by a phobic-attitude avoidance." "We stay immature, we go on manipulating the world, rather than to suffer the pains of growing up." "We would rather suffer being self-conscious, being looked upon, than to realize our blindness and get our eyes again."

The organization in the intermediate zone, caught in the vicious circle of neurotic organizational behavior, seems to be stuck and unable to break out of its predicament. The organization continues to manipulate the world through its fantasies rather than suffer the pains of growing up and taking responsibility for its predicament.

The organization is phobic—afraid to make the changes necessary to face inner and outer reality.

4. *The organization expends energy on its delusion.*

The organization that is living in the fantasy world will be dissipating a major part of its energy on its own maintenance, rather than channeling the energy to achieve its goals and outputs.

Organizations, like other open, living systems, need to use part of their energy input to "maintain themselves," to "repair breakdowns in their organization," for "their processes." In organizational theory concepts, this is called channeling energy into "task," or "output," or "goals," and into "maintenance," or "process," or "people."

> They had started out as a group of young doctors who had graduated together and decided to create a different kind of hospital. It would treat the whole person and not only an illness. People would be given individual personal attention. The quality of the treatment would not be affected by the patient's ability to pay. It would be on the cutting edge of medical science.
>
> Thirty years later reality proved to be different. Many other doctors who had joined the staff throughout the years had not had the founders' dreams. There were difficulties in finding and training nurses to suit the ideals of personal treatment. Serving the broad needs of the community made it difficult to be on the cutting edge. Financial considerations and hard-headed administrators also played their part.
>
> The hospital was like other hospitals—no better and no worse. People were treated as in other hospitals, and all that remained of the founders' dreams were the good intentions. Most of the founding group was still in the hospital; many were unhappy and frustrated. But it was difficult to swallow the hard facts of reality so they created their own illusionary reality. They put it this way: "Yes, we know that things are not as we would like them to be but see what we have achieved, look at the special relationship we have with our patients." "People are not numbers; we treat them as individual human beings." "You can always be sure to get the best treatment here." "We never turn anyone away."
>
> It did not matter that the facts of life were different; the delusion held. Reality is painful, so why face it.

Organizational functioning necessitates channeling the organization's energies in both directions, that is, to both "task" and "maintenance." The organization produces its outputs, achieves its goals, and at the same time maintains itself as an integrated system.

The organization needs to store a surplus of energy to be able to divert it where needed. Bowler (1981) points out that because of the constant demand on use of energy in control, maintenance, and production, there must be a constant backlog of net or stored energy. "This is essential because steady state systems are constantly subject to stresses requiring adequate supplies of energy in various places at various times" (p. 37).

As an organization dysfunctions more, it needs to divert more of its stored and excess energy into coping with the results of its own dysfunctioning. De Board (1978) illustrates how, at the group level, as the group uses more of its defense mechanisms, it has less available energy for its primary task. Levinson (1972) writes that all coping activities cost energy. As the organization's equilibrium becomes progressively more precarious, the organization will apply increasing energy to shore itself up. Organizational energy is dissipated in attempts to maintain integration and effective functioning under a set of conditions that makes this a difficult task. As the declining organization is functioning in a dysfunctional mode, it needs to invest more and more of its energy in maintaining its integration. In a systems model of organizations, Beer (1981) points out that if there is good fit between a system's components, relatively little energy need be spent in social maintenance activities. The more an organization functions integratively with components resonating to each other's needs and to those of the organization, and the organization resonating to the needs of its parts, the less the organization needs to invest in its own internal maintenance. The less the integration between the components, the less they resonate to each other and to the organization's goals, the more the organization needs to invest energy in its own maintenance, at the cost of reducing its ability to attain its objectives and goals. A simple example of this statement is that the more an organization invests energy in dealing with internal disputes and destructive conflicts, the less energy it has left to pursue its production goals.

Another common example of the dissipation of energy in declining organizations is the "fire-fighting" mode of management. Living in a fantasy world, and ignoring and distorting feedback, the organization attends to matters only when things break down. The organization is not proactive, and is not even reactive; it does not react to feedback but only to breakdowns. In ignoring earlier feedback warning signals, a factory does not attend to production difficulties until the production line literally stops functioning. When this happens the factory deals only with getting the line moving again, without attending to the underlying causes of the disruption. The organization is not consciously being tricky or evasive. Its avoidance of reality, although basically sincere, stems from a narrow range of alternatives. Management in this mode is one of "putting out fires." But before one fire has been put out, a number of new ones have started burning fiercely. The organization is in a never-ending rush to deal with one breakdown or crisis after another.

Levinson (1972) describes the "squeaking wheel" philosophy concerning incoming information, in which the organization gets information only when it has a problem. The organization living in the intermediate zone is beyond the "squeaking wheel" (which is more like feedback); it deals only with "broken wheels." The organization in the intermediate zone rushes from one crisis to another. Management is overwhelmed with putting out everyday fires: here a resignation, there a breakdown in a marketing outlet; here the departure from the organization of an essential specialist or manager, and there a disruption of relations between two departments. Before some kind of short-term solution can be found for one problem, three new problems have appeared over the horizon. The feedback of organizational dysfunctioning is not attended to until the deviation goes beyond the tolerance level of the organization. When it reaches this stage, it has become a breakdown or a crisis, and the organization is forced to pay attention to it. Levinson writes:

As the organization becomes increasingly disordered, it acts less successfully on its problems. It also achieves less returns for its investments in its coping activities.

The decreasing efficiency of these counterbalancing activities is characterized by increasing amounts of energy invested, increasingly less successful coping effects that provide fewer results and less gratification. (pp. 347–348)

Organizational energy is invested in maintaining a façade and bolstering an artificial "face." The organization is not being its real self. It is not investing its members' energy in organizational objectives and members' needs as they arise or change. The organization is dissipating energy trying to maintain what to the outside is a false reality, covering up and blocking from its own awareness countervailing facts and tendencies. The organization is stifling and deadening emotional and motivational energy that strives to give expression to affect and needs that are not included in the organization's fantasy image. All this serves to maintain the status quo of the intermediate-zone fantasies.

FORMS OF ORGANIZATIONAL DELUSION

Perls suggested that a person's fantasies may take a number of forms. Some of the forms he mentions are:

1. *Avoidances.* A person escapes the present that is causing pain by becoming submerged in the past or projecting into the future.
2. *Fantasied self-image.* A person creates a false image of self in order to avoid the pain of confronting the present real image.
3. *Playing games.* A person substitutes games for genuine contact with others such as "smile and smile" or "comparing."

Developing from the foregoing an analogy to the organizational level suggests the following as examples of some of the common forms of organizational delusion.

1. *Avoidances.* An organization "escapes" from a difficult present-day reality by submerging itself in delusions about its past and projecting itself into the future.
2. *Fantasied self-image.* An organization "escapes" from a painful present-day self-image by creating a fantasied self-image.
3. *Playing games.* An organization's parts substitute "games" for genuine contact with each other.

The forms and content of organizational delusion are probably manifold. The three forms described here are given as examples, because they are commonly met and easily recognizable.

Avoidances

While Freud placed the greatest emphasis on resistance, Perls placed the greatest emphasis on *phobic attitude, avoidance, flight from.* Perls saw people as wanting to avoid unpleasant situations, as determined to avoid pain and suffering even when the latter were needed to attain maturity and responsibility. If the present, the "now," is painful, people are ready to throw the now overboard and avoid the painful situation. The unpleasant "now" can be abandoned and replaced by a fantasy world of the past and the future. Parts of the person that cause painful feelings can be disowned.

Organizations seem to follow similar patterns of avoidance. When the present situation is painful, an organization can escape from it into the past or the future. David Bohm (1981) sees this structure of self-deception to be pervasive in individuals, groups, organizations, and societies. In Bohm's view behind the self-deception lies a drive for perfection. He sees this self-deception fantasy as an integral aspect of neurotic functioning. "Self-deception arising in this way means that . . . people will not generally be capable of facing their actual problems. And thus the individual will tend to get caught in neurotic disorders" (p. 437). Bohm suggests that this process of neurotic self-deception can, in the long run, lead groups to a tendency to disintegrate from within.

Living in the past

Describing a person escaping the present, Perls (1969) wrote:

Lack of contact with the present, lack of the actual "feel" of ourselves, leads to flight either into the past (historical thinking) or into the future (anticipatory thinking). . . . Often the past becomes a 'consumation devoutly to be wished for.' In short, we develop a retrospective character. (p. 92)

Some organizations also live only their past without having a present or a future. When an organization creates a delusion built on the past, the past becomes the only reality. In this case the past is glorified; it is the yardstick by which the present and future are measured. Everything is viewed within the context of the past. The organization sees the roots of the past as far more substantial and meaningful than the outgrowth of today or the promise of the future.

The past may assume a special aura as a time when all was fine and of special value. People say: "Those were the times. "Do you remember how we used to. . . ?" "It will never be like that again." "Things were not like this then." The organization's fantasy may be selective; it can choose to remember all in the past that has a positive connotation and forget that which has negative associations. Perls (1980) wrote: "Nietzche once said, memory and pride were fighting. Memory said it was like that and pride said it couldn't have been. And memory gave in" (p. 179). The same may happen to organizations. Memory may "give in" as to the reality of what happened in the past. Levinson (1972), in his compendium of symptoms for diagnosing organizational health or pathology, writes about the organization that lives in the past. In this kind of organization, the members talk about its glorious history or refer to the organization's traditions as the basis for their perceptions. Levinson illustrates this? "Much of the talk at Dalton State Hospital is in terms of past glory.... Old timers recall the changes and newer employees pick up the aura of the past from them. The present, by contrast, is not as good" (p. 281).

In organizations living in the past, some of the following patterns of behavior may occur.

★ The past may be venerated and glorified in contrast to the present, which may be regarded as if it were less worthy of attention.

★ Most organizations uphold traditions and understand the present in the context of their past. In organizations living in the past, this may be brought to the extreme in the resources and energy devoted to celebration of occasions from the past, anniversaries, and upholding traditions.

★ Present-day achievements may be belittled in comparison to past successes.

★ Societies maintain records of their past in museums' archives, and so on. In organizations living in the past, this activity may be given major priority and many resources may be allocated to it.

★ Present-day problems may be belittled and/or ignored and what is of importance may be seen to have taken place in the past.

Living for the Future

"All of us look backward and forward, but a person who is unable to face an unpleasant present and lives mainly in the past or future, wrapped up in historic or futuristic thinking, is not adapted to reality" (Perls, 1969, p. 95).

As in the above, very much like Perls' (1969) prospective character who "loses himself in the future," an organization may lose itself in the future. The fantasized future may be an illusory world, an intermediate zone, that blocks contact between the organization and reality. In this case what is happening in the organization and the environment might be ignored in the light of what is to take place in the future.

Organizations allocate resources to planning for the future. Managers are taught and trained to attempt to forecast future trends. Strategic planning for the future is advocated by many business colleges. An organization that ignores trends that are developing and may affect its future may find itself not equipped to face a changed reality (Ackoff, 1981). In times of environmental turbulence and "future shock" (Toffler, 1971), organizational adaptation necessitates some form of planning for the future. Planning for the future needs to be differentiated from neurotic absorption in the future. The former is a healthy organizational function, and the latter a pathologic activity. In the pathologic form of living in the future, present reality, today's problems, everyday life, what is happening now in the organization, and changes occurring in the organization's environment all may be blocked from awareness or assume different proportions in the light of the promise of events that will take place in the future.

The utopia of tomorrow might be a world of delusion in which company lives, without attempting to contact today's reality and face the dilemmas, issues, and problems of the present. Present problems might be belittled, distorted or ignored for the sake of "the future of the industry" or "the growth of the company." Robert Townsend, quoted by Bibeault (1981), notes that overexpansion is the number one mistake management made in declining companies. A growth or diversification myth, in which the organization ignores inner and outer reality and deflects and distorts information, may lead the organization to investing all its resources in the future. A company living in a fantasized future may allow itself to deviate in the present for the sake of the future. "The end justifying the means" comes very much to life in organizations that live in a future fantasy. Delorean allegedly was willing to enter a gigantic cocaine transaction to ensure the future of his car industry.

Social reform, revolutionary, and religious organizations are prone to accepting the pattern of neurotic behavior associated with living in the future. Forms of social movement that strive to create and bring about "a better world" may lose touch with present reality and substitute in its stead the promise of a better world in the future. The history of radical movements can provide many examples of this. In our times the Bader-Meynhoff gang in Germany and the Red Brigades in Italy are willing to rob, kidnap, and murder for the sake of achieving what they believe will be a better world. An extreme manifestation of this pattern was in the collective suicide of the Jones' sect in Guyana.

Sometimes an organization lives in two fantasy worlds, the past and the future. Only the present does not exist. The organization glorifies its past and fantasizes a revival of that past in the future. The here and now of the present are ignored and not contacted. There are a past and a promise of a future, but there is no grounding in the reality of the present. In Perls' terms there is a hole instead of the present.

Creating a Fantasy Image

"The patient has taken great pains to build up a self-concept. . . . It is often a completely erroneous concept of himself, each feature representing the exact opposite of its actuality" (Perls, 1980, p. 50).

As an individual in the above passage, an organization can avoid contact with its inner reality by creating a fantasy self-image. This self-image need not have any connection with reality; it need not map reality. In fact it can be "the exact opposite of its actuality." The organization may be a failure and can build a self-image of achievement. Fantasy may replace reality. The function of the fantasy self-image is first and foremost to block the pain of genuine contact with reality and replace it with a make-believe world of myth.

Organization members need to collude in order to preserve a fantasized self-concept for the organization. Most of them need to accept the delusion, or it cannot be maintained.

The fantasy self-image can be about what the organization is like. It can be a fantasy about how others regard it, what valuable goals it achieves, its role in society, its conditions of life, its interpersonal culture, and so on.

Argyris and Schon (1978) differentiate between individual images and organizational maps. The continued efforts of individual members to know the organization are the images. Maps are the shared descriptions of organizations, which individuals jointly construct and use to guide their own inquiry. These could be, for example, diagrams of work flow or compensation charts.

People in organizations act on the basis of these maps and expect certain outcomes. When there is a mismatch of outcome to expectations, the organization members may respond by changing their images and maps so that expectations and outcomes are in line.

Argyris and Schon see the maps as media of organizational learning. An organizational fantasied self-image is not a medium of organizational learning; on the contrary, it is a barrier to organizational learning. The difference between the organizational map and the fantasy self-image is that in the former the organization is in contact with reality and thus the map increases learning, whereas the fantasy obstructs reality and obliterates organizational learning.

Some organizational theorists call the fantasy self-image a façade. This term might lead to confusing the fantasy self-image with what Marquis (1970) calls the corporate image.

Levinson (1972) writes about an organizational facade.

St. Agnes' Hospital presents a façade of innocent self-sacrificing dedication, an institution struggling against sickness, death and economic odds and, therefore, deserving of adherence and support. This serves simultaneously as a bulwark for its activities and to mask the underlying gradual disintegration of the institution. Had economic and social circumstances outside the hospital not changed, it could have continued its work effectively for that mode of adaption served it well for many years. But that virtuous stance toward the outside, a reflection of deeply held values, makes it impossible for the organization to look at what is now transpiring and to change its modes of action to deal with the fractionation of its three major components: employees, medical staff and nuns.

To decrease confusion it might be worthwhile to differentiate among four concepts: image, façade, self-image, and fantasied self-image.

The organization (corporate) image, as defined by Marquis, is the sum of the impressions of the organization in the public consciousness.

The organization façade may be reserved for those cases when the organization awaringly creates a false image to serve its own ends. An example would be that of a company trying to play the role of public benefactor when its sole purpose is increased profits.

The organization self-image is the picture of the organization in the eyes of its members. This is what Argyris and Schon (1978) call organization maps.

The fantasy self-image can be reserved for those cases in which the delusion-based organization maps are maintained without intention and awareness by the members even when they do not match reality.

A CASE OF LIVING IN THE PAST

Mills was an old family company in a coastal city. For years the company had been an important supplier of food and other necessities to ships and fishing boats. The firm had a long tradition in its field and the name held an aura of solidity and style among the public. The company was considered to be a good, old-fashioned, family company.

The senior manager prided himself very much on being the consul for a middle-sized European country. In earlier days the consulate had been very busy, but as the city's importance as an important port diminished, the consul now very seldom was called upon. Somehow in the public's eye he managed to get across that he was fulfilling an important and oft-needed function. The junior manager was loosely connected with an organization working for the benefit of fishermen. The company rented office space to the organization and was both in its own and in the public's eyes seen as working for the benefit of that organization.

The longtime employees talked a lot about old times when there was a lot going on. They recalled incidents when they had all worked very hard, when companionship and cooperation among members were great. They talked about the big ships they had been on and related stories about the men on board. They seemed unaware that when they talked about their daily work, their excitement disappeared.

Many of the younger employees were dissatisfied with how the company was run. Offices and shops were deteriorating. Colors were dark and walls badly needed paint. (The company also sold paint.) The younger employees who had an opportunity left the company. For years there had been a lot of talk about building a new building on a lot the company owned at the waterfront. And there was a lot of dreaming about how nice it would be with office space overlooking the harbor. How easy and convenient everything would be with new equipment.

The company was actually in decline, but building plans got bigger, and employees looked forward to moving. They seriously believed that moving into new locations would bring new life into the organization. When the new building was finished eventually, they boasted about it being the tallest building in town, which it was at that time. In the eyes of the public this showed again a good company.

Business, however, did not prosper. The city did not any longer have the former importance as a seaport. Times had changed.

After a few years in new localities, the company had to go out of business. The fantasy had not taken economic reality into consideration.—*I. Flagtvedt*

Organizational Games

> "I now see the neurosis as consisting of five layers. The first layer is the cliche layer. If you meet somebody you exchange cliches, "Good morning," handshake and all the meaningless *tokens* of meeting.
>
> Now behind the cliches, you find the second layer, what I call the Eric Berne or Sigmund Freud layer, the layer where we play games and roles" (Perls, 1976, p. 59).

Perls saw games playing as a superficial, as-if kind of activity, a synthetic relationship that substitutes for genuine contact between people. Perls described this kind of relationship as a phony, synthetic existence.

Some of the games Perls mentions are "the comparing game" and "the fitting game." The fitting game is one of fitting reality to one's theories. "We look upon reality and see where does this reality fit into my theories, my hypotheses, my fantasies about what reality is like" (Perls, 1976, p. 63). This description of the fitting game is very close to Perls' other descriptions of the neurotic tendency to fantasize and distort reality to fit the fantasy.

Just after graduating from college I was hired as a receptionist/secretary in a hospital laboratory. The atmosphere in my work environment was filled with frustration and mistrust. The communication was almost non-existent. The only message that I got was that our work was very, very important and that the leaders of our unit were very, very busy. They were so busy in fact that they couldn't even stop to tell me just what it was that I was doing and how it fit in with their mission. I did know that I had to expect to work alone at least one weekend a month, and that if I didn't respond exactly as I was expected to, a patient's life might be threatened. With this added anxiety, I tried even harder to establish what I did and how it fit in with the rest of the operation. It was only after a very frustrating and unhappy three months that I was told that my area had to do with the billing function for emergency laboratory work. My superiors had deluded themselves into believing that they truly dealt with emergency medical practices. There was never a mention of the billing process itself.

It was no wonder, as I look back, that my position was one of great turnover and was rarely filled for more than a month or two. The delusion and exclusion of relevant information had kept the unit in a closed system, one which exemplified many symptoms of neurotic organizational behavior.

A number of organization theoreticians have written about organizational games. Gregory Bateson (1972) uses the concept "double bind" to describe a situation in which a person is caught in a no-win game and the rules of the game cannot be discussed. Bateson advanced his theory of the double bind to account for the etiology of schizophrenia. Argyris and Schon (1978) use the concept on the organizational level. They suggest that limited learning systems are predictable generators of situations such as these:

> They require, as a condition of membership, that individuals assume the double layers of vulnerability inherent in camouflage and games of deception. They then put a taboo on discussion of these conditions and on the processes by which one has gotten caught in them. (p. 119)

Argyris and Schon give as an example a staff member of a government agency who experiences a world of ambiguity, fears punishment for delays he is not responsible for, fears the consensus-seeking process and is afraid to avoid it, feels he does not understand the problem, and believes he cannot raise all these issues with others in the organization.

From a different viewpoint the same authors define games as schemes and procedures designed to achieve the purpose of maximizing lifetime income and minimizing the probability of being held responsible for major errors. The results of games of this kind are that management does not receive important information and lower levels systematically alter orders given to them, and both hide the fact that they know what the other is doing. Argyris and Schon suggest that it would be worth inquiring into how the games at different levels interact to create a cumulative equilibrium of increasing dysfunctionality.

Villere (1981) deals with organizational games from the viewpoint of transactional-analysis theory. Accordingly games are irrational actions and their primary outcomes are negative. They promote power achievement, poor morale, hurt feelings, distrust, and poor communications.

Villere's version of organization games has similarities to Bateson's double bind. Beneath the presented surface of complementary transactions is a conflicting ulterior purpose. The game is maintained by not confronting and disclosing the ulterior purpose. If the ulterior negative purpose were to be disclosed, the game would have to be discarded. On the individual level, Perls (1976) wrote about the comparing game, the "more than game": "My car is bigger than yours, my house is bigger than yours, I'm greater than you, my misery is miserabler than yours . . ." In almost the same words, but in the organizational context, Villere (1981) writes "mine is better than yours," ". . . how our bike was faster than their bikes, how our house was bigger than their houses" (Villere, 1981).

To summarize the different views on organizational games, this definition may serve an integrative purpose. An organizational game may be defined as a repetitive series of transactions among organizational components. The transactions have dysfunctional outcomes for the organization but the organization's components collude in not confronting the situation and continue with the transactions.

PROPOSITIONS AND DEFINITIONS

The following have some clinical and research support but are dealt with primarily theoretically.

★ In organizational neurosis the organization creates a delusion that is in fact a false mapping of reality.
★ Members of the organization collude in maintaining the delusion.
★ The organization maintaining a delusion may ignore feedback signals as to deviations of essential variables beyond their limits.
★ These deviations arise from organizational actions based on a false mapping of reality inside and outside the organization.
★ Incoming information that conflicts with the organization's delusion may be blocked from awareness, distorted, or given a different meaning.
★ The organization in a delusion may get caught in a vicious circle; it is maintaining dysfunctional patterns of behavior, and not taking action to change these, thus leading to further aggravation in its dysfunctioning.
★ The organization in a delusion may dissipate more of its energy in coping with the results of its own dysfunctioning.
★ The organization in a delusion may dissipate more energy to maintain internal integration.
★ The organization in a delusion may dissipate more energy in dealing with breakdowns.

★ Some of the forms an organization's delusions may take are avoidances, fantasy self-image, and playing games.

★ Forms of organizational avoidance are living in the past and living for the future.

★ An organization may attempt to evade confronting present-day problems by living in the past and aggrandizing it.

★ An organization may attempt to avoid confronting present-day problems by directing most of its attention to the promises of the future.

★ Social reform, revolutionary, and religious organizations are more prone to adopting the pattern of living in the future.

★ An organization may combine different delusions, for example, living in the past and in the future.

★ An organization may create a fantasy self-image of itself to avoid seeing its present-day reality.

★ An organization's fantasy self-image is a false mapping of the organization's reality in the eyes of the organization's members.

★ Organization members collude in maintaining the fantasy self-image.

★ Genuine contact between an organization and its environment or among an organization's components may be replaced with organizational games.

★ An organizational game is a repetitive series of transactions among organizational components that have dysfunctional organizational outcomes, yet are continually maintained without confrontation.

CHAPTER 8

CONTACT AND WITHDRAWAL

OVERVIEW

The preceding chapter dealt with the various dysfunctional forms that organizational delusion can take.

This chapter deals with the homeostatic process of contact and withdrawal. Contact is when an internal reality, individual or organizational, meets the external reality of the environment. Withdrawal is the opposite condition. This process is disrupted in organizational neurosis. The forms this disruption takes will be detailed in the next two chapters. This chapter attempts to conceptualize the fluctuations of contact and withdrawal on the organizational level.

The process of homeostasis, as understood in Gestalt therapy, is described at the individual level. Homeostasis, as it is maintained in organizations, is seen to have great similarity to the Gestalt therapy descriptions.

Contact and withdrawal have various connotations in Gestalt therapy. These different connotations are surveyed and compared. An analogy of contact and withdrawal on the organizational level yields five forms of organizational fluctuations: fluctuations of dissipative structures; the input–output cycle; opening and closing; the task/maintenance cycle; and the work cycle.

The organization is conceptualized as a living, fluctuating, pulsating system.

THE HOMEOSTATIC PROCESS IN GESTALT THERAPY

"The homeostatic process is the process by which the organism maintains its equilibrium and therefore its health under varying conditions. Homeostasis is thus the process by which the organism satisfies its needs. Since its needs are many and each need upsets the equilibrium, the homeostatic process goes on all the time. All life is characterized by this continuing play of balance and imbalance in the organism. When the homeostasis process fails to some degree, when the organism remains in a state of disequilibrium for too long a time and is unable to satisfy its needs, it is sick. When the homeostatic process fails, the organism dies" (Perls, 1980, p. 5).

In this passage Perls describes the basic life process of homeostasis and its disruption in neurotic behavior and death. A need arises within the organism and the organism contacts the environment to satisfy the need. When the need has been satisfied, the organism returns to its steady state until another need arises. Alternatively a change occurs in the environment, disturbing or arousing the organism. The organism takes action to deal with the change and returns to its steady state. In both cases some change, internal or external, creates a stress that can only be alleviated by the organism taking action in contact with its environment.

A way of seeing this process is that of *self-regulation*, in which a changing organism interacting with a changing environment is constantly maintaining a steady state of adjustment. "We might call the homeostatis process the process of *self-regulation*, the process by which the organism interacts with the environment" (*Ibid.*, p. 6).

The homeostatic process can also be viewed as one of closing the gestalt. A need or tension has developed and it must be attended to, or it will pressure the organism. When the need has been attended to and satisfied, or the tension has been relieved, the gestalt is closed and the organism may now attend to other business.

The organism has many needs and a number of them may create pressure at the same time. The organism needs to find a way to fix priorities (Perls, 1980).

Human beings have thousands of . . . needs on the purely physiological level. And on the social levels there are thousands of needs. The more intensely they are felt to be essential to continued life, the more closely we identify ourselves with them, the more intensely we will direct our activities to satisfying them . . . (p. 7)

The organism, therefore, has to create priorities and it attends first to what it sees are its dominant survival needs. "The healthy organism seems to operate within what we call a hierarchy of values. Since it is unable to do more than one thing properly at a time, it attends to the dominant survival need before it attends to others" (p. 8).

The dominant survival needs become the figure and the organism channels its action to satisfy it. The dominant survival need becomes the gestalt that demands closure. "The dominant need of the organism, at any time, becomes the foreground figure and the other needs recede, at least temporarily, into the background" (p. 9).

To achieve closure, satisfy its needs, and relieve tensions, the organism must be able to determine priorities between its needs and be capable of interacting with the environment in a manner that will achieve need satisfaction. "For the individual to satisfy his needs to close the gestalt, to move on to other business, he must be able to sense what he needs and he must know how to manipulate himself and his environment" (p. 9).

HOMEOSTASIS IN ORGANIZATIONS

Perls was aware that the homeostatic process applied not only to the individual, but also to organizations. In a well-known passage describing the ideal community, Perls (1980) writes: "The principle of homeostasis, of self-regulation, also governs such a society. As the body responds to its dominant needs first, so would the society respond to its dominant needs first" (pp. 26–27).

In his descriptions of the homeostatic process, Perls used concepts and terms suitable to the level of the individual organism, with which he was dealing. Open system theory applies the homeostatic process to different systemic levels, including the individual organism and the organization. It therefore uses concepts that can be applicable at different levels. Except for the differences in terminology, the descriptions of the homeostatic process in Gestalt therapy theory and in open systems theory are almost identical.

Cannon (1939) coined the term "homeostasis" to avoid the static connotation of equilibrium and to stress the dynamic properties of physiological systems.

The coordinated physiological processes which maintain most of the steady states in the organism are so complex and so peculiar to living beings . . . that I have suggested a special designation for these states, *homeostasis*. The word does not imply something set and immobile, a stagnation. It means a condition which may vary, but which is relatively constant. (p. 24)

Buckley (1967) suggests using the term *steady state* when dealing with the organizational level to express "not only the *structure-maintaining* feature, but also the *structure-elaborating* and *changing* feature of the inherently unstable system" (pp. 14–15).

When Cannon coined the term *homeostasis*, feedback theory had not yet reached its present level of development. It was Ashby (1960) who brought forward the evidence that homeostasis is a condition that is maintained by feedback. Ashby proposed the definition that a form of behavior is adaptive if it maintains its essential variables within physiological limits. He demonstrated the use of feedback mechanisms as signals to return the organism to its steady state in which these variables were within their limits. Von Bertalanffy (1968) elaborated on the characteristics of the steady state in open systems: "The composition remains constant, but in contrast to conventional equilibria, this constancy is maintained in a continuous exchange and flow of component material."

The steady state the system maintains with the environment "prevents variations in the environment from destroying systems" (p. 49). There is a range of stability for each of the system's numerous variables and the feedback processes keep these variables within their range of stability. When any of these variables goes beyond its range of stability, this constitutes stress and creates strain within the system.

Miller (1978) notes that the steady state is restored by the system "in order to relieve the strain of the disparity recognized internally between the feedback signal and the comparison signal" (p. 53).

Throughout the 1970s and into the 1980s, the homeostatic-steady-state, open-system approach has become the dominant theoretical view of organizations. Most of the major organization theorists (e.g., Katz & Kahn, 1978; Buckley, 1967) deal with organizations from such an approach. A majority of the organizational behavior textbooks use this approach as their organizing principle.

Cummings (1980, p. xvi) contributes a clear concise summary of the properties of these steady-state, open systems. Specifically open systems are:

1. *Hierarchical*—that is, they are both an independent framework for organizing lower level parts and a dependent member of a higher level system.

2. *Negentropic*—that is, they can replenish themselves by importing energy from their environment, transforming it into products or services, and exporting the product back to the environment.

3. *Partially bounded*—that is, they selectively relate to their environment, maintaining necessary exchanges while excluding others.

4. *Self-regulating*—that is, they maintain their internal integrity and environmental exchanges by using information about the consequences of their behavior to control future behavior.

5. *Equifinal*—that is, they can reach a final state from differing initial conditions and in different ways; hence they can change to match emerging conditions.

The detailing of these properties of open systems applied to organizations illustrates how much similarity there is between them and between the properties of homeostatic organisms described in Gestalt therapy.

CONTACT AND WITHDRAWAL IN GESTALT THERAPY

The homeostatic cycle of interacting with the environment to satisfy needs and relieve tensions is one of contacting the environment to satisfy the need or relieve the tension and then withdrawing to decreased contact with the environment, assimilating the new and attending to internal dynamics. We make a distinction between healthy psychological withdrawal and the neurotic behavior of the individual or group engaging in an intermediate-zone activity such as the "Ain't it awful" syndrome (Perls, 1980).

Contact and withdrawal, in a rhythmic pattern are our means of satisfying our needs, of continuing the ongoing process of life . . . contact and withdrawal . . . are descriptions of the ways we meet psychological events, they are our means of dealing at the contact boundary with objects in the field. (p. 23)

Contact and withdrawal allow a person to become aware of needs and to determine priorities among them; to contact the environment to satisfy them and then to withdraw to consummate the satisfaction and become aware of another need. Contact and withdrawal are a constant rhythmic process of opening and closing gestalts. "Contacting the environment is, in a sense, forming a gestalt. Withdrawing is either closing it completely or rallying one's forces to make closure possible" (Perls, 1980), p. 23).

In these passages Perls uses the term "contact" in the sense of the organism facing outward, relating to and interacting with its environment. "Withdrawal" then means the organism is facing inward and relating internally. In this sense contact and withdrawal can be understood as an organism opening and closing itself to environmental inputs and stimuli. "During the day when we are awake, we are in touch with the world, we are in contact with it. During the night when we are asleep, we withdraw, we give up contact. In summer we are usually more outgoing than winter" (p. 23).

In his earlier writings Perls had a different version of contact. "Primarily, contact is the awareness of, and behavior toward, the assimilable novelty" (Perls et al., 1951, p. 230). By this definition an organism interacting with its environment to export its outputs or acting to change the environment in any way would not necessarily be in contact with the environment.

Perls does not attach any evaluation, either positive or negative, to contact or to withdrawal. "Withdrawal per se is neither good nor bad . . ." "The same thing applies to contact. Contact itself is neither good nor bad . . ." (Perls, 1980, p. 21).

The Polsters (1974, Chap. 5) see contact as "the meeting function between ourselves and that which is not ourselves." They write about "the possibility of being in contact with oneself." They suggest that this kind of contact can happen because of the possibility a person has to be, at the same time, observer and observed. It appears that what the Polsters call "being in contact with oneself" would be regarded as "withdrawal" under the terms of Perls' definitions. It could, however, be considered a legitimate form of contact of one part of the self with another. The Polsters also write about making contact with memories and images. This again would not fit any of Perls' descriptive definitions of "contact," either as opening to and interacting with the environment, or as behaving toward novelty in the environment.

Another meaning, sometimes given to contact in Gestalt therapy, is that of direct sensory mediated interaction with a person or an object. This is differentiated from noncontactful interaction, in which a component of imagery or thinking comes between the person and the sensed object. A review of Gestalt therapy literature makes it apparent that the concepts of contact and withdrawal are used in a number of different ways. Perls himself uses the concepts he coined with different meanings.

Before attempting to develop analogies for these concepts at the organizational level, it might be advisable to clarify the different meanings at the individual level.

Table 8-1 lists the different meanings of contact and withdrawal in Gestalt therapy literature. It is not within the purpose of this work to examine the overlap of these definitions. They are detailed to demonstrate that the terms can be understood in different ways, which is necessary before creating analogies to the organizational level. In looking for organizational analogies, it will be more in the direction of the first four definitions. They have in common a cyclical fluctuation between two phases, which are, in some sense, opening and being active outward and closing and focusing inward. In contact the environment is figure and internal activity is ground. In withdrawal internal activity is figure and the environment is ground.

The rhythmic quality of the cyclical fluctuations of contact and withdrawal expresses a dynamic state of alternation between two phases. This describes conditions such as inhaling, exhaling, inhaling, exhaling, and so on, or biting, digesting, biting, digesting, and so on. Phase one is followed by phase two, followed by phase one, and so on.

In this sense the last two definitions are not part of a contact and withdrawal cycle. They define only one phase, without specifying a movement to a second phase. These definitions of contact have no polarized definition or description of withdrawal. They carry an evaluative overtone, especially in the Polsters' writings. Contact is evaluated as healthy and adaptive, while interaction without contact is regarded as unhealthy and unadaptive. This is so, because the Polsters use contact as sensory-mediated interaction versus, for example, fantasy-mediated interaction. In this context it is understandable that contact is regarded positively. However, this might be a source of confusion if contact were contrasted with withdrawal. It might lead to the implication that withdrawal is maladaptive or unhealthy.

Contact and withdrawal will be used in their nonevaluative

Table 8-1
Different Meanings of Contact and Withdrawal

No.	Essence	Description	User
1	Rhythm of need satisfaction	Contact as interacting with the environment to satisfy a need or relieve a tension. Withdrawal to assimilate and integrate and become aware of another need.	Perls
2	Opening and closing boundaries	Contact as opening boundaries to the environment. Withdrawal as relatively closing them.	Perls
3	Focusing outward and inward	Contact as focusing on and interacting with the environment. Withdrawal as internal focusing and interaction.	Perls, Stevens
4	Diurnal, weekly, and seasonal rhythms	Contact and withdrawal as diurnal, weekly, and seasonal rhythms of activity and inactivity.	Perls
5	Contact as assimilating and rejecting novelty	Contact as assimilating novelty and ejecting unassimilated novelty. Withdrawal is undefined.	Perls, Hefferline, and Goodman
6	Contact as sensory-mediated interaction	Contact as sensory mediated, both with the environment and inward. Withdrawal is undefined.	Polsters

sense as being neither good nor bad, but both necessary and complementary aspects of the same process.

Contact will not be used in the sense of sensory-mediated interaction as in definition 6. This is the way the Polsters, and sometimes Perls, use the term. Contact, in the first four definitions, may be illusion/fantasy mediated. Contact and withdrawal will refer to the *direction* of focusing awareness and directing energy (outward or inward) and not to the quality of that awareness (reality or illusion mediated). A person becoming sensorily aware of parts of the body and directing energy toward them will be withdrawing and not contacting the body, as the Polsters would have described it.

CONTACT AND WITHDRAWAL AT THE ORGANIZATIONAL LEVEL

Concepts analogous to contact and withdrawal have been advanced in both systems theory and organization theory. The theory of fluctuations of dissipative structures is regarded as an important advance in the understanding of open systems and their change. Again, from a systems theory approach, the continuous repetitive cycle of input, transformation, and output has become the basic model of a majority of organizational theorists.

At the level of the individual, the organization, and society, a number of scholars have postulated a regular oscillation between states of opening and closing boundaries.

From a different viewpoint, the organization fluctuates regularly between dealing with its *outputs* and its *maintenance*, or as others describe this, between *tasks* and *people*. The work cycle of organizations fluctuates between periods of activity and inactivity.

The Fluctuations of Dissipative Structures

Prigogine received the Nobel prize for his work on dissipative structures. The Texas University computer confirmed his mathematical predictions about the role of fluctuations in producing new dissipative structures.

Prigogine's work (1980) deals with open systems in which the structure exchanges energy with the environment. Dissipative structures are nonequilibrium, unstable, and continuously fluctuating systems. A dissipative structure can be anything from a chemical solution to a person, an organization, or a society. The more complex the system, the more it needs to dissipate energy to maintain its complexity. When the fluctuations pass a critical level, they are amplified by the system's many connections, and can bring the system into a new, different state. This new state is more complex, more connected, more ordered, even less stable, and works according to a different set of rules. With each new state, there is greater complexity and instability and greater potential for change.

When a system is perturbed by increasing fluctuations, the number of interactions increases and elements of the system interact with each other in new ways.

When the system moves to a new state, it reorganizes itself. This reorganization, called *self-organizing*, may be by nonlinear processes. Prigogine gives an example from freeway traffic. When there is little traffic, the driver can drive in a linear mode, with minimal slowing and lane changing because of other cars. When traffic is heavy, all the cars begin to affect each other—the driver being driven by the system. This is a nonlinear process of competition between events.

Prigogine has related his theory of fluctuation to problems of social systems and organizations. He has suggested that it violates the law of large numbers. Fluctuations attributable to a minority in an organization can cause it to shift into a new order.

The fluctuations to which Prigogine refers are the fluctuations of all the system's variables along the continuum of their critical range. An example would be body temperature changing from low to high and back within its regular limits. It is not one variable fluctuating, but many variables fluctuating simultaneously and being interrelated, thus affecting each other—and this causes fluctuations in the system itself. Lippitt (1982) gives an example:

The financial resources available to an organization such as a voluntary agency will fluctuate, but through a complicated process of self-regulation the organization is able to maintain itself in a more or less steady financial state, unless, of course, resources decrease beyond some critical point.

Prigogine's theory of dissipative structures gives support to the conceptualization of the homeostatic process as put forward in

Gestalt therapy and to its parallel concept in systems theory—the steady state. The theory of dissipative structures describes how one steady state changes into another.

The Input–Output Cycle

To judge by current textbooks, it appears that the majority of organization theorists base their model of organizational dynamics on an open systems model of input–transformation–output. Basically this model is analogous to the pulsation of contact and withdrawal in the sense of alternating between focusing on the environment and then focusing inward.

The input–output model is graphically illustrated in Figure 8-1. The organization contacts the environment to derive from it resources that it needs to continue functioning and develop and to sense changes in the environment that might affect it. The organization transforms the inputs of matter-energy and information it receives from the environment into outputs, which it will export to the environment. Part will be exported and part will be used (dissipated) to maintain the organization's internal processes. The outputs to the environment ensure continued organizational

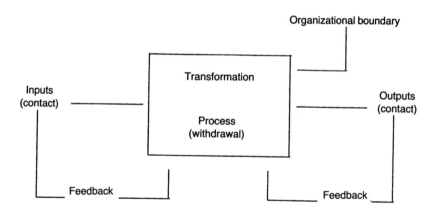

Figure 8.1
Input—output model of an organization

existence as they supply an environmental need for which the environment is willing to furnish the organization with the resources it needs.

An individual may maintain a "parasitic" relationship with the environment in the sense of not contributing to it while being supplied by society with all the necessary resources. An example would be a completely invalided person maintained by a social institution. The considerations are humanitarian and the term "parasitic" refers to the quality of the relationship, with no evaluation connotations. In the relationship of organizations to their environment, or of part of an organization to the total organization, parasitic relationships are less common than on the individual level. Most societies are reluctant to supply resources to organizations that do not contribute value in return. A parasitic relationship generally takes place when the parasitic system has some kind of symbolic value to its suprasystem, or when its outputs are difficult to evaluate and measure.

Contact may be seen as the input and output of the cycle. The organization opens its boundaries to interact with the environment—to export its output, to get feedback on the fit between the output and changing environmental needs, to obtain the resources it needs, including information. Contact serves to warn the organization of impending dangers and alert it to the possibility of new opportunities in the changing environment.

The organization is not only reactive to environmental stimuli, or proactive in actively seizing environmental opportunities, but it actively affects and changes its environment. It attempts to change environmental conditions to suit its own needs, even to the point of creating its own environment. An industry attempts to create consumer tastes for its new products. It develops new sources of supply for its raw materials and works on changing legislation in its favor. An organization may attempt to change the environment with which it interacts by changing its physical location or its customers. In Perls' terms it not only changes itself, but also the environment.

Withdrawal is the transformation process part of the cycle. It may be understood as "internal contact." The organization integrates the inputs it brought in from the environment and makes them part of itself. Simultaneously the organization transforms part of these inputs into a different state and exports them to the environment. To do this the organization needs to be in contact with its components and subunits. It needs to be able to sense what each subunit needs in order to fulfill its function effectively and develop itself. The organization needs to integrate the inter-action of the subunits to ensure continued effective organizational functioning.

This condition could also be conceptualized within the Polsters' definition of contact as in "being in contact with oneself." Parts of the organization could be making contact with one another. Such contacts could be vital to the survival of the organization, as when the marketing division gives feedback on environmental needs to the R&D department, or when blocks to communication within parts of the organization demand attention in order to facilitate the contact necessary in building a team.

Alternating between contact and withdrawal, the organization needs constantly to monitor its feedback mechanisms on the state of all relevant variables in the environment and within its bound-aries. It is easier to discern the fluctuation of the contact and withdrawal process at the individual level than at the organiza-tional level. The individual can pay attention to only one figure at a time. If the environment is figure, the individual has difficulty withdrawing and simultaneously attending to internal matters. The alternation between contact and withdrawal is *sequential*.

Organizations can maintain a division of labor, with part of the organization interacting with the environment to obtain resources (contact) and, as we have described, part of the organization en-gaged in transforming inputs into outputs. The fluctuations be-tween the external and the internal are less discernible. Basically, however, the alternating sequence exists because the transforma-tion process is dealing with inputs acquired earlier and not those inputs that are being acquired simultaneously. The outputs—the organization contacts the environment to export—need first to be transformed through internal processes. Therefore, although the entire process seems to flow, it is made up of overlapping cycles of contact and withdrawal.

The input–output model of open systems seems to be the closest to contact and withdrawal, as the rhythm of need satisfaction on the individual level, as described in Gestalt therapy. Like the pulsation of the amoeba, the opening and closing of the sea urchin, or breathing and eating in human beings, the never-ending cyclical rhythm of input–transformation–output is the life mechanism of organizations. This cycle is the model used in sociotechnical ap-proaches to organizational change. The flows of matter-energy-information through the cycle are discerned and bottlenecks identified. Alternative ways of structuring the flows are experimented with. As a result changes are brought about in the work flow or the technology or the decision-making procedures or the structures of the organizations. Cummings' (1976) sociotechnical intervention strategy exemplarizes the use of this approach, which is based on the input–transformation–output model.

Opening and Closing

A further analogy to contact and withdrawal is the concept of "opening and closing." Various scientists (Jantsch, 1975; Lippitt, 1982; Klapp, 1975) have described the fluctuations between opening and closing as a basic natural process of human life at both the individual and the social level. Perls saw the pulsation of opening and closing as the natural rhythm not only of individuals, but also of societies. (Klapp (1975) developed an open systems model of contact and withdrawal in which the system is in a continual oscillation between relative openness and closedness—resilient adjustment to intakes of information and states of entropy. Klapp challenges the conventional belief that openness is always better than closedness. He points out that systems theory has emphasized homeostasis in living systems as a balance between intake and outgo. He brings support from information overload theory, the study of creativity as an inner change in configuration and not a recombination of pieces flowing in from outside, and the spasms of closing and opening found in all societies.

Klapp describes the process of opening and closing as "not only a feature of organizations but as part of a natural tide or rhythm throughout the living world" (p. 252). Aliveness or adaptability is not continual intake, but sensitive alternations of openness and closure:

In such a view, closing is not a setback to growth and progress but evidence that the mechanisms of life are working, that the society has resiliency. Opening and closing can be seen as a way to gain information while defeating entropy. (pp. 252–253)

On the organizational level, opening and closing may be viewed as an alternation between self-identification and collective identification. The closing stage buttresses the "we" identity, and the opening stage opens the organization to wider identifications. All organizations are open systems, and therefore open to the environment. What are called open organizations close themselves in different ways, and at different points, than closed organizations.

An open society oscillates within a range different from that of the closed one, on a continuum stretching theoretically from high solidarity (cohesiveness, morale, esprit de corps, etc.) at one end to total alienation at the other. (p. 254)

Openness is not more adaptive than closedness. The organization needs to oscillate constantly between relative openness and closedness—resilient adjustment to intakes of information/ entropy. Klapp points out that oscillating between opening and closing does not imply synchronicity. The opening and closing of subsystems may be out of step with the total system. A department may tend to openness when the company is swaying into closedness.

Task and Maintenance Cycle

While the cycle of opening and closing was treated mainly from a systems theory perspective, the task/maintenance cycle leads back to group and organizational theory and research.

In the analysis of group and organizational dynamics, theorists have stressed the importance of the dimensions of task and maintenance. Bales (1963) drew attention to these dimensions of group activity and postulated that a team needs two leaders, one for each function. The task leader would be responsible for fulfilling the group's tasks (outputs, goals, work, etc.). The maintenance leader would be responsible for the socioemotional aspects of group functioning, and would take care of maintenance (process, people, etc.).

Although they utilized different names, various leadership theories have stressed these dimensions as the two basic aspects of leadership. Examples of this are: "concern with production" and "concern with people" (Blake & Mouton, 1978); "goal emphasis and support" (Bowers & Seashore, 1966). Reddin's (1970) managerial styles are also based on the two dimensions.

Bales not only differentiated between the two dimensions of task and maintenance, but also postulated that they did not take place simultaneously and that leadership fluctuated between attending to one and then the other.

Coming from Berelson and Steiner's (1964) inventory of scientific findings is this summary:

In general, there is an alternation within groups, especially those having tasks to perform, between communications (interactions) dealing directly with the task and communications dealing with emotional or social relations among the members—the former tending to create tensions within the group and the latter tending to reduce them and achieve harmony. (p. 349)

The task/maintenance cycle at the group and organizational levels might be the analogy of focusing outward and inward at the individual level.

The Work Cycle

Most organizations function within the rhythm of a period of activity alternating with another period of inactivity. This coincides with the cycle of day and night and the cycle of workdays and weekends. In effect a time period of work, production, and goal activity alternates with a period of renewal of human energy and machine and human maintenance.

The past 20 to 30 years have seen the development by individuals of alternate work schedules, such as flex-time, part-time work, and division of work activity between two workplaces. Cohen and Gadon (1978) point out the plethora of different work schedules developing in organizations. Indeed, individual work schedules need not coincide (although they need to be coordinated) with the organizational work cycle. The organization as a whole, however, generally does maintain daily and weekly work cycles.

The different periods in the organization's work cycle coincide with the stages of contact and withdrawal. The period of work activity and production may be viewed as the period of contact. The period of inactivity, revival of energy, and maintenance could be viewed as the period of withdrawal. From this standpoint most organizations have two regular cycles of contact and withdrawal. One of these is based on an alternating cycle of day and night, and a second, with larger intervals, is based on the weekly cycle of weekdays and weekends. Some organizations also maintain a third cycle of even larger intervals based on the yearly cycle. A variety of institutions (industries and schools, for example) have a few weeks or months a year when they completely close down.

The daily, weekly, and yearly cycles of work and inactivity are maintained simultaneously and are not alternative ways of fulfilling the same function. The daily cycle is a short-wave cycle, superimposed on the medium-wave weekly cycle, which is superimposed on the long-wave yearly cycle.*

The work cycle at the organizational level coincides in some form with the diurnal and weekly rhythms at the individual level.

Summary of Organizational Cycles

A recapitulation of organization's various cyclical fluctuations (see Table 8-2) leads to a different image of organizational dynamics than that generally depicted in the textbooks.

The dynamics of pulsation, oscillation, fluctuation, and cyclical change appears to be an integral aspect of organizational functioning. The organization, like all other living systems, maintains its homeostatic steady state in a continuing process of fluctuating cycles of different kinds and durations. Waves of shorter cycles intersect with medium-length waves, and they, in turn, oscillate on waves with longer cycles. No studies have, as yet, examined the relationship between the different cycles, the degree of resonance between them, and how the organization is affected by different degrees of resonance between different kinds of cycles.

All of these cyclical fluctuations appear to have as the focus of their two phases some aspect of what Gestalt therapy terms contact and withdrawal. In the contact-like phase, the organization focuses on, interacts with, and opens itself to the environment, and expends energy on working for goals geared to environmental needs. In the withdrawal phase, the organizations, which are outwardly inactive, face inward to transform; to integrate and maintain parts; to deal with internal processes, production, and members' needs; and to replenish energy. In the withdrawal cycle, however, could be a micro, within-organization, contact phenomenon among its subsystems.

---

*The yearly cycle might be superimposed on an even longer cycle. This might be what is termed the organizational life cycle (Kimberly & Miles, 1980). The organizational life cycle refers to a series of sequential stages most organizations pass through between their birth and termination. At present there is not agreement among scholars as to the definition of these stages. Nevertheless, while yet insufficiently substantiated at present, it seems likely that the stages alternate between primacy of external focus to primary of internal focus, and so on.

There seems not to be one basic cycle of contact and withdrawal. Instead a variety of intersecting cyclical fluctuations of differing function and duration maintain the rhythmic homeostatic balance of life. There can even be a deliberate choice at some moment when there is internal contact until ready to move out into the world. In the Growtowski Laboratory Theatre of Poland, before presenting a new work, withdrawal from public contact was systematically required of all members.

Table 8-2
Cyclical Fluctuations in Organizations

Name of Cycle	Description of Cycle	Scholars
Fluctuations of dissipative structures	a. Perpetual short-term fluctuations of an organization's variables, between their critical limits. b. A long-term qualitative shift into new internal order.	Prigogine J. G. Miller
Input–output cycle	The organization as an open system continually receiving inputs from the environment, transforming them, and exporting outputs to the environment.	Cummings Katz and Kahn
Opening and closing	Organizations going through repetitive cycles of alternatively opening and closing their boundaries to the environment.	Klapp Lippitt
Task and maintenance cycle	Task teams (in organizations), and possibly some organizations, oscillating between centrality of task functions and maintenance functions.	Bales
The work cycle	Organizations alternating between periods of work and periods of inactivity on a daily, weekly, and yearly basis.	Cohen and Gadon

The chapter has examined the various forms in which the fluctuations of contact and withdrawal manifest themselves in organizations. The next two chapters will discuss the ways these fluctuations are disrupted in organizations displaying neurotic organizational behavior.

PROPOSITIONS AND DEFINITIONS

The following have varying degrees of theoretical, clinical, and empirical support. They relate, as usual to both organizations and their subunits.

★ The organization maintains itself in a steady state while exchanging matter-energy and information with its environment.
★ The organization maintains this steady state through a continuous process of fluctuation of its variables within the limits of their critical range.
★ The organization imports inputs of matter-energy and information from the environment, transforms these, and exports outputs to the environment.
★ The organization dissipates part of its energy to maintain its own internal complexity.
★ When the organization's variables fluctuate beyond the limits of their critical range, a restructuring of the organization in a new, qualitatively different order may take place.

(All of the above, derived from systems theory, are well supported by empirical research.)

★ Organizations fluctuate between focusing their awareness and energy inward and outward.
★ Organizations fluctuate between periods of being more open and being more closed to their environment.
★ A healthy organization fluctuates between periods of being relatively open to the environment and periods of being relatively closed.

(The above have some, but not sufficient, theoretical, clinical, and empirical support.)

★ Organizations fluctuate between periods of goal-centered activity and periods of maintenance-centered activity.

(This proposition has some theoretical support but no clinical or empirical support.)

★ Organizations maintain work cycles of activity and inactivity, based on daily, weekly, and yearly cycles.

(This proposition is strongly supported by clinical observation.)

★ The organization is in a constant process of fluctuation, with cycles of different kinds and duration intersecting with each other.
★ These cyclical fluctuations have two phases; one phase is focused on the environment and the second phase is internally focused.

CHAPTER **9**

THE DISRUPTION OF CONTACT AND WITHDRAWAL

OVERVIEW

The preceding chapter dealt with the homeostatic process of contact and withdrawal, at the individual level and the organizational level. Perls' conceptualization of contact and withdrawal was analyzed and seen to present a number of different meanings. At the organizational level, the fluctuations of contact and withdrawal were seen to consist of possibly five kinds of cyclical fluctuations—the fluctuations of dissipative structures, the input–output cycle, opening and closing, the task and maintenance cycle, and the work cycle.

Perls' insight was that neurotic behavior involved disruption of the contact and withdrawal cycle. In this chapter Perls' treatment of this disruption will be described and then the organizational level will be examined to see if the disruptions occur also in that context. An attempt will be made to see if the contact and withdrawal cycles are disrupted when an organization displays neurotic behavior. In what way are these cycles dysfunctioning in neurotic behavior? What forms do these disruptions take?

An endeavor will be made to address these questions and to suggest a series of propositions concerning organizational neurosis and the disruption of the contact and withdrawal cycles in organizations.

CONTACT AND WITHDRAWAL AND NEUROTIC INDIVIDUAL BEHAVIOR

Both contact and withdrawal are essential aspects of the same process of learning and adapting common to all living systems. The lack of either contact or withdrawal, an overdose of either of them, or a regular imbalance between them is part of system dysfunctioning.

In his earlier definitions of contact, Perls saw it as the creative and dynamic adjustment of the organism and the environment. At that period he understood contact in the sense of behavior toward novelty, accepting the assimilable and nourishing and rejecting the unassimilable and toxic. From this viewpoint Perls (Perls et al., 1951) wrote: "Abnormal psychology is the study of the interruption, inhibition, or other accidents in the course of creative adjustment" (pp. 230–231).

Furthermore: "Since the real is progressively given in contact, in the creative adjustment of organism and environment, when this is inhibited by the neurotic, his world is 'out of touch' and therefore progressively hallucinatory, projected, blacked out or otherwise unreal" (p. 231).

What Perls is saying is this:

—The ability of the individual to adjust creatively depends on the quality of interaction with the environment.
—A person who is sufficiently in touch with reality will be able to maintain a creative adjustment to the environment.
—As the fantasy world comes between the neurotic and reality, he/she is unable to adjust creatively.
—This inability to adjust creatively (contact and withdrawal) intensifies the fantasylike quality of the neurotic's relationship to the environment.

Much later Perls (1980) described the construct somewhat differently.

Are you all there or are you at home attending to some unfinished business, and where are you in your awareness? Are you in touch with the world, are you touch with yourself, are you in touch with the middle zone—the fantasy life that is interfering with being completely in touch with yourself or the world? (p. 195)

The neurotic's fantasy life dislocates the ability to maintain the homeostatic process of contact and withdrawal.

We now see something else about the neurotic. His contact and withdrawal rhythm is out of kilter. He cannot decide for himself when to participate and when to withdraw because all the unfinished business of his life, all the interruptions to the ongoing process have disrupted his sense of orientation, and he is no longer able to distinguish between those objects or persons in the environment which have a positive, and those which have a negative cathexis; he no longer knows when or from what to withdraw. He has lost his freedom of choice, he cannot select appropriate means for his end goals, because he does not have the capacity to see the choices that are open to him. (p. 24)

The neurotic's behavior is ineffective. When a fantasy life creates a barrier between the person and reality, the neurotic is unable to maintain an effective rhythm of contact and withdrawal. Perls (1980) writes:

One of the characteristics of the neurotic is that he can neither make good contact nor can he organize his withdrawal. When he should be in contact with his environment his mind is somewhere else and so he cannot concentrate. When he should withdraw he cannot. (p. 21)

DISRUPTION OF CONTACT AND WITHDRAWAL AT THE ORGANIZATIONAL LEVEL

At the individual level, when neurotic mechanisms replace reality mapping, the homeostatic process of contact and withdrawal is disrupted. At the organizational level, when delusion interrupts, or distorts the flow of feedback—about what is happening inside the organization and what is occurring outside it—the organization's homeostatic adaptive ability is disturbed.

The problem is compounded by the very nature of the homeostatic process itself. This is not a simple process of keeping one set of variables in equilibration, but of maintaining multiple conflicting equilibrations (Litterer, 1973).

The many regulating systems have individual equilibrium points. However, the same conditions do not produce equilibrium in them all. On the contrary, the optimal conditions or stable conditions for one are unstable for another. . . . As one system takes action to bring itself into equilibrium, it upsets the equilibrium of another. . . . The consequences are that organizations are continually churning internally as subsystems struggle for equilibrium against their reciprocally disturbing influences. (p. 269)

A nursing college has the fantasy that it is an excellent college with good staff, good quality of education, good relationship to the field of cooperation, and a very good group of students, and educates excellent nurses.

This fantasy is mostly based on the fact that:

1. There is a large number of applicants for the 40 yearly student places, (1200–1600 applicants).
2. Very few students drop out during the three years of training.
3. Most of the students get good grades on their papers and all are passing in their practical training.

Even though the nurses in the field of students' practical training give information to the college supervisors that students do not have the desired interpersonal relationship with staff and patients, and they are not doing the nursing care according to the objectives at that level, the supervisors give the students good grades.

The teachers are also reporting to the leadership and complaining about students' absence from classes, students' superficial knowledge and poor nursing care—and yet they give students good grades on their papers.

Instead of checking out the real message of the double-bind information from the nurses, supervisors, and teachers, the leadership filters or blocks an awareness of this essential information.

From the double messages, the leadership is in confusion, and unable to take action for needed changes.—*S. Kateraas*

When the organization's neurotic mechanisms distort, deflect, filter, or block the organization's awareness of essential feedback on these processes, the organization may lose its ability to take effective action to satisfy its needs and react to both internal and external changes that demand response. The organization may have difficulty in maintaining its essential variables within their limits and in returning to a steady-state dynamic equilibrium. The organization may run into problems of adaption, for as Berrien (1968) has pointed out: "Adaptive systems are those which maintain their essential variables within those limits necessary for survival within the environment in which they exist" (p. 63).

In this process the organization may suffer harm or hurt, and if matters become worse, the organization may get caught in the vortex of a disintegrative cycle. Bowler (1981) writes:

A stress becomes a crisis when there is no available reaction for equilibration. In such situations, the system either acquires a new pattern of response or suffers some degree of injury or disintegration. (p. 38)

As Berrien (1968) writes, it is the feedback mechanisms that cope with a wide variety of disturbances that would otherwise upset the steady state of the system. "It is the feedback mechanism that accounts for the automatic maintenance of homeostasis" (p. 64). When this mechanism is disrupted by fantasy, the contact and withdrawal cycles get "out of kilter." In the initial phase, the neurotic mechanism blocks the information flow from feedback mechanisms. Possibly the first information to be affected is that of the fluctuation of the organization's variables between their critical limits. This might take the form of what Bowler (1981) describes as "serious distortions of interpretive information in order to make perceptions (feedback) less stressful" (p. 122).

The organization's steady state is maintained by feedback messages to the organization's control subsystems when any of its continually fluctuating variables reach their critical limit. For example, when the organization's expenditure is too high, or production afflicted with two many deficiencies, or between-departments tension reaches too high a level, feedback messages reach the organization's control system and the organization balances the situation by taking action to remedy the conditions. This action returns the organization to the steady state within the critical limits it can sustain without severe stress or damage.

It was more than two years after Bell took over the management of the institute that reactions began coming in from the clients. Bell had been an excellent scientist but was a bad manager. The managerial function seemed to aggravate some basic insecurity and paranoia. Her managerial style was erratic and unpredictable—one day aggressive, demanding, and entrepreneurial; the next day manipulative and seemingly affectionate. She seemed to see all initiatives of others as attempts to usurp her authority and replace her.

Scientists who had been used to a great deal of autonomy found themselves, like children, being told what to do. Some of them who had been the institute's mainstay found themselves unwelcome in policy decisions. As a result they resigned themselves to inactivity and passivity in these areas and concentrated solely on their professional activities. Asking no one's advice, Bell took on a number of projects of a kind the institute had abstained from involving itself with in the past. Boundaries became unclear: "What do we do, and what don't we do?" A crusade against younger members of the staff Bell thought were not dedicated enough led to job insecurity. People were not sure "if we will belong or not." The manipulations had disrupted the boundaries. The climate that developed was one of tension and conflict and it was difficult to differentiate what was interpersonal and what were substantive differences over professional approaches or policy.

The discontent and demoralized climate in the institute affected clients only after quite a time. First a few, then more and more, reports came in about mismanaged projects and disappointed clients. New applications for the institute's services began dwindling. Mention of the institute's name began sometimes to be accompanied with a cynical remark. From a condition where there had been a waiting list of clients, the institute found itself needing to decrease staff—for lack of projects. Financial pressures continued to increase.

When a neurotic mechanism blocks feedback information flow, the organization's control systems might not receive information that critical limits have been passed or this information may be distorted, filtered, repressed, or deflected in some way. The organization may be unaware that it is stressed. Bowler (1981) notes:

There may be stresses on systems that are not perceived, not recognized as stresses, and perhaps not perceived at all by the control subsystems of a system. The energy-matter information may be beyond the range of the system's receptors. It may be received as meaningless noise or distorted for assimilation into existing maps which interpret it as routine stress or insignificant, that is, not requiring a response beyond recognition. (p. 194)

Some variables passing beyond their critical limit may have a ripple effect on other critical variables of the organization. For example, a severe shortage of income or low motivation may affect many aspects of an organization's functioning. The organization may suffer damage in the sense of its future functioning being impaired by what has happened. An example would be defective products, which not only lead to loss of present customers, but also deter customers in the future. Another example is labor dissatisfaction, which is seen as meta-grumbles when in fact it is serious enough to cause a strike. The dysfunctioning of the feedback cycles, thus leading to disruption of the fluctuation of the organization's variables beyond their critical limits, might be in the initial phase of the disruption of the contact and withdrawal cycles.

Together with the disruption in the fluctuation of the organization's variables beyond their limits, two other cycles may begin to dysfunction. The "opening and closing" and the "task and maintenance" cycles may suffer from lack of reality-based information.

GUM DEPARTMENT STORE, MOSCOW, U.S.S.R.—A CASE STUDY IN FROZEN PATHOLOGY

To buy a pair of shoes in the Gum Department Store on Red Square, you must do the following: (1) stand in line at the shoe counter and wait to see the shoes, pick out the color, establish the price, size, etc.; (2) stand in another line leading to a cashier to pay for the shoes and obtain a receipt; and (3) stand in line again at the shoe counter to exchange the receipt for the shoes. This system is extremely inefficient and wastes countless hours of time, yet it is a system which has been going on for years.

Several "neuroses" are occurring at the same time at Gum. First, there is virtually no feedback—the store management and the consumer know of no other way in which a store could be run. Therefore, there is little or no complaining. It is a tightly closed system with no demands for change. The store and the consumer are not in touch with reality as they are seeing reality through economic and cultural filters that prevent the formation of alternatives. Creative adjustment depends on quality contact with the environment. With our Western mentality we would see the obvious effect such a system would have on profits and would streamline it immediately or lose the business to our competitors. Gum Department Store has no competitors (a virtual monopoly) and thus no impetus to change.—*R. Drickey*

The organization may lose its ability to control its boundaries effectively. In lacking dependable feedback, the organization may have problems in dealing with how much, when, and to what to open and close its boundaries. This may take a variety of forms, such as opening boundaries too much when they should be more closed; closing too much when the boundaries should be more open; having difficulty discriminating to whom to open and to whom to close the boundaries; and hanging on to what should be closed out. These various forms of difficulty with opening and closing boundaries will be detailed later in this chapter.

The task and maintenance cycle of organizational functioning may also be affected by the distortion of feedback. The organization may run into difficulties in defining its needs and deciding to which of them to grant priority. There may be problems of choosing and putting into effect the actions needed to attain its objectives. Lacking a sensitive mapping of conditions within the organization, internal maintenance may not be taken care of. The balance between task and maintenance may not be maintained, as when an industry is only geared to production, and ignores workers' needs. These various forms of imbalance in the task and maintenance cycle will be detailed in the next chapter.

THE PHASES OF ORGANIZATIONAL DYSFUNCTIONING

The remaining two cycles to be affected by the disruption of reality feedback communication are the input–output and work cycles. The hypothesis developed here suggests that the development of organizational dysfunctioning as a result of neurotic fantasy may pass through two phases.

Phase One: The neurotic mechanism blocks reality-based feedback, thus leading to fluctuations in the organization's variables beyond their critical limits.

At the same time, lack of dependable feedback leads to disruption in the organization's ability to control the opening and closing of its boundaries. The lack of reality-based feedback also causes difficulty for the organization in equilibrating its task and maintenance cycle to ensure attainment of organizational goals and satisfaction of individual needs. (This disequilibration will be dealt with in the next chapter.)

Phase Two: In this phase of a declining organization, its input–output and work cycles are noticeably affected to an extent that might endanger continued functioning and adaptability. The fluctuations of critical variables beyond the organization's tolerance level may lead to a reorganization and qualitative shift in the organization's internal order in the direction of increasing entropy.

> Bolton General Hospital passed through phase one of neurotic organizational behavior and then moved into phase two of a declining organization.
>
> In phase one the hospital got bogged down in a climate of outdated, inefficient bureaucratic procedures. Doing things by the book stifled all individual and team initiative and creativity. Bureaupathology made attempts to get things done or innovate an impossible task. Putting decisions into action got bogged down in a mine of bureaucratic obstructions. Management and many of the staff lived in the delusion of the period of the hospital's beginning, when for a time it had innovated new medical procedures. Present-day problems and difficulties, and the hospital's inefficiency and low-energy climate, were ignored in light of the achievements of the past. Many of the hospital's "essential variables" were fluctuating beyond their critical limits. Bed occupancy was going down, expenses were going up, patients' complaints were increasing in number and severity, and dissatisfaction among the staff was rife. Some of the most capable managers, doctors, and nurses were leaving, and fewer young talented doctors were applying for jobs. This condition continued for some years throughout a number of management changeovers.
>
> Phase two became apparent when the inefficient functioning, staff discontent, low work morale, and negative selection in personnel began seriously to affect treatment effectiveness, bed occupancy, and the hospital's financial solvency. Attempts to deal with the financial crisis by layoffs and cuts in fringe benefits led to disruptions in labor relations, strikes, and worsening crisis. The disruption in services further damaged the hospital's reputation and image in the community and among the staff. The hospital developed a failure self-image, which, in turn, lowered work morale even further and contributed to an atmosphere of cynicism, lethargy, and gloom, and further deterioration.

It is hypothesized that most organizations displaying neurotic organizational behavior do not necessarily move on to phase two. Not all manifestations of neurotic behavior lead to disruptions of the organization's productive ability and to cyclical disintegrative crises.

According to Prigogine's theory of dissipative structures, at certain points fluctuations lead to the reorganization of the system. This reorganization is at a new level of greater complexity (differentiation and interdependence between components) and negentropy. It is suggested, here, that maladaptive systems, at the level of declining organizations, move in a polarized direction. They move into an order of decreasing complexity, decreasing interdependence among subsystems, and greater entropy. Their direction is in accordance with the second law of thermodynamics, toward increasing entropy. In other words, declining organizations behave as nonliving systems. They are unable to revitalize themselves and maintain integration with the energy they derive from the environment. Declining organizations move from one cycle to another in the direction of increasing disorder and less integration (disintegration).*

It is necessary, at this point, to clarify what makes the movement from phase one to phase two such a crucial occurrence. Movement into phase two means disruption of the organization's input–throughput–output and work cycles. In other words, *phase two means that dysfunctioning has developed in the production subsystems, the functioning of which is an essential condition for continued organizational existence.*

The hypothesis is that organizations have a sense of self-preservation that guides them, even when dysfunctioning, to maintain their essential functions. While neurotic behavior may affect other, less life-sustaining aspects of organizational functioning, the organization will attempt to preserve and not impair the essential functions that are a condition for its survival. The organization's survival depends on producing outputs the environment wants sufficiently to provide in exchange for the inputs the organization needs for continued functioning. As Burke (1980) writes: "Organization must not only take from the environment more than it uses but it must constantly arrange for accurate feedback from the environment to ensure that the organization's output is accomplishing what the organization intends" (p. 218).

In declining organizations the organization's control systems are no longer receiving this feedback, and the production process is running down. The environment is not receiving valued outputs, essential inputs are not coming in, and entropy is developing.

The organization, even the declining one, knows that if production is impaired so that outputs are not valued by the environment, it may be denied essential inputs necessary for continued

---

*Possibly this distinction between neurotic organizational behavior and declining organizations may be applied, using Prigogine's conceptualization, to the distinction between neurotic and psychotic individuals. This, however, is not the subject of this work.

functioning. The organization therefore will do all it can to shield the input–throughput–output production and work cycles from being impaired.

> The publishing department of a large independent educational institution included a subgroup whose responsibility was producing a magazine. The function of this magazine was to keep friends, alumni, and others aware of ongoing activities and projects in the organization.
>
> Former professional editors made up part of the magazine team. It was their ambition to make their product into a high-circulation, glossy news-and-views organ. In reality they had neither the personnel nor the budget to carry this out. As a compromise they decided to publish it just six times yearly, and as circulation and income increased, they would expand the number and length of issues.
>
> Very early on the group came up against the amount of work required to produce even a small-scale magazine. As well as becoming strained and overworked themselves, they were coexisting in a publishing department also very much under strain. The desire these people had for a highly professional magazine was so strong, however, that they continued to strive for it.
>
> At management meetings to which this magazine subgroup sent a representative, the question would arise whether it was appropriate for the magazine to continue with its ambitious format, given that it not only strained the magazine group to produce it, but also the publishing department to print it. The group refused to admit to strain, as one tactic to remain as they were. Another tactic was to counter by saying, "We can't function without support; you're undermining the institution's having a means of communication with its alumni." The hysterical note effectively stopped all discussion of better ways to produce a magazine.—*C. O'Connor*

Organizations do all they can to protect their essential production processes. Thompson (1967) describes ways in which organizations buffer their production core from environmental variations. He details different methods the organization uses to protect its technical core. An example would be to keep sufficiently large inventories to ensure steady production even in times of shortage. Another method is that of "smoothing," for example, offering inducements to customers for using services during difficult periods. Another approach is to absorb volatile changes with extreme organizational flexibility. Whatever the approach, the purpose is to protect the technical core, to ensure continuance of an effective input–output cycle, and to buffer the steady fluctuation of the organization's work cycle.

The hypothesis brought forward here is that an organization

will do all it can to shield its input–throughput–output and work cycles from being damaged by its own neurotic behavior.* While dysfunctioning will appear in other aspects of the organization's functioning, for example, relationships and norm maintenance, the organization will attempt to protect its essential production functioning from its own dysfunctioning. Possible exceptions to this are organizations whose input/output ratio cannot be measured, and whose survival thus does not depend on their efficiency. Some public service institutions qualify for this category. Another possible exception is the subsidiary organization that is maintained by the corporate organization for reasons other than profit—prestige, for example.

The hypothesis about the organization shielding its production subsystem from its own neurotic behavior explains why organizational neurosis does not always lead to organizational disintegration. It is possible to discern what is described here as neurotic organizational behavior in many organizations. But not all of them have problems in their production subsystems, and not all of them will disintegrate because of such problems.

Although there are differences in how tightly an organization's subunits are coupled, all parts of a system are connected in some way with each other; all in some way affect each other. In organizations it is not easy to segregate a subsystem completely from pathology in other subsystems or in the system as a whole. Therefore, it is to be expected that in organizations displaying neurotic behavior, the production subsystem will somehow be affected; there will be some spilloff of the organization's pathology on its input–output cycle. Nevertheless, this, generally, seems to be confined to a level that does not endanger continued organizational functioning. The mechanisms by which an organization does this need to be studied and explicated. Organizational survival is in jeopardy when the pathology disrupts the input–output cycle to a degree that essential inputs from the environment are no longer forthcoming and available.

To summarize up to this point: When delusions and fantasy block reality feedback, the organization loses awareness of the fluctuations of some of its variables beyond their critical limits. Lack of dependable feedback may also lead to malfunctioning of

---

*This probably happens at the individual level as well. The neurotic might attempt, as much as possible, to shield his/her work role from his/her own neurotic functioning. This has clinical support but needs empirical investigation.

the boundary control cycle of opening and closing, and the task/maintenance cycle.

The organization will probably attempt to protect its production (input–output and work cycles) from the effects of its own dysfunctioning. As long as an organization succeeds in doing this (protecting its outputs from dysfunctioning), it will be defined as displaying neurotic behavior as distinct from the next phase, which will be called a declining organization.

At a certain point, the reverberations of the fluctuations of essential variables beyond critical points may bring the organization into a qualitatively different state. This state, found in declining organizations, is marked by repetitive entropic disintegrative crises, and the input–output balance with the environment is proceeding in a direction that will endanger organizational existence.

DISRUPTION OF THE CYCLE OF OPENING AND CLOSING

Control of the organization's boundaries with the environment is a critical function. Various organization theorists have devoted research to the organization–environment interfaces and the control of boundaries to ensure adaptivity and organizational health.

Alderfer (1980) suggests that there is a curvilinear relationship between an organization's boundary openness and the organization's vitality. Vitality is seen as an organization's tendency toward survival and growth. Both extremes—wide-open boundaries that permit infiltration of harmful inputs and tightly closed boundaries that bar essential inputs—were shown to be detrimental to organizational vitality. Niv (1980) deals with organizational disintegration, its roots and types. He researched communes that had adapted and communes that had disintegrated. Among the communes that had disintegrated, Niv differentiated between two types. Some disintegrated because they were too closed to essential environmental relationships. This kind of disintegration may be called stagnation. Another kind of commune was assimilated into the environment because it was too open to environmental relations. The Shaker colonies are an example of the stagnation process that stems from closed boundaries. The Amana villages are an example of assimilation. In 1932 they decided to split into a church and a business enterprise, which, though economically successful, ceased to function as a commercial organization.

Klapp (1975) suggests that opening and closing are not a matter of quantity of indiscriminate information flow. Openness does not imply indiscrimination as to what is admitted and what is barred entry. A business might diversify investment without being venturesome in labor relations. An industry might welcome technological innovation and resist managerial or structural novelties. He writes: "Openness might be characterized as readiness to look around a gestalt while widening the range of scanning as artists try to do" (p. 255).

Klapp suggests thinking of opening and closing as part of strategy to get the most of the best information and least of the worst noise "depending on a trade-off in the signal-to-noise ratio." When the environment burdens the organization with information overload, it needs to close. The oscillation between opening and closing can be seen as moves to gain variety or redundancy as needed by the particular state of the system.   From the point of view of the system, both opening and closing may be functional and dysfunctional. Klapp suggests the following alternatives (see Figure 9-1). He writes:

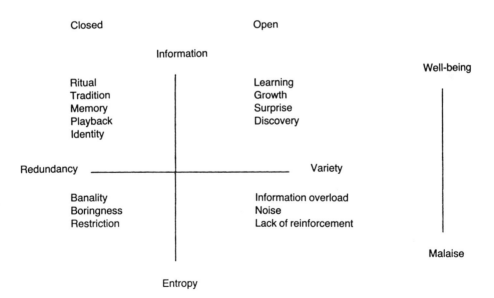

Figure 9.1
Kinds of opening and closing in systems

Oscillation between opening and closing is the normal way to play the game. Good moves take one into advantageous sectors. Mistakes, opening or closing at the wrong time or to the wrong things may place one in deep trouble. (p. 256)

"Bad" closing (lower left section) necessitates an oscillation to the "good" opening (upper right section). "Bad" opening (lower right sector) demands a swimg to the "good" closing (upper left sector). Bad opening means "being overwhelmed by noise or signals of amounts and kinds that a system cannot use for its own growth. . . ."

Using many examples from organizations and taking a systems approach, Klapp has in effect elucidated Perls' concepts of disruption of the contact–withdrawal process in the sense of opening and closing boundaries.

An organization may be affected negatively (malaise, entropy) by opening and closing if:

—It closes itself to inputs it should be open to.
—It opens itself to inputs it should be closed to.
—It closes itself too much when it should be more open.
—It opens itself too much when it should be more closed.

FORMS OF DISRUPTION OF OPENING AND CLOSING

Disruptions of the cycle of opening and closing may take a variety of forms. Three of the most prevalent forms of disruption in organizations are:

1. Excessive closure.
2. Excessive opening.
3. Inability to discriminate.

Excessive Closure

"As pathological as the complete withdrawal, the ivory tower or the catatonic stupor" (Perls, 1976, p. 65).

Complete withdrawal in an open system is impossible. It would mean the system would be a closed system devoid of inputs and outputs. Open systems, such as individuals and organizations, cannot close themselves completely, as this would mean termination of their existence. Nevertheless, organizations do withdraw and close themselves to a degree that, while being harmful, allows the organization to continue functioning.

De Board (1978) describes how disengagement from reality leads to organizational withdrawal and excessive closure, possibly leading to termination.

If, for instance, an old, established family firm realizes that its product and methods are no longer appropriate to the 1970s, the anxiety may be so strong that energy is withdrawn from managing the boundary and used in a whole variety of defense mechanisms to avoid the real issue. For a time these will protect the firm from the need to change and adapt, but unless it eventually faces up to this harsh reality, it will inevitably go bankrupt. (p. 141)

Miller's (1978) categorization refers to (1) lack of matter-energy inputs, and (2) lack of information inputs. Lack of matter-energy inputs would mean, for example, that the organization has closed itself to a degree that it is not receiving sufficient people as employees or as members, and this is disturbing its effective functioning. Another example is that the organization is not open to new technology that is needed for it to compete for markets. Lack of information inputs might mean that the organization has closed itself to information that might demand a change in its way of functioning, in production methods, or in managerial style. Another example might be that of a social movement that is closed to information that might disrupt the priorities of its value system. This often happens in political parties with strong ideological commitments.

Alderfer (1981) illustrates how organizations with overbounded, nonpermeable, rigid boundaries lose vitality and have difficulty adapting to their environment. He differentiates among eight dimensions of overboundedness: authority is often rigid; roles are defined too specifically; communication is distorted; members' energy is blocked by system boundaries; members attribute negative qualities to others and feelings are supposed to be sublimated; the overbounded organization has problems responding to change although it is relatively wealthier than underbounded systems.

Niv (1981) describes the disintegration of communes that comes as a result of excessive closure. The resulting lack of resources, as in the case of the Shakers, leads to disintegration of a kind that Niv calls stagnation. This usually takes the form of physically abandoning the commune.

Levinson (1972) includes in his list of maladaptive and disruptive activities "withdrawal into organizational self; giving up the community, professional associations" (p. 542). He illustrates withdrawal with the example of a church that withdrew from its environment: "If West Hills Mennonite Church had any harmful effect on the environment it would be only in the form of withdrawal which deprived those who might have been helped by what the church had to offer" (p. 329).

Within the framework of this work, it is not possible to deal with the organizational conditions that favor withdrawal in particular as a form of neurotic reaction. Probably the degree to which the organization is what Miller calls totipotential contributes to the choice of this type of reaction. Most organizations deal only with a segment of their members' lives and cannot close themselves to outside influences brought in by their members from their other role activities. Jantsch (1975) points out that one of the differences between social systems and individual systems or organs lies in the partial membership of the organization's subsystems. People can belong concurrently to many organizations, and each organization deals with only a segment of the person's life, while "cells are not multiple members of different organs." Jantsch sees this multiple membership of people in different social systems as a driving energetic force that activates and energizes organizational change and evolution. It seems reasonable to suggest that organizations that deal only with a partial segment of their members' lives have greater difficulty in withdrawing. The possibility of closing oneself to outer influences increases the more the organization is totipotential; that is, to which it covers most of its members' needs and roles. The more totipotential an organization is, the more it assumes responsibility for different segments of its members' lives. Goffman (1961) called organizations of this kind total institutions, such as ship or a residential college. It seems that total institutions are able to withdraw more completely than other organizations, and also are generally more self-sufficient.

Excessive Opening

Excessive opening is the polarized pathology of excessive closing. Klapp (1975) has pointed out that there is a conventional bias that openness is always better than closedness. It is therefore necessary to clarify that too much openness can be just as maladaptive as too much closedness.

Miller (1978) has devoted two categories of his eight forms of system pathology to excessive opening: (1) excesses of matter-energy inputs and (2) excesses of information inputs. Excesses of matter-energy inputs can be seen, for example, as too many students in a university, beyond the institution's coping ability. Excesses of information inputs can result, for example, in an organization that is unable to process the flood of orders from its customers. Another example would be that of an organization losing control of its inventory. Miller has devoted a series of studies to the subject of information overload at a variety of system levels, such as organisms, groups, and organizations. An interesting finding is that at different levels the systems use the same adjustment processes to deal with the information overload. These processes are as follows (Miller, 1978):

Omission—failing to transmit certain randomly distributed signals in a message. Queuing—delaying transmission of certain signals in a message. Filtering—giving priority in processing to certain classes of messages. Abstracting—processing a message with less than complete detail. Multiple channels—simultaneously transmitting messages over two or more parallel channels. Escape—acting to cut off information input. Chunking —transmitting meaningful information in organized "chunks" of symbols rather than symbol by symbol. (p. 123)

Inability to Discriminate

"This contact and withdrawal from the environment, this acceptance and rejection of the environment, are the most important functions of the total personality. . . . We . . . see them as aspects of the same thing, the capacity to discriminate. This capacity can become confused and function badly. When it does, the individual is unable to behave appropriately and consequently we describe him as neurotic" (Perls, 1980, p. 23).

To deal effectively with its environment, an organization needs to be able to differentiate between what it should accept and what it should reject from the environment. It needs to be able to discriminate between what is growthful and what is harmful for it. The growthful can be assimilated, and the harmful rejected.

Furthermore, if the system is unable to discriminate and it accepts harmful inputs, it will suffer as a consequence. Bowler (1981) points out that if what flows in and dynamically reacts is too inconsistent with the existing patterns, there will be change, and possibly some destruction. Even more, if the organization is unable to discriminate this may lead to its disintegration. Bowler writes that there must be order and discriminatory judgment of some kind if individuals and society are not to disintegrate.

When illusion replaces reality mapping and feedback cycles are distorted or ignored, the organization may lose its ability to appreciate differences. It may have difficulty in discriminating when and from what to withdraw. It may be unable to see with what and when to make contact. In these cases the organization may be unaware of noxious developments in its environment; it may open itself to toxic inputs of matter-energy and information and may be incapable of proactively exploiting advantageous opportunities.

A breakdown in the organization's ability to discriminate will allow harmful or excessive inputs of some kind to disrupt the steady state. Miller (1978) describes the inability to discriminate as a pathology. In his terms it is called an inappropriate form of matter-energy. An example of this would be an organization that accepts unsuitable members or employees. Another example would be the introduction of a production technology that is harmful to the employees who implement it.

Klapp (1975) describes the organization's need to discriminate in its interaction with the environment: "Opening and closing are not a matter of amount of information flow. The notion of a gate swinging ajar or slamming is not meant to imply indiscriminateness in what is admitted or barred" (p. 254).

Open systems planning (Merry & Allerhand, 1977, pp. 117–124) is an approach that has been developed to sensitize organizations to changing demands from relevant domains in the environment. Participants in the process become aware of signals from the environment they formerly did not discriminate. One industry that had a large export market in the past was insensitive to changes in the countries to which it was selling. It was ignoring changing governmental regulations and currency values—and recurring distress signals from its agents in these countries. Another industry, which made parts for medical equipment, continued year after year to produce the same product, ignoring signs of decreasing demand because of better-quality and better-priced items offered by competitors.

"Hanging on" is a common form of the inability to discriminate. Perls (1976) described it this way: "Many people rather hang on with their attention to exhaust the situation that does not nourish. This hanging on to the world, this over-extended contact is as pathological as the complete withdrawal" (p. 65).

Hanging on can take the form of the organization continuing to maintain a certain relationship with its environment long after that relationship has lost any meaning or purpose. The Anti-Tuberculosis League continued to function for years long after that disease had completely disappeared from the Western world. The railroad system in the United States hung on to its original services long after they had lost their competitive ability. Industries hang on to outdated products long after they have lost their market value.

PROPOSITIONS AND DEFINITIONS

The following have varying degrees of theoretical, clinical, and research support.

★ Living in an intermediate zone of illusions and fantasy may decrease an organization's ability to receive feedback.
★ A decrease in an organization's ability to receive feedback may block its awareness of the fluctuations of some of its variables beyond their critical limits.
★ Fluctuations of some of an organization's variables beyond their critical limits may create a ripple effect among other organizational variables, negatively affecting organizational adaptability.

(The above propositions are generally supported by systems theory and the clinical observations of some organization theorists.)

★ A decrease in an organization's ability to receive feedback may decrease its control of the opening and closing of its boundaries.
★ A decrease in an organization's control of the opening and closing of its boundaries commonly may take these forms: (1) excessive closure; (2) excessive opening; (3) inability to discriminate.

★ In excessive closure the organization will close its boundaries to a degree that bars inputs of matter-energy and information the organization needs for effective functioning.

★ In excessive opening the organization opens its boundaries to a degree that allows inputs of matter-energy and information that are harmful to the organization's functioning and/or development.

★ An organization unable to discriminate will not differentiate between matter-energy and information to which it should open its boundaries and matter-energy and information to which it should be closed.

(The above propositions have support both in organizational theory and research.)

★ Disruption of the input–output cycle and work cycle may endanger the organization's essential inputs from the environment.

★ As not receiving essential inputs may lead to disintegration, organizations attempt to protect their input–output and work cycles from the effects of their own dysfunctioning.

★ In the first phase of neurotic organizational behavior, organizations may maintain a pattern of neurotic behavior over a period of time without this necessarily leading to noticeable disruptions in their output–input and work cycles.

★ In the second phase of a declining organization, dysfunctioning spreads throughout the system, affecting the work cycle and the input–transformation–output cycle.

★ In this second phase, fluctuations of an organization's variables beyond their critical range may lead to qualitative shifts in the organization's internal order in the direction of increasing entropy.

(The above propositions need empirical verification.)

CHAPTER 10

THE DISRUPTION OF THE TASK/MAINTENANCE CYCLE AND REVERSING THE DECLINE OF ORGANIZATIONS

OVERVIEW

The former chapter dealt with the disruption of contact and withdrawal and the links between this disruption and organizational neurosis. It was suggested that organizational dysfunctioning develops in phases, delaying effects on the organization's outputs, in order to ensure survival.

The various forms of disruption of the cycle of opening and closing were described and detailed.

This chapter continues the description of contact and withdrawal disruption in organizations. The cycle dealt with here is that of task and maintenance.

A model of blocking this cycle that was developed in Gestalt therapy is conceptualized in organizational terms.

The chapter continues with an elaboration on this model by describing the three major ways an organization can block its task/maintenance cycle: by blocking awareness, by blocking energy, and by blocking action.

As energy is not conceptualized with sufficient clarity in organizational literature, a large section of the chapter deals with organizational energy and its blocking.

The final section reports some preliminary research on the transformation of declining organizations, indicating what elements may be necessary for reversing the decline.

BLOCKING THE TASK/MAINTENANCE CYCLE

The task/maintenance cycle was specified as occurring in task teams and possibly in organizations. This cycle takes the form of the system alternating between dealing with its maintenance (socioemotive needs) and its task (production needs).

The dichotomy of task/maintenance has been recognized by many organizational theorists under a variety of names: goal emphasis/support (Bowers & Seashore, 1966); instrumental/expressive (Gouldner & Gouldner, 1963); concern for production/concern for people (Blake & Mouton, 1978).

Debate, research, and conflicting theories and research findings exist as to the relationship between attendance to task/maintenance and organizational effectiveness and health. An integration of the different approaches that might receive support from most of them today could be worded thus: marked inattendance of an organization to either its maintenance or its task needs will result in organizational malfunctioning. This formulation moves attention from the desired mix to the process by which an organization blocks itself from satisfying its maintenance or task needs.

At the individual level, Perls conceptualized contact and withdrawal in the form of a cycle. The organism becomes aware of a need, feels excitement, and thus mobilizes energy to attend to the need. The organism then takes action to satisfy the need, and following this, returns to the state of repose until another need arises. The new need arises from the interaction of the organism, or a part of the organism, and the environmental context in which it finds itself at that moment. Perls has elaborated on how an individual may block any phase of this cycle and thus disrupt the homeostatic cycle of contact and withdrawal.

Zinker (1977) has developed this approach into a model with the phases of the contact and withdrawal cycle drawn in a circle. He has also conceptualized what happens when each phase of the cycle is blocked.

A simplified model of the contact and withdrawal cycle could be illustrated as in Figure 10-1.* This model can be used to help a person become aware of how he/she blocks the contact–withdrawal cycle of satisfying needs. At the organizational level, the same model may be used to examine how an organization blocks satisfaction of its task/maintenance needs. The model points to the three major possible ways of disrupting the satisfaction of needs:

1. Blocking awareness of needs.
2. Blocking energy mobilization.
3. Blocking action taking.

In many aspects there is much similarity between Gestalt therapy thinking on the foregoing and that of others influenced by Lewinian-field theory. Therefore, the reader may find that some

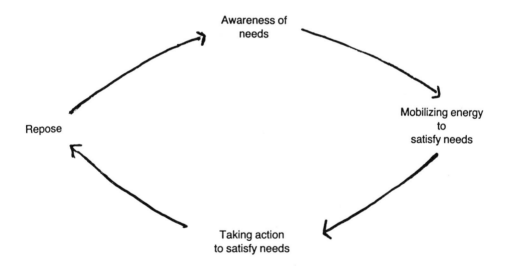

Figure 10.1
The contact and withdrawal cycle

*Suggested by David Richo.

parts of the following paragraphs have much in common with other presentations of this subject.

BLOCKING AWARENESS OF NEEDS

Perls (1976) describes the blocking of awareness of needs in terms of desensitizing the sensoric system. He writes:

If excitement cannot flow into activity through the motoric system, we try to desensitize the sensoric system to reduce this excitement. So we find all kinds of desensitization: frigidity, blocking of the ears, and so on—all these roles in the personality that I talked about earlier. (p. 69)

What Perls is saying is that, in neurotic behavior, when the organism will not deal with its needs and tensions by taking care of them in action, it tries to deaden its own awareness of these needs and tensions. A feeling of bottled-up excitement that cannot find relief is, at the least, uncomfortable. In order not to be in this condition, the organism attempts to eliminate the source of the excitement by desensitizing itself to inputs that may create the condition.

In organizational terms desensitization may take the form of the organization decreasing its awareness of communication and feedback, or diminishing or devaluating their significance for its inner and outer needs.

Both organizations displaying neurotic behavior and healthy organizations have blockages in awareness of needs.

Very often even healthy organizations are not totally aware of their own needs. Ineffective communication channels, one-way communication downward, a climate of insufficient trust and openness, and other factors have been found to create conditions in which an organization is insufficiently aware of and sensitive to the needs of its members or clients. De Greene (1982, p. 13) has identified this list of things that can go wrong with flow and feedback of information:

Misidentified as to source.
Incorrect at the source, even though the source is correctly identified.
Attentuated in transition, perhaps through filtration.
Amplified in transmission.

Noisy, that is, wanted signals or content may be difficult or impossible to extricate from the unwanted signal or content . . . the introduction of random elements or by purposeful action.

Delayed in transmission.

Incomplete when received.

Misperceived by the receiver.

Refused or suppressed.

It is not by chance that a great deal of the consulting work done with organizations is spent in unclogging feedback, opening communication channels, and helping the organization to become aware of and sensitive to its needs. Forms of ineffective communication are common in many organizations. While problems in the flow of feedback of information may cause healthy organizations to be not completely aware of their needs, they are deeper and more compounded in organizational neurosis. Living largely in the intermediate zone and lacking reality-based feedback, the organization displaying neurotic behavior almost always blocks awareness of its own socioemotional needs and, at later stages of neurosis, of its task needs.

The chapter on mechanisms of organizational delusion and fantasy (Chapter 7) dealt in detail with the various ways in which an organization can live in the intermediate zone, blocking awareness of what is happening inside itself and in the environment. Some of the common mechanisms for doing this were described.

When a healthy organization is confronted with information on needs of which it has been unaware, the reaction will generally be one of discovery, acceptance, acknowledgment, and ownership. The "confrontation meeting" (Beckhard, 1967), individual interviews and group feedback (Merry & Allerhard, 1977) and open systems planning (Jayuram, 1976; Merry & Allerhard, 1977) are all organizational development processes aimed at assisting an organization become aware of needs to which it has not been attending. In organizational neurosis the problem of blocking awareness of needs is more complicated. The organization is blocking awareness of its needs and does not know it is doing this. But even more, when the organization is confronted with reality-based information, it very often (1) does not accept the information and (2) avoids owning its blocking tactics.

This can be done in a variety of ways. Some of the most common ways are denial, dimunition, and devaluation. These avoidance tactics may take the following forms.

Denial—unawareness of and denying the existence of signals relating to the existence of unsatisfied needs. An example would be (in a dissatisfied organization): "People here are satisfied; we have no problems."

Dimunition—acknowledging there are some signals relating to needs, but not acknowledging their intensity or spread. An example would be (in a dissatisfied organization): "Yes, there is a little grumbling, but it is on the fringe among the permanent malcontents."

Devaluation—acknowledging the signals, but not giving them their deserved importance. An example would be (in an extremely dissatisfied organization): "Yes, there are many complaints; have you ever met an organization without them?"

Some consultants, when expecting avoidance tactics, deal with them by first confronting them before returning feedback to the organization. One way of doing this (developed by one author) is to display a list of avoidance tactics and have the organization's management discuss whether any of these reactions are found in there. An appropriate list might be as follows:

★ We have no such problems.
★ We have some problems, but they are not serious.
★ We have such problems, everyone has them.
★ We have such problems, but no one can deal with them.
★ We have such problems, but we cannot deal with them because we (have a wooden leg, etc.).

The management team is invited to add to this list its particular sentence and to discuss how widespread any of these reactions are in the organization.

BLOCKING ENERGY MOBILIZATION

Energy in Gestalt Therapy

Before dealing with the blockage of energy mobilization, it is necessary to clarify what Perls meant by energy. The concept of "energy" occurs in Perls writings with a number of different meanings, therefore, the connotation according to which it will be used here requires that it be made manifest.

The concept of energy to which Perls seems to have devoted most interest is that of the excitement or vitality created by the emotions that leads to action. The following passages exemplarize this use of the concept (Perls, 1980).

The force which basically energizes all our actions. That force seems to be emotion . . . emotions are the very language of the organism; they modify the basic excitement according to the situation which has to be met. Excitement is transformed into specific emotions, and the emotions are transformed into sensoric and motor actions. (p. 24)

This use of the concept of energy is the one Perls stresses in his later writings. It is this concept of energy to which Perls alludes when he speaks about mobilizing energy or, in contrast, blocking energy flow in the homeostatic cycle.

In this conceptualization, energy in individuals is seen as a force, an excitement, a vitality, that is aroused by a need or a tension. This excitement may then develop into the form of a particular emotion. The energy in the form of an emotion is then transformed into sensoric or motoric action.

This excitement-energy can be blocked by either sensoric or emotional desensitization. The form of desensitization called sensoric desensitization was described in the former section dealing with blocking awareness. It now remains to deal with emotional desensitization.

As Perls (1980) puts it:

One of the most serious problems of modern man is that he has desensitized himself to all but the most overwhelming kind of emotional response. To the degree that he is no longer capable of feeling sensitively, to that degree he becomes incapable of the freedom of choice that results in relevant action. (p. 85)

Miller (1982) explains how living systems import matter-energy from the environment, use it for their processes, and return part of it to their environment. The matter-energy of the input is lower in entropy than that of output. It is this process of living systems that allows them to maintain a steady state and repair themselves.

Bowler (1981) points out that these processes require a continual supply of energy that comes directly or indirectly from the sun. Solar radiation becomes available to living systems as photosynthesis. Living systems utilize energy in many forms and store and package it. Because of its constant use in control, maintenance, and production, there must be a constant backlog of stored energy.

This is essential because steady state systems are constantly subject to stresses requiring adequate supplies of energy in various places at various times. This necessary flexibility of the energy supply requires adequate storage and distribution of "packaged energy" and, hence, the steady state system's balance is always "off center" toward an excess of energy. (p. 47)

Because of this excess of energy, a living system is always active; it is always "fired up." Bowler suggests that this produces a restlessness in the system.

In any case, it is clear that while a living system must equilibrate, its goal is never a state of equilibrium. The steady state requires, rather, a fluctuation between relative rest and relative activity, not passive waiting for a stimulus to which it can respond. Its own inner conditions are as much the cause of its activities as anything in the environment. (p. 38)

These statements of Bowler are worth noting both as a background for the phenomena of contact and withdrawal, and for understanding how a living system is energized.

Except for its use in systems theory, energy in organizations is recognized by practitioners who work and consult with organizations. Books and articles on organizational consulting and organizational development use the concept of energy. Possibly, in dealing with the realities of organizational life, it is difficult not to pay attention to such a striking phenomenon as the level of energy of an organization.

Levinson (1972) diagnoses the energy level of organizations, the rate (consistent or variable) with which they discharge energy, and points and periods of peak energy. Speaking about an organization's energy level, he writes:

What is the pace of the organization? With what degree of enthusiasm or lethargy does it pursue new products, different markets, innovative technology? How aggressive is it in its competitive efforts? . . . the degree of "vigor" of an organization. (pp. 240–241)

Steele and Jenks (1977) refer to energy as a dimension of the organization's climate. They build their approach to consulting

around energy as one of the most important dimensions of organizational life. Beer (1981) connects energy to human effort and
motivation as possibly one of the most important kinds of energy
in organizations. He writes:

Entropy, or a running down of the system, will occur to the extent that
energy is not continuously imported and converted into valued outputs
that allow reinvestment and further development. For social systems, the
most important maintenance source is human effort and motivation. Thus
the motivation of people in the organization becomes just as important
a source of energy as financial and other energy/matter resources. (p. 77)

Ways of Blocking Organizational Energy

Organizations have various ways of blocking the expression of
their energy. Two of the common ways of doing this are:

1. Dampening emotional expression.
2. Blocking personal expression.

From the days of the Hawthorne experiments (Roethlisberger
& Dickson, 1939) the human relations approach to organizations
has been to theorize, research, and explicate the relationship between an organization's functioning and how much it attends to
the needs of its human components. Probably, in reaction to the
extreme "task" orientation of the Taylorian scientific management
approach, the earlier formulations of the human relations school
were excessively "people/maintenance" oriented. With passing years
both the contingency and systems approaches have righted the
balance. Contingency therories have elucidated the conditions under which either task or maintenance needed to be attended to.
System theories replaced one way causal-linear explanations with
the complexity of the mutual interaction of a system's variables.
The picture that emerged was that organizations needed to attend
both to task and to maintenance, varying their attention according
to contextual-situational conditions.

After each consulting day with Brayburn Company, I felt as if all my
energy had been drained out of me. I knew beforehand that this would
happen, but could do little about it. The climate of the place was infectious.
The low-energy, dreary, almost hopeless consultation with the CEO was
guaranteed to quell any energy and enthusiasm I had brought with me.

He spoke in such a dragging, tired, lifeless way that all problems seemed insurmountable. He epitomized the climate of the company. The place was tired, low key, bored, unenergized, and sort of hopeless.

Years of grappling endlessly and unsuccessfully with mounting problems, internal conflicts, demoralizing scandals, low efficiency, high turnover, and decreasing income had led to hopelessness. The company was in a state devoid of all energy and motivation to do anything. People had resigned themselves to things remaining as they were or getting steadily worse. Those who remained could not be aroused and there seemed no way to ignite their enthusiasm. The place was without energy, without hope, without motivation—resigned to its dull, listless struggle to continue existing in its own dreary lifeless way. But people knew that even that barren existence would not have been possible without outside resources supporting the company. They also knew that the flow would end one day.

Nevertheless it needs to be pointed out that in most cases where there is an imbalance, it is generally in the direction of neglect of people/maintenance and not of task. Environmental reaction generally ensures that an organization will take care of its task dimension. Neglecting outputs as a task function can have an immediate effect on essential inputs. Berrien (1968) makes a case for the relative stability of the ratio between task and maintenance. Using different concepts, he argues that the upper limits of maintenance and the lower limits of task "are normally under the control of the super system." Contrariwise, the lower limits of maintenance and the upper limits of task are normally controlled by the subsystem. The force field created between these opposing forces maintains the relatively stable ratio between task and maintenance. In many cases it seems that this stable ratio has an imbalance that favors task and neglects maintenance. This situation appears to create conditions that block organizational energy by dampening emotional and personal expression.

Low-energy systems are organizations in which people invest little motivation, interest, and excitement in their activities. There are very little initiative, proactiveness, enthusiasm, and creativity. There is an air of lethargy, tiredness. It is extremely difficult to arouse people to do anything. It is as if everything has already been tried out and found hopeless. Nothing is worth their energy. Motivated and high-energy people find it difficult to function in this type of organizational climate. They leave the organization, and the energy level is even further lowered. The implementation of decisions may be aborted when difficulties and resistance are met. The sustained effort needed to ensure any difficult change may not be maintained.

Bottled-up feelings, emotions, and affective excitement may lead to organizational desensitization. If the emotional excitement of the people in the organization cannot flow freely, the organization may desensitize itself "to all but the most overwhelming kind of emotional response." An organizational climate may develop that is insensitive to feelings, emotions, attitudes, motivations, and the entire gamut of the affective domain. The organization may lose the ability to sense what its members are feeling, and what people in other bodies with which it is in contact are feeling. With this loss of sensitivity to feelings may come a loss of valuable information that could serve well in making organizational decisions. In a certain sense, the organization becomes incapable of the freedom of choice that results in relevant action.

A low-energy organization may have blocked its own awareness to a whole range of information sources. It may not know what people feel about and how they relate to each other and to that part of the organization to which they belong. The affective aspects of human functioning may be regarded as irrelevant to task achievement. Being irrelevant and illegitimate, they will not be monitored to follow changes. Therefore, when changes do occur, the organization may be unaware of them. It may not pay attention to warning signals that could have engendered coping activities aimed at containing and isolating an upcoming, developing crisis. Matters may reach a breaking point without giving the organization a chance to take defensive action. A variety of organizational development approaches have recognized the value of reinstating awareness to feelings and granting legitimacy to their disclosure and flow in organizational life. Schein's (1969) process consultation, McGregor's (1964) theory X and theory Y, Likert's (1967) system 1 to system 4, and Blake and Mouton's (1978) managerial grid are all examples of applied behavioral science approaches to resensitizing organizations to the human aspects of their functioning, especially in their affective and social manifestations.

In the 1950s and 1960s, the burgeoning human potential movement developed the sensitivity training group (T. group) approach. Based on interpersonal feedback in group settings and a norm of disclosing feelings, attempts were made to transfer this to the organizational setting. After years, some practitioners concluded that this approach, which was developed for strangers in a temporary, isolated workshop setting, might not be appropriate for members of staffs and teams who permanently worked together interdependently in the organizational context.

Since this early effort, the attempts to change an organization's climate to one of more open expression of feelings has taken a number of forms. Argyris (1978) went a step beyond "human relations" to understand the implications for process consultation that was not based on sensitivity training. Two other possibly promising directions are (1) norm changing and (2) experiencing disclosure in the context of confronting organizational problems. In norm changing the consultant assists the organization in attempting to work directly on becoming aware of and changing the organizational norms that are supporting the blocking of emotional expression. This approach has been developed by Neale Clapp. The second approach commonly used by many consultants is experiencing disclosure in the context of confronting organizational problems. This approach encourages and legitimizes the expression of feelings in dealing with organizational problems. Management and members experience this in meetings facilitated by a consultant. An example of this approach is "role negotiations" as developed by Harrison (1972) and Merry and Allerhand (1978).

In Everglades the climate was one of low energy. Organization leadership had for some years directed the organization in a task-oriented style. The leadership was composed of young managers with a very strong task orientation and little patience and experience in dealing with the complexities of human relations. They wanted to "get things done," "increase productivity," "raise outputs and cut expenses." Most of the young managers had received their socialization in managing and directing as officers in the army. They brought with them the army style of hierarchical structure, commands that were obeyed, and clearly defined task objectives. Feelings and relations did not enter into their equation of running an efficient organization. For some time the new style they introduced did result in more efficient procedures and higher outputs. But at the same time, people were becoming more and more frustrated with the brusque, insensitive, rough way in which their affairs were being handled. Most individual requests that needed delicate handling and sensitive attention were treated roughshod, without any sensitivity as to how people were affected. The style was one of matter-of-fact, no-nonsense achievement-oriented decision making. People's feelings were of no concern and, in fact, were not accepted as information that needed to be considered.

The result was that many people in the organization stopped bringing requests, suggestions, and initiatives to the organization's decision-making bodies. A number of older, influential people who had formerly been active in the organization moved to the sidelines, preferring a stand of noninvolvement and noncommitment to being active, and hurt in the process. The organization had for years encouraged creative nonconforming people to express themselves and had developed conditions that nourished new ideas and novel directions. Soon all this had changed. People who were "different" soon found themselves disregarded and second-rate citizens in the organization. People were hurt and frustrated with policies and decisions that took no account of their feelings and relations.

After a time the initial surge of productivity tapered off. People who were hurt became demotivated, and this found expression in work outputs. More and more people "moved to the sidelines," resigned to be inactive rather than be hurt. Gradually the energy level ebbed lower and lower. Bottled-up emotions, given no legitimate channel of expression, turned into lethargy, boredom, and a measure of anxiety. Rather than being hurt by insensitive remarks, decisions, and policies, some people developed an armor of insensitiveness to what was happening around them. Frustrated, unhappy, and feeling unable to change things, many of the old-timers withdrew into their own private or family world.

When the consultants were finally called in "to see what was wrong," matters had deteriorated considerably. The climate of the organization was one of low energy and deadened vitality. People seemed to be bored with life and uninterested in anything. Nobody spoke about efficiency. People seemed to be anxious about their future and the future of the organization. But beyond this anxiety it was difficult to arouse any feeling and excitement to initiate change.

Blocking Personal Expression

Blocking personal expression in organizations decreases people's motivation and lowers the energy level. It means not recognizing organization members as people, but seeing them only as role bearers. In practice this takes the form of not accepting that people are individuals, are different from each other, and have different styles of behaving and performing organizational activities. This involves not accepting that organization members have different needs and personal priorities, and these are often not confluent with organizational imperatives. No legitimacy is granted to people who wish to find an outlet for their individual potential, skills, and abilities within the framework of the organization's work and activities.

People are expected to behave alike and as stipulated by the organization's rules, regulations, procedures, and norms. They are expected to fulfill their obligations and perform their duties as defined in their job description. People are seen as "hands," and are not to express other facets of themselves while performing in organizations. Aspects of a person that stem from family life and other relationships and activities have no place in organizational life.

Many organizational theorists have researched and analyzed the effects of blocking personal expression on the level of people's motivation, for example, McGregor (1964), Walton (1978), Katzel (1981), and Luthans (1981).

Steele and Jenks (1977) point out that the more an organization makes people feel that someone or something else is in control of their fate, those most capable of maintaining a high energy level will leave. As a change strategy to reengender excitement and energy, Steele and Jenks suggest "legitimizing people's expression of different sides of themselves, rather than encouraging and rewarding the stereotyped behavior they often feel is the 'right' way to behave" and "encourage members to use the skills and interests that are most alive for them" (p. 99).

From a systems theory perspective, Jantsch (1975) points out that entropy is usually high when a system's members cannot express themselves, as in a dictatorial system. To the degree that the creativity of an organization's members can enfold and contribute freely to the life of the system, entropy decreases.

The *extremely bureaucratic organization* may stifle personal expression because the latter does not fit into its conception of ideal organizational functioning.

The apathy-preserving dysfunction of rules may support a norm of maintaining a low energy level in the organization. Steele and Jenks (1977) and others have written about directly lowering the energy level in the organization by creating norms concerning how much work is "enough," how hard to work, and how much effort to put into organizational activities. The phenomenon of organizations in which hard workers are called "rate busters," and are punished for this, is not too uncommon.

In the bureaucratic organization, control is ensured by rules and regulations that are programmed to cover all eventualities. These are buttressed by a system of rewards and sanctions to discourage deviance. People are expected to be treated in an even-handed manner, in accord with the organization's regulations. This creates difficulties in acknowledging individual differences and particularistic needs. As Merton explains, people are depersonalized without regard to their differences.

People in bureaucracies may be confined to a narrow range of behavioral choices. The tendency is to keep to the rules, as doing something out of the accepted mode may lead to sanctions. Individual initiative, originality, and creativity may be discouraged if they depart from the accepted way of doing things.

In bureaucracies all decisions need to be examined in the light of their creating a precedent that might be repeated later. The tendency therefore may be to avoid decisions that might create costly precedents and open the door to new demands. This leads to difficulties in satisfying individual needs that do not fall within the accepted rules.

The depersonalizing aspects of bureaucracy, when carried to the extreme, can lower the motivation of the organization's members and with it the level of energy in the organization.

The extremely task-oriented organization may also block personal expression and lower the level of organizational energy. Blocking personal expression may take the form of the organization's seeing itself first and foremost as being in the service of its task goals. People in the organization may be regarded only as serving the purpose of achieving these goals. They may be treated in an instrumental mode, in the sense of recognition being given only to those of their aspects that are deemed to serve the purpose of achieving the organization's goals. People may be treated only as "working hands" or "role bearers."

The extremely task-oriented organization may ignore all aspects of human functioning except those that seem directly related to production. The individual, the personal, the relational, and the affective domain of human living and expression may be completely blocked from organizational awareness. Feelings, emotions, personal needs, aspirations, and dreams may be regarded as having no relevance to organizational life. The social aspects of human living in terms of personal relationships, affection, aversion, closeness, support, dislike, belonging, liking, or attraction may not be recognized as having any bearing on organizational functioning. In the extreme, people may be treated as artifacts that may be used, moved, and controlled according to organizational needs, with no thought given to how they feel about this.

Treating people as instruments and artifacts clashes with the psychological needs they have to satisfy to attain job satisfaction. When a task-oriented organization frustrates the satisfaction of these needs, motivation may decrease and the energy level may go down.

The critically evaluative organization may stifle its members' energy. Such an organization constantly monitors its members' behavior and evaluates them critically. Organizational norms are maintained by members keeping an eye on each other. Each individual's behavior is under the critical surveillance of others. People are exposed to the evaluation and criticism of others. It is accepted as legitimate, in the organization, for people to voice their negative evaluations of other members. The criticism may take the form of direct negation or ignoring. Sometimes people have little privacy as most aspects of their lives may be seen as related in some way to organizational functioning. Personal morale, family life, social relations, child rearing, life-style, and so forth, are all possible subjects of organizational surveillance.

The critically evaluative organization may be found in the form of a small, tightly knit community, and sometimes in social movements. This is not the typical climate of most modern organizations, which claim control of only a small part of their members' life space.

Organizations that monitor only a small part of their member's lives may also use a critically evaluative fear-based strategy. McGregor (1960) called this approach "theory X." Theory X is based on the idea that people will not perform the work required by an organization unless they are motivated by fear that they will lose pay, esteem, and so on. Gibb (1961) researched and analyzed the demotivating effects of a defensive climate. In a defensive climate members attend first to their own self-preservation. Gibbs described evaluation as a typical behavior found in a defensive climate.

Boredom

An organizational climate of boredom may be a symptom of an organization blocking energy by dampening personal expression. An atmosphere of boredom may signify that in their work the organization's members are not really in contact with what is important to them. The members of such an organization may appear to be lethargic, disinterested, apathetic, listless, and not to care for anything. People may go about their daily chores in a tedious humdrum manner with dull eyes. It is as if nothing will be able to excite or enthrall them.

Perls (1950) wrote:

Boredom occurs when we try to stay in contact with a subject that does not hold our interest. We quickly exhaust any excitement at our disposal;

we get tired and lean back. We want to withdraw from the situations. (p. 22)

When an organization is in genuine contact with the needs of its members and allows them to express themselves in organizational activities, it is alive, throbbing, excited, and invigorated. It is conceivable that the organization can facilitate an awareness by the members of their part in their own boredom, as it arises, and what alternatives exist. Peter Vaill (1978), in describing this as a high performing system, in effect described it in terms of what is here called a high-energy system. People light up to things; their interest can be stimulated and their activities may be invigorated. In low-energy organizations, people seem so bored that it is extremely difficult to enliven them and engage their interest.

Boredom may be accompanied by cynicism. The cynical outlook expresses a lack of hope and belief that life in the organization can ever be improved. It is possible to meet the knowing smile of "I've seen this before and anyhow nothing is going to help." People may be hiding their feeling of hopelessness behind a cynical outlook. Cynical remarks may be a cover for the frustration and pain of disbelief in the value of any action geared to change the status quo.

The combination of boredom and cynicism is deadening to any genuine effort aimed at helping the organization break out of its low-energy dysfunctioning mode. Change projects need energy and excitement to move things. Boredom and cynicism can break all attempts to begin a process of organizational renewal.

Organizational consultants have recognized the phenomena of boredom, apathy, and cynicism as being major stumbling blocks in the way of organizational renewal. Therefore, strategies of helping the organization regain the capability of healthy functioning attempt to deal with the low-energy phenomena in the first stages of organizational renewal. The premise is that the change effort will not develop without a flow of organizational energy.

The organization is assisted in becoming aware of how it is blocking its energy as a client is made aware in Gestalt therapy. The organization is helped to regain the ability to make genuine contact with its inner and outer reality. In Gestalt terms, if living in the intermediate zone has disturbed the organization's ability to make genuine contact, this function needs to be regained for meaningful change to come about.

Medcom was a social service agency that did not grant legitimacy to personal expression. This approach was rationalized by an ideology that gave priority to social service and rational needs over individual aspirations. Individuals were expected to identify with social services and to find personal satisfaction in living a life that served such needs. Legitimacy was not given to an individual's personal goals that did not coincide with social service needs or rational goals.

Personal growth was seen as a narrow, narcissistic, egotistic orientation to life, in contrast to "self-commitment," which was seen as a worthwhile, full life, putting social service ideals into practice. Demands for personal expression, individual fulfillment, and personal growth, not only in terms of social ideals, were seen as echoing California life-styles unsuited to the reality of the organization. Personal growth and expression were described as the latest passing fad of an affluent society in which people having everything spent all their time in narcissistic endeavors.

Members were expected to channel their career paths according to the needs of the agency. People whose interests lay also outside the organization found that they were not welcome as members in Medcom. People were obliged to accept work roles and managerial assignments even when vehemently opposed to doing so. The accepted view was that the individual had to bow to organizational needs. Work had to be done, services had to be given, and therefore people might have to engage in activities to which they objected. The organization saw its strength in being able to impose decisions even when they were contrary to an individual's wishes.

The agency would make decisions that would lead to losing capable members if it felt that these decisions were necessary to serve a social service need. Talented people whose personal plans clashed with the organization's demands left it to choose another style of life.

For many years during its earlier days, the majority of Medcom's members were completely identified with its social service goals. During those years the strong identification and commitment to the organization's goals served it well and assisted it in developing into a large, thriving agency. But changes took place as many of the basic goals were achieved, and members began to pay more attention to and to be more concerned with their own personal individual satisfaction in their work role and other activities. New members who joined lacked the ideological fervor of their predecessors; brought up in different times, many were more interested in study, travel, personal careers, and a satisfying family life than in serving social ideals.

More and more the channels of personal expression of the organization's members clashed with organizational needs and demands. The organization prevailing in these clashes led to frustration of personal plans and personal expression. The organization had not changed. It continued behaving in the way that served it well in the past. But times had changed and the members had changed.

After some years energy began to ebb out of the system. Motivation went down and down, and with it the agency's vitality and excitement. Many of the members followed their daily routines in a frustrated, unhappy, bored, and listless manner. Excitement, interest, vitality, and energy were seldom seen or felt. Routine duties were carried out but motivation, commitment, and energy were on a continual decrease.

Low motivation began to lead to increasing difficulties in organizational functioning. The reaction to this was a backlash of even stronger and more severe demands for individual conformity to organizational imperatives. A vicious circle was set in motion, creating an ever-widening gap between organizational needs and demands and the members' personal expression, thus blocking organizational energy more and more.

BLOCKING ACTION

Perls wrote about blocking action. He saw this as stopping a natural process: "This is done by interrupting the ongoing process, by preventing ourselves from carrying out whatever action is appropriate" (Perls, 1980).

Perls detailed a number of ways in which a person can block action taking. Some of these revolve around the inability to differentiate the particular need that has to be acted on; others reflect the inability to take effective action.

In the first case, the individual is aware of needs, and also has the energy to translate the needs into action, but is unable to create a priority between needs. "The neurotic has lost the ability (or perhaps he never developed it) to organize his behavior in accordance with a necessary hierarchy of needs" (Perls, 1980, p. 19).

Inability to differentiate may also take the form of having difficulty in defining which need is dominant (Perls, 1980).

If through some disturbance in the homeostatic process the individual is unable to sense his dominant needs or to manipulate his environment in order to attain them, he will behave in a disorganized and ineffective way. (p. 19)

This passage points to another way of blocking action. The person has been able to create a hierarchy between needs and has identified a dominant need, but is unable to manipulate the environment in order to satisfy the need (Perls, 1980).

For the individual to satisfy his needs, to close the gestalt, to move on to other business, he must be able to sense what he needs and he must know how to manipulate himself and his environment, for even the purely physiological needs can only be satisfied through the interaction of the organism and the environment. (p. 9)

As Perls understood it, to put intention into action, the individual first must clarify the intention and then be able to persist with the correct action. Having lost this ability, the neurotic cannot create priorities and deal with each need separately in its own time. The neurotic, unable to concentrate on personal actions, cannot become involved in what he/she is doing and is unable to persist and stick with it.

He must learn to discover and identify himself with his needs, he must learn how, at every moment, to become totally involved in what he is doing, how to stick with a situation long enough to close the Gestalt and move on to other business. (p. 19)

Zinker (1977) writes about the interruption between mobilization of energy and action. He describes this form of blockage by using the metaphor of a person spinning his wheels and unable to act on his impulses. The person may be mobilized, yet is unable to use his energy in the service of activity that gets him what he wants.

Zinker refers to neurotics as people who are often unable to put the most basic feelings and energies into action. He describes some of the ways neurotics do this, such as wishing instead of acting. He refers to people who "wish away their lives with 'if onlys'." Another way is deflecting; that is, keeping busy wastefully (for example, watching TV) instead of taking action that has to be taken. Zinker also writes about the person who does not take action for fear of the results. This person breaks the energy as it builds for fear of failure and ridicule, or the disappointment or disapproval of others. Many of the clients with whom Zinker worked got stuck in a morass of ideational self-deceptions and rationalizations.

Blocking Action in Organizations

The organization may be aware of its needs and may mobilize the energy for action, yet block the action itself.

Perls was aware that not only individuals, but also organizations, interrupt the natural process of taking action. He wrote about a society or a community responding in action first to its dominant need.

Quite often it is to this phase of interrupting action that most management consultants address themselves. Many consultants spend a large part of their consulting time on training managers to take effective action on their decisions. "Time planning" and "management by objectives" are two of the popular change technologies geared to closing the gap between intention and action. Lippitt and Lippitt (1978) see the gap between intention and effective action as a major block to organizational change.

Levinson (1972), in diagnosing an organization, examines the "quality of its action." By this term he refers to the form and consequences of the organization's behavior. Some of the dimensions of these are the degree of directness with which an organization confronts its problems, the organization's flexibility in suiting its action to the problem, the degree of planning and timing in action, the degree of persistence in the action taken, the degree of effectiveness in the sense of how well the action works, and the degree of constructiveness or destructiveness in terms of the organization's long-term goals.

The two major interruptions of action Gestalt therapy finds at the individual level may also be found at the organizational level. These are:

1. Inability to identify priorities.
2. Inability to take effective action.

Inability to Identify Priorities

This is a common phenomenon in organizational functioning. This inability may take the form of the organization's "threshing about" in all directions without dealing with its crucial problems. In Gestalt terms this may be described as the organization not delineating its dominant needs. This phenomenon is familiar to people who have consulted with and observed many organizations, and points to neurotic behavior.

One of the initial phases of an organizational renewal project is that of problem sensing and prioritizing. Information is collected by individual interviews, group sessions or questionnaires, observations, and hard data. This leads to a list of the major problems and issues confronting the organization. This in turn is followed by a series of meetings at which the organization prioritizes the problems in the order in which it will take action on them. Choosing priorities among the issues correctly is a crucial factor in determining the success of a renewal project, and generally this is achieved in a well-functioning organization. If the organization begins dealing with irrelevant problems, it may be spinning its wheels, unable to take effective action where needed. This generally leads to aborting the entire renewal project in its first stages, and often is a symptom that organizational neurosis is behind all this.

Such organizations seem to be unable to develop a workable effective list of priorities among their problems. The organization appears to be incapable of prioritizing its need in a way that will deal effectively with its crucial problems. It can block effective action in a number of ways. For instance, items given first priority are basic existential issues that are an irresolvable part of organizational life—such as "individual autonomy and organizational goals," or "participation in decision making," or "the individual's commitment to organizational needs." The organization may give these issues top priority and choose project teams to deal with them. Generally the results are negligible, while energy and time have been invested in unchangeable existential dilemmas.

Another way of blocking is to choose problems that can be dealt with only at a later stage after other problems have been solved. An example of this is an organization that is economically unviable giving first priority to a huge investment to improve the working environment when the organization is unable to raise capital to develop its production capability. Another way of evading crucial issues is to grant first priority to minor irrelevant problems that are not going to make a difference either way. This needs to be differentiated from a tactical approach, which might begin with problems that can be dealt with relatively easily. A consultant might recommend beginning with easily manageable and visible problems to bolster confidence. This differs from blindly giving priority to minor irrelevant problems.

Inability to Take Effective Action

Some organizations cannot find ways to interact effectively with their environment to satisfy their dominant needs. In Perls' terms they are unable "to become totally involved" in what they are doing; they seem to be finding it difficult "to stick with a situation long enough to close the gestalt and move on to other business."

The organization seems to have difficulty in getting totally involved in its actions. It is not involved in them sufficiently to culminate the activities in an effective solution. This may be true because the organization's attention is fragmented. Sometimes the difficulty lies in maintaining a sustained effort to the degree needed to attain objectives. Levinson's (1972) dimensions of the quality of an organization's action refer also to the degree of persistence in the action taken. Some organizations appear to lack this persistence, signaling thereby that neurotic behavior is affecting action.

Inability to take effective action may take the form of hopping from one problem to another, jumping from one activity to another. Levinson (1972) gives this example:

Dalton State Hospital becomes excited about one project, then another. There is a fadlike quality to this activity. Committees are born and die; no one misses them; they just peter out. Part of this is due to staff turnover; more, to a lack of consistent direction and urgent demands from the administration. (p. 245)

People do not seem to have the staying power needed to finish dealing with matters. The result may be many unclosed, troublesome issues and frustrated members. Managers in this kind of an organization often develop a managerial philosophy to suit the conditions. One manager put it this way: "The best policy with many major problems is not to take action. Either things will work out without your intervention, or they will not. In any case, you can do little to change things, so why expend the energy and why make the effort?" In Gestalt therapy terms, there is a block here between the sensoric and the motoric subsystems.

Action-taking change strategies such as management by objectives attempt to ensure effective action by breaking goals up into clearly defined, concrete, attainable, and measurable objectives. These objectives need to be attained at preordained dates by specified individuals. Another popular approach, developed by Kepner and Tregoe (1981), attempts to forestall action failures by preparing for all possible eventualities that may block effective action. Lippitt and Lippitt (1978) suggest that a key function of the consultant is to develop the skill necessary for increasing the probability that the action taken will be successful rather than abortive.

All of these approaches take a rational attitude toward action blocking. The premise is that if an organization is not taking effective action, its members need to be trained in methods of doing this. These methods seem to be effective when what is lacking in the organization is skill and know-how. It is questionable whether these same approaches can help an organization when action blocking is not the result of lack of training but is one aspect of a syndrome of neurotic organizational behavior. Clinical observation of organizations displaying neurotic behavior suggests that the rational methods do not give results. New approaches need to be developed to deal with action blocking when it is part of neurotic behavior syndrome.

TRANSFORMING DECLINING ORGANIZATIONS

How awareness, energy, and action can be unblocked, thus reversing the decline of organizations, is described in the data of the following research. In 1984–1985, one of the authors and his colleagues* made a study of declining organizations that had succeeded in transforming themselves and returning to healthy, adaptive functioning. What we were looking for were common features and dimensions in the process of recovery and revitalization.

The findings of this study, which have not yet been published, were based on material collected by interviewing individually at least ten persons in each organization, who were involved either as active central participants leading the change, or as consultants. Together with hard data acquired by other means, all the information was analyzed; this is a summary of the major findings. All of the following are characteristics, events, and features we found to be common among declining organizations that had revitalized themselves.

1. *The transformation of the organizations was led by a new group of young managers.*
    —The transformation was *not* led by the *older, former* group of managers that had headed the organization during its years of decline.

*We are deeply indebted to L. Mokedi, D. Atid, and Z. Mizrochi for their innovative contributions to this study.

—The transformation was not led by their assistants or by young managers who had held central posts during the time of decline.

—The transformation was led by a completely new group of *young* managers who were not identified in any way with the organizational failure.

—They were a coalition of young managers who had grown up in the organization, with strong personal ties to the older leadership, and a number of young talented managers who had joined the organization recently.

—These together became *a leadership group* with strong informal and formal ties among them.

—Two orientations were very strong in this group; the first was to the economic aspects or organizational functioning. In other words, some of the people were experts on the economic policy aspects of organizational functioning and were very up to date in this area.

—The other orientation was to people. Most of the managers were "people oriented"; they understood and accepted people's needs and recognized the role of the organization in satisfying them.

2. *What was their relationship to the former leadership?*
     —The relationship between the new leadership and the old leadership was a complicated balance of *revolt and continuity*.

—On the one hand, the new group honestly honored and respected the old-timers. The members described themselves as continuing the way the others had paved. They made special efforts to express their respect at ritual occasions and ceremonies.

—On the other hand, they were very clear-cut and decisive in changing everything that they felt needed changing, even when it reflected unfavorably on the policies of their predecessors.

—The old-timers did not resist the change. They accepted the new leaders and seemed to give them a mandate to do what needed to be done. They sometimes "gritted their teeth," but they did not resist or sabotage the changes and the new leadership.

3. *How did the change in leadership come about?*
     —In each organization the particular circumstances were

different, but what was common was that this occurred after a major crisis in the organization.

—Some *special incident* that epitomized the crisis happened, and following this the young leaders met in some way and decided to take matters in their hands. There was a *meeting of some kind*. In each of the organizations a decisive meeting was held at which the following occurred.

—They decided to revolt against the failure pattern and create a new, healthy pattern of functioning, completely different from the former pattern.

—The ways in which they became the central leadership were different in the different organizations, but in all of them they did become the leadership after some time. The "blessings" of the old-timers helped this takeover.

4. *How the organizational delusion was changed.*

—At the very earliest stages, there was a *conscious decision* by the new group to begin working on changing the organization's image.

—They did not condition the change in image by first bringing about other major changes. They worked on changing the image *without* the organizational reality changing basically before that. They *reframed reality.*

—They used all sorts of approaches to transmit the messages that: "We are not a failure." "We are O.K." "We can stand on our own feet."

—They communicated the messages in various ways, both to the organization's members in words, and outward to other bodies in their environment, including their suprasystem.

—Inwardly they initiated a number of very *visible* physical changes in the organization's facilities, grounds, or buildings, or in the quality of some services given to organization members. These were not necessarily very expensive changes, but they were very visible to all members of the organization and symbolized the change taking place.

—Outwardly they took a stand in matters that denied their failure status.

—They reframed the way organization members saw their particular circumstances so that conditions that formerly were seen as hindrances were now seen as advantages (e.g., physical location).

—They initiated a variety of ceremonies, rituals, and symbols aimed at raising morale, and honoring and acknowledging the contributions, of various sectors of the organization's populations.

5. *The economic viability of the organization was a major focus.*

—The organizations had been dysfunctioning for years and were being supported economically by their suprasystems. A major long-term effort was aimed at changing this.

—In each of the organizations, one of the first steps taken was to close down unsuccessful economic ventures and departments that had been dragging the organizations down for years.

—This was done tactfully and humanely but decisively, and though it involved much pain, it was accomplished fully; the organizations were relieved of heavy economic loads they had carried for years.

—Concurrently each organization developed new economic ventures that promised high yields in the future. (In these organizations this took the form of a new industrial line and other new projects.)

6. *Relating to people was involved.*

—The organizational management began to relate to and deal effectively with *people's needs* that had been severely neglected through years of decline, crisis, and lack of resources.

—While resources were still scarce, a major effort was made to *legitimize people's rights* to have the needs for which the organization was responsible be met by the organization. Whether the needs involved work satisfaction, better working conditions, social benefits, or something else, the organization recognized the needs and did its utmost within its means to satisfy them.

—A major effort was made to change the norm from "each person trying to get the most for him/herself from the organization to a norm that "the organization willingly supplied people's needs that were its responsibility."

—The organizations paid much attention to the special needs of different kinds of people. For instance, special efforts were made to create conditions amenable to the older population, or married women, and so on. New social services such as counseling, social workers, and the like were introduced.

—A variety of social and cultural activities were encouraged and developed, and the organizational agenda was a hive of intense activities, serving the interests and tastes of the different kinds of people in the organization.

7. *Human Resources were developed.*

—Much energy was invested in efforts to *attract to* the organization capable and talented people who could and would contribute to it and its standards.

—Resources were invested in living accommodations and other facilities and conditions that were needed to attract, hold, and absorb the new people.

—Thought and efforts were devoted to do all that could help to integrate the new people into the social and economic fabric of the organization.

—Simultaneously a new policy of *encouraging study and development* was initiated. People were encouraged to develop themselves professionally and personally. Raising the level of personal, work, and professional education and training was regarded as a worthwhile investment.

—Special attention was paid to the training and education aimed at developing new management and leadership and deepening and widening the knowledge and skills of the present management. This was done through both in-house training, consultation, counseling, and workshops, and outside courses and study.

8. *Organizational functioning was reversed.*

—Soon after coming into office, the new management took a number of steps to rebuild and *revitalize the organizational structure* and return the organization to an effective functioning mode.

—Each of the organizations, in its own way, involved many of the people in the organization in different kinds of meetings and workshops aimed at *renewing communication* among sectors of their population and *identifying issues* that needed attention.

—Needed functions that were not carried out, or were neglected, were located, and problems that needed to be taken care of were identified. Then the necessary structure to deal with them was created, whether by delegation to an individual manager, or by a committee, or by creating a new committee of project team.

—The new management tended to decentralize organizational structure by spreading out and delegating responsibility throughout the organization.

9. *The need for help from outside the organization was analyzed.*

—At a certain point, a decision was made by the new leadership to move from dependency to autonomy. The direction chosen was from a condition of dependency on outside help ("They'll maintain us") to a condition of standing on their own feet ("We will do it on our own").

—There was a move from being closed to the environment, in the sense of not maintaining contact with relevant outside organizations, to a direction of *opening up and maintaining genuine contact* with the outside world.

—This move led to the development of leadership and managers with wider horizons and wider network of ties outside the organization—all of which enriched the managers' contributions to their organization.

—At some point in the revitalization process, the suprasystem to which each organization belonged, which had helped it during the time of decline, decided to make a basic evaluation of the organization's condition.

—The review allowed the suprasystem to see that it had a dependable leadership to deal with. As a result the suprasystem decided to invest *financial and other resources* to assist in the organization's program of recovery and renewal.

—These resources played an important role in helping the new leadership put into practice its plans for revitalizing the organization. This help from outside was given over a period of a number of years.

—In all cases the assistance of applied behavioral science played a part. In some of the organizations, an outside consultant played a major role in working with the new management. In one of these, management said that the transformation would not have taken place without the help of the consultant. In another organization some of the managers themselves were thoroughly grounded in applied behavioral science.

10. *The change process was ritualized.*

—The full process of change takes place over a period of five to ten years, in which certain *turning points are marked by ritual and ceremony.*

—The change begins with a traumatic meeting of highly symbolic, mythical, ritualistic quality. Everyone remembers this meeting.

—After years, during one of the later stages of recovery, another important ritualistic ceremony or occasion celebrates and institutionalizes the achievement of success.

—This celebration has a number of functions. It honors and says goodbye to the old-timers.

—It is also an internal celebration of achievement and success and strengthening of the new positive self-image.

—And it is aimed outward to environmental bodies, communicating to them and receiving from them acknowledgment of the new status of the organization.

SUMMARY

The transformation of a declining organization to a well-functioning one is characterized by the following.

1. The transformation is led by a new group of young managers who are not seen by others as identified with the organization's decline.

2. The new leadership pays honor to the former leadership, and in turn is supported, or at least not resisted, by the latter.

3. The decision to commit themselves to leading a transformation project is taken by the new leaders at a meeting, after a major incident during a period of crisis.

4. The new leadership makes a conscious decision to change the organization's delusional image. It does this by communicating a different positive image within the organization and outside it, and making meaningful, concrete, visible changes that symbolize this.

5. Returning the organization to economic viability is a major focus of the efforts of the new leadership. New productive economic ventures are embarked upon.

6. The new approach is characterized by a "people" orientation that relates to individual human needs and attempts to satisfy them in the organization.

7. Much energy is devoted to developing human resources.

This is done by bringing in new people with capabilities and encouraging the development of those already in the organization.

8. Effective functioning is renewed by revitalizing the structure, taking care of undealt functions and issues, and widely involving people in responsibility.

9. At a certain point, recognizing the transformation, the organization's suprasystem decides to assist the change with a major investment of resources.

10. Different turning points in the change process are marked by rituals and ceremonies that symbolize the transformations taking place.

It should be pointed out that all of these propositions are tentative as they are generalized from the findings in a small number of organizations. We have had much difficulty in finding declining organizations that succeeded in renewing themselves. Generally decline leads to demise. The organizations we were able to locate had been saved from disintegration by the support of their suprasystem—their mother organization.

We will need a larger number of different kinds of "renewed" organizations to verify these propositions. The fact that we did find these similarities in the organizations we studied raises hope that similar findings will come up in a larger number of organizations.

Although the reorganizations we studied were of a specific kind, many of the procedures for decline reversal could apply to all organizations.

A number of the approaches of the managers are based on Gestalt principles, but specific mechanisms for carrying out the activities are not explicated. The following chapter presents specific Gestalt-based activities that hypothetically might have been used, or at least could have been used, by the new managers in the transformation.

PROPOSITIONS AND DEFINITIONS

There is some theoretical and empirical support for the following.

★ Maintaining an appropriate balance between attendance to task and attendance to maintenance is a built-in source of tension in organizations.

★ Marked inattendance to either task or maintenance needs will result in organizational malfunctioning.

★ Imbalance in attendance will mostly be in the direction of more attendance to task and less attendance to maintenance.

★ Inattendance to task or maintenance needs may be conceptualized as a process either of blocking awareness or of blocking energy or of blocking action.

★ Blocking awareness of needs often takes the forms of denial, dimunition, or devaluation.

The following have wide support from systems theory and research:

★ Organizations import energy with lower entropy and export energy with higher entropy. (Energy is defined as the ability to do work.)

★ The energy is used in the processes of production for outputs and for maintenance (integration and repair of the system).

The following have less support and need research:

★ Surplus energy is stored for use when needed, thus creating an active-excess state of potential to action in all organizations.

★ Organizations differ in their energy levels and in their distribution of energy among task, maintenance, and surplus.

★ The motivation of an organization's members may be a major factor affecting its level of energy (i.e., its ability to do work).

The following have support in organization theory and research.

★ Organizational energy may be decreased by decreasing the expression of emotions in the organization.

★ Organizational energy may be decreased by decreasing the personal expression of the organization's members.

★ The extremely bureaucratic organization decreases personal expression, and therefore organizational energy.

★ The extremely task-oriented organization decreases personal expression, and therefore organizational energy.

★ The critically evaluative organization decreases personal expression, and therefore organizational energy.

The following has support only in clinical observation:

★ A climate of boredom is one symptom of an organization blocking personal expression and lowering organizational energy.

The following is based on preliminary research.

★ It seems possible to reverse the trend in declining organizations based on a transforming second-order change where energy and action have been unblocked.

CHAPTER 11

USING GESTALT IN ORGANIZATIONS

BACKGROUND

It appears to be possible to develop organizational change approaches and technologies by creating organizational-level analogies from Gestalt therapy (Burke, 1980; Alevras & Wepman, 1980). Theories, techniques, and interventions applied in Gestalt therapy to help neurotic individuals may possibly be developed for use at the organizational level for organizational neurosis. Some examples of doing this have already been demonstrated.

Nevis (1980) has suggested an alternate approach to organizational diagnosis built on Gestalt therapy perspectives. From a Gestalt therapy approach, there are the following reservations about the usual diagnosis process: (1) overemphasis on the past and cause–effect relationships in contrast to what is happening in the here and now; (2) overemphasis on a rational analytic model that restricts awareness; (3) overemphasis on intellectual understanding before moving into action; (4) too little use of participant observation and unobtrusive measures in collecting data; (5) a focus on illness rather than on health.

The Gestalt therapy approach differs from the usual diagnostic mode in a number of ways: (1) Diagnosis and intervention are intertwined. Diagnosis is not seen as a separate step prior to intervention. (2) There is an emphasis on gaining the client's trust more than on collecting a substantial amount of information. (3) The consultant's sensations, feelings, and internal states are seen as important data. (4) The responsibility for the diagnosis is not taken from the client. In dealing with an organization, the Gestalt therapy approach would advocate that the consultant use a combination of active, directed awareness with open, undirected, receptive awareness not biased by preconceived models. The consultant would attend to what he/she "cares about," listen to what the client cares about, selectively share assessment data, and work on integrating his/her energy with the energy of the client.

A Gestalt therapy approach to management development has been explicated and empirically tried out in a number of organizations (Herman, 1972, 1976; Herman & Korenich, 1977). This approach to authentic management differs from the usual human relations approach on these features: (1) a focus on recognition and mobilization of the individual's strength and powers; (2) a sharpened awareness of what the individual does and how; (3) an intensification or dramatization of "problem behavior" until a change of relationship takes place; (4) consideration of aggressiveness and conflict as valued vitalizing forces; (5) an emphasis on the individual's own feedback; (6) an emphasis on strengthening the person's competence and autonomy; (7) acknowledgment of the importance of increasing awareness of present behavior and completing it; (8) keeping values up front even when this means less disclosure; (9) an emphasis on increasing the individual's competence; (10) involvement of the consultant as a participant, a director, and an activist.

The authors utilize a number of Gestalt therapy approaches to improve communication in the organization. This is done by introducing the organization to the difference between "about," "should," and "is" as modes of communication. Good contact based on awareness and boundary recognition is used to facilitate more authentic relationships. Gestalt therapy approaches have also been found to be effective in increasing collaboration (Karp, 1976).

In addition to the items listed by Nevis, Herman, and others, we would add the following comments on how Gestalt interventions and strategies could be used at the organizational level. These present one overview of some potential uses of Gestalt. They are only touched on as illustrations of the breadth of the possibilities in using Gestalt therapy within an organizational context.

When we speak of using Gestalt therapy with organizations or at the organization level, the fact remains that we ultimately are going to be using this approach with individuals or groups of individuals.

In this chapter we will present *some* of the principles and approaches to Gestalt therapy that may be applied to examine and remedy neurotic organizational behavior. We emphasize "some" because this book has as its major emphasis the use of Gestalt to study the structure and functioning of organizations, especially when they exhibit neurotic behavior. If pervasive and intense enough, such behavior can lead to the decline of an organization, and we have indicated the possibility of reversing this trend. This volume is not a comprehensive "how to" book. We recommend the forthcoming work in this series by Ed Nevis, entitled *A Gestalt Approach to Organizational Consulting*. We will, however, present examples here, drawn from the practice of Gestalt therapy, which illustrate the potential Gestalt has for working with neurotic organizational behavior, and possibly declining organizations.

Because of its broad repertoire of therapeutic interventions and change strategies, Gestalt therapy as a systems theory holds special utility for increasing and maintaining the health of organizations. At this point we also cannot say whether these approaches are primarily for first-order or second-order change. We would like to assume that, if applied continually and totally, the likelihood of a dramatic second-order change is possible. Such a possibility, when combined with other interventions, seems indicated by the preliminary findings presented in the previous chapter. We can say with some confidence that these suggestions can be used in the typical ongoing daily situation in organizations. Even here a cumulative effect could promulgate second-order shifts in a declining organization. Our primary intent, however, is to minimize the development of pathology in organizations that otherwise might shift from a healthy, productive condition to one of decline. We focus on prevention, but are also aware that Gestalt therapy approaches can be used to deal directly with the neurotic organizational behavior that can emerge from time to time in any organization, whether this behavior be on the part of subsystems or the organization as a whole.

In this chapter we present two stages.

Stage One: *Making clear resistance to engaging with a problem predominant at the moment, and helping personnel to make a commitment to working on the problem situation.*

Stage Two: *Acting on tasks and maintenance of the organization, including emerging problems, to improve the overall functioning of the organization.*

There are elements common to both stages so there may very well be some overlap. And in practice, making a distinction between these stages could be an artificial separation.

GESTALT INTERVENTIONS

Stage One: Gestalt Therapy Approaches to Resistance

A major concern of any change agent whether manager, trainer, consultant, or in some other role, is overcoming resistance to change. The Gestalt approach is initially fully to explore the parameters of the resistance without attempting to make changes. This is based on the Gestalt principle that when one experiences "What is," "What is" changes. A consequent step can be making interventions to increase awareness that alternatives exist and choices can be made, followed by action.

The work of John Enright presents what is essentially a Gestalt approach to five sources of "resistance," wherein he applies Gestalt tactics and strategies to clear up resistances of an individual client. They make what is implicit explicit. In organizations these five steps hold promise for both the external consultant and someone who works from within the organization—either as a troubleshooter or in a management position responsible for part or the whole of the organization's functioning. The five steps provide the following checklist that can be followed in sequence or used as separate interventions, dependent upon the situation.

1. Acknowledging the willingness to be present in the "therapeutic" or problem-confronting situation.
2. Identifying the actual or experienced problem.
3. Determining whether the problem is perceived as having a solution.
4. Discovering whether the person in the consultant, trainer, or management role is perceived as a person with whom those involved want to work to solve the problem.

5. Finding out if there are any competing intentions or countervailing factors.

What follows is an elaboration of these steps.

*Step 1. Acknowledging the willingness to be present in the
"therapeutic" or problem-confronting situation.*

Essentially this step is directed toward evoking a response to
the question "Do you want to be here?" The "here" is being in
the present situation, ready to engage in work on the problem
situation with the change agent, whether manager, trainer, consultant, or in some other role.

The change agent will have to assess how many personnel need
be committed to pursuing the problem situation—a majority, a
minority, a plurality, and so on. Such a decision will depend, of
course, on the nature of the overall situation, including the problem
situation, the role of the unit involved, and the policies of the
organization in terms of carrying out task and maintenance functions of the organization.

Ultimately what the change agent is after is a clear "yes" or
"no" to the question, "Do you want to be here now?" In processing
this step, the change agent must listen carefully to the responses,
not necessarily in terms of the content of the statements, but
especially to the quality of emotional engagement as revealed by
the voice as emphasized in Gestalt training. The word "yes" can
be halfhearted, intensely committed, or even mean "no!" The
change agent has to be clear as to what the organizational options
are for a negative response, whether made directly or implicitly.
If the rules of the organization demand participation and provide
no option for personnel but to be there, then there is a likelihood
that individuals either must be fired or tolerated with a potential
reaction of, at best, inertness or neutrality, and, at worst, devious
sabotaging behavior. If the organization does allow for the option
of being there or not, then the change agent can be in the same
role as that of the therapist who works with the individual.

When the therapist in working out this step discerns that the
client does not really want to be there, the therapist can say "goodbye," send the client on to another therapeutic situation, or some
other alternative. It is important that the therapist provide the
individual client with an option; the client who decides to remain
in the situation explicitly has taken responsibility for the decision.
One would hope that the same option could occur within the
organization. Personnel who are there because they have decided
to be there are going to be more fully functioning and committed

than those who, for whatever reason, are there reluctantly. We do not necessarily mean altruism here. It may very well be that people are there because they want to earn more money or receive the approbation of their superiors, but what we are after is the conscious commitment represented by the statement, "Yes, I want to be here now."

The change agent will find this step worthwhile pursuing until an explicit commitment is made, otherwise there may be trouble later. If nothing else, the change agent, by not completing this step, will have the most responsibility for what happens from here on, instead of sharing that responsibility with those involved in the problem situation.

Step 2. Identifying the actual or experienced problem.

After the personnel involved in the unit of the organization, collectively representing a subsystem or the organization itself, have made a choice through step 1, they can move from acknowledging this choice to experiencing the problem situation. If in the situation, personnel are only intellectually involved in the problem because it is really someone else who has power to impose it on them, or the problem is perceived as being some other unit in the organization, again, they can go through the motions without any intrinsic involvement. What may be needed here is either further clarification or a redefinition of the problem so that it can become the unit's problem—not only "thought" of as a problem, but experienced as such. Sometimes rules, decisions, or judgments can be "swallowed whole" in the introject sense and, as a result, the problem or problem situation does not belong to those involved but is internalized in an introject mode out of the feelings of insufficiency or lack of power. From a Gestalt perspective, the more total the experience, the greater is the potential for growth and change.

Within the organization the change agent, who would be in a role equivalent to that of a therapist with an individual, could ask basic Gestalt questions, such as "What is happening with you now?" "Whose problem is this?" "What are your feelings now?" Directed toward personnel in the subsystem, or the organization as a whole, the questions would be used to help those involved acknowledge that they chose this problem as a real problem for them at that moment. Comments, or even thoughts, such as "The stockholders are expecting it of us," or "Management wants us to get involved in this project," have to be confronted in terms of whether those present are actually *willing* to be involved in the specific problem-solving process, and further to consider how they may be a part of the problem situation in question.

From a Gestalt point of view, personnel who don't "own" that the problem is theirs, or that they are actually in a problem situation, will function at a low level of involvement, making only a surface commitment with no intrinsic and meaningful activity on their part. What will occur instead is a kind of window dressing, going through the motions with minimum involvement. If there is actually to be engagement of personnel, or even the potential for intrinsic involvement, this can occur only through an awareness focus on what is happening from moment to moment. If, by chance, there is little trace of intrinsic involvement, then the organization, or the representative of the organization, must face that fact and respond accordingly. Either personnel will, as a consequence of the awareness clarification process, "own" the problem as theirs, or another real and more pressing problem that may be lurking in the background can begin to emerge. From a Gestalt point of view, it is what is experienced that needs dealing with, not what "should" be there. The point here is (1) to clear up and focus on how the problem or problem situation exists for those involved and (2) through this clarification process, in Gestalt therapy terms, make what is implicit explicit.

Confusion can prevail within the context or frame of the problem. Different elements can compete for the attention of the individual involved or for the organization or subsystem of the organization. To move on requires developing a focus where one issue or situation is acknowledged to be the primary problem of the moment. As a consequence of this awareness, the organization or the subsystem can begin to act instead of using energy for dissembling or for struggling with confusion. Until this clarity and priority are achieved, confusion or competing interests and demands can immobilize functioning. This is not to deny that problems can have complicated interrelationships with other elements within or outside the organization, or even with other problems in the organization, but until the real problem engaging the concerns of the personnel at that moment is brought into awareness to be dealt with, moving on to these complications is not possible because of immobilization.

Step 3. Determining whether the problem is believed to have a solution.

If the unit is exhibiting middle-zone or intermediate-zone activity where personnel have created a state in which the implicit message can be pinned down to "Oh, we've tried this over and over again and nothing happens but if someone wants us to continue doing it, we will go through the motions" or "We might as well be playing the game, there's nothing better to do," etc., the consequences are obvious. Until this belief is confronted through Gestalt exploration, there will be little chance that the personnel of the unit involved can truly believe that something will happen. Because of the effect of the self-fulfilling prophecy, anything happening will not be the consequence of the efforts of the unit involved. There have been studies that have clearly demonstrated that until one can conceive, one will not perceive. The old saw that "When I see it, I'll believe it" should actually be stated as "When I believe it, I'll see it." Until the personnel of the unit have some confidence in their capability, or, in Gestalt terms, are in touch with what is available for problem resolution (their internal and external resources), the unit cannot mobilize its energy and resources to get on with the task.

The leader or trainer can help the unit explore these internal and external resources so that the self-definition of the unit as capable of working through the problem situation is experienced and internally integrated.

Step 4. Confronting the question: "Am I as leader, consultant, manager, a person with whom you believe you can work as a unit to deal with this problem situation?"

Sometimes the mere confrontation will bring about a resolution. In some cases within the organization, this could be delicate. The leader or consultant must be skilled in terms of not using extrinsic factors such as role or power inordinately to influence response. What is obvious is that there is actually authority in the leader's or consultant's role. In this case the leader needs authentically to communicate a shared responsibility for the problem, and thus the shared power in this particular situation, as opposed to what might otherwise be true in a different functional context. This may not be amenable to development in the instance of the situation, and may have to be a consequence of a longer overall pattern of relationship. What will help will be to make the special context of the present situation clear in contrast, perhaps, to a more generalized situation in the organization. Thus we have the comment, "Well, people, I know you see me as district manager, but in this case we're in this together. You may have a little difficulty in making the switch, but I'm going to do everything I can to convince you that I'm here because you want me to be here, and if not, we'll get somebody else to do this job, and I mean it. Doing something about the problem is that important." An essential element for the believability of this statement is that the speaker believe it. The content of the words will not communicate as much as the quality of the voice. Authenticity must be communicated, and for this to happen, the speaker must be authentic.

Based on what we have written earlier about contact, being "present" in terms of an awareness of self, a sense of self derived from an experience of self, is crucial for real contact to be made. Otherwise the listeners will not really "hear" the statement. An increased experience of self can be made available through Gestalt training. Managers and others can move from a manipulating role, whether deliberate or from middle-zone functioning or an organizational role mythology, to authentic contact and consequent communication.

Step 5. Finding competing intentions or countervailing factors.

If the previous four steps have been accomplished, the chances are for a relationship where people will feel freer to admit hidden issues, such as "If we solve this problem, we may work ourselves out of a job." These are important to consider, or all the efforts necessary for the accomplishment of the task for the organization will be sabotaged. It will be an example of a unit of the organization functioning in the Gestalt metaphor of an underdog role where management becomes the top dog. In the "top-dog–underdog" situation, top dog is the part that makes demands; it is full of "shoulds." Underdog is the saboteur who somehow, in devious ways, cancels out the demands of the authority, top dog. This is a simplistic formulation but it helps in terms of conceptualizing what frequently goes on within the power structure of the organization. Sometimes a problem can actually be a solution. Gestalt intervention can make what may be implicit explicit, acknowledging what having the problem does *for* the unit instead of what it does *to* the unit. Having a problem can be used to avoid dealing with what, consciously or not, is fantasized as an unfaceable situation. "As long as we have this problem, then we cannot, and thus we do not have to, deal with this other 'overwhelming' situation."

The competing intentions or countervailing factors, when simply brought into awareness in a nonthreatening, nonjudgmental context, can be more readily assessed. Through the act of awareness and being made explicit, sometimes the competing intention will disappear. If not, at least it can be dealt with, and more intelligent and reality-based commitments and decisions can be made for action.

As Enright points out, sometimes dealing with just one of these five steps will facilitate a change from resistance to getting on with what needs to be done. Certainly the five steps present a process for "clearing the decks for action." Most important is that this process of making what is implicit explicit, in Gestalt terms, can free organizations or subsystems for constructive action. The organization or subsystem can thus take responsibility in the Gestalt sense for (1) having the ability to respond, and (2) owning that they themselves as a unit are doing or not doing what needs to be done. Once this is brought into awareness, the organization is ready to act in a freer and more creative way. The research reported in the previous chapter on the activities of new managers reversing the decline of their organizations seems to support this statement.

Within the theory of Gestalt, resistance is sometimes defined as an assistance. What is meant is that, when there is resistance, it is derived from what the unit experiences as the only alternative to a situation. The resistance is imagined to be exactly what is needed at that moment with nothing else to be done. By going through the process described, the situation is illuminated. Options and choices can now come into existence.

Most important, the process itself can be learned, and thus can be more readily repeated in the next problem situation.

Stage Two: Gestalt Therapy Approaches to Task, Maintenance, and Emerging Problems

The steps included are not comprehensive. They are provided to illustrate the further use of Gestalt therapy approaches in organizations and can be utilized as a guide or a checklist for the change agent.

Steps

1. Separating out, or differentiating, what is happening outside the organization and for what, through the activities and values of its members, the organization is responsible.

2. Examining the interaction of these two factors, including the effect of outside forces on the internal pathology.

3. Describing the "boundary phenomenon" of the organization as the interface between what is outside and inside the organization.

4. Describing the nature of the internal pathology in terms of what individuals are doing by themselves, from the CEO down through the hierarchy of management and supervisorial levels to the work force.

5. Examining the nature of the internal pathology in terms of the interactions among the individuals when it is supported by the authority or power structure of the organization, formal or informal.

6. Exploring how this situation is colored by individuals' needs, both real and imagined.

7. Carrying out a further exploration of the situation in terms of how it is affected by individuals' perceptions of what the organization needs when these may be impacted by individuals' unfinished situations.

8. Beginning to enhance the awareness process within the organization.

9. Using the awareness process to help separate an individual's material from the organization's.

10. Using the awareness process to experience what the individual's material is and what some other individual's material is, and how this can affect subsystems of the organization.

11. Using the awareness process to differentiate between what is said and what is actually done.

12. Learning to use descriptive feedback in contrast to evaluative, assessing, or judgmental feedback.

13. Examining the structure of the organization, including definitions of what and how things are to be done and values and tasks of the organization that may be in conflict with the external reality of the environment in which the organization exists.

14. Examining how personnel in the organization may be operationally denying any of the above, influenced by unfinished individual gestalts, and neurotic perceptions and activities, individual or collective, distorted by some construed organizational definition.

15. Exploring the organization to discover whether there is some part or parts of the organization in terms of subsystems or individuals that are responsible for the distortion.

16. Learning to describe, without evaluation, the immediate demands of the environment along with, and in contrast to, de-

mands of a more long-range nature, and using the awareness process for this.

17. Discovering, as part of the awareness process, how individuals in the organization, as individuals or collectively, may have allowed themselves to become immobilized as a consequence of constructing pseudorealities.

18. Mobilizing energy for change.

19. On the basis of the awareness process, selecting alternative behaviors to meet actual organizational needs, both immediate and long range.

20. Selecting from these alternatives that which is most appropriate for action.

21. Building in metaprocesses within an open-system format.

22. Building in an occasional meta-metasituation systematically to check out processing effectiveness.

Many of the 22 steps were used in the research on how declining organizations were changed in the preceding chapter. This will become clearer in the elaborations that follow.

Before showing how Gestalt therapy can be used for each of these 22 steps, we will delineate two settings for Gestalt interventions, each determined by the situational context. Either (1) the interventions are used in a training or a consulting situation, where the situation is reproduced or replicated in a different place so that approaches such as role playing are to be used, or (2) the Gestalt interventions are made within the actual organizational situational context. There are advantages and disadvantages to both.

If one is using replication, then certain elements that may be significant in the situation that could be having an influence on organizational personnel and on the organization's functioning could be neglected and thus missed in the replication—for example, the smells from the cafeteria at 11:30 in the morning. However, using Gestalt strategies or interventions in a replicatory mode provides opportunities for "stopping the action," to process what is going on, or to take time to reflect on what is happening, and so on.

The advantage of working in the actual situation, on the other hand, is that elements that otherwise might be forgotten (forgetting is a common form of avoidance) are less likely to be overlooked. The skillful change agent, as consultant, observer, facilitator, or manager, will be able to make what is implicit explicit, recapturing

what might otherwise be lost in transferring the intervention process outside the work context. And working in the actual situation
does not preclude the opportunity to process later outside the
work situation. Other things being equal, we would predict that,
wherever possible, Gestalt strategies and interventions should be
introduced directly into the work context. We have a qualifier for
this, and that is the readiness on the part of the personnel to
benefit from Gestalt intervention strategies. The facilitator needs
to take into consideration the reality of readiness, and will probably
have to begin with trust-building interventions before moving into
more impactful strategies. If the change agent has an ongoing
working relationship with personnel, then trust building will become an intrinsic part of that relationship.

The following is a hypothetical sequence that can be used as
a checklist or guide to maintaining a healthy growth for the in-
ternality of the organization and enhancing its interactions with
the environment. The steps can also be used to identify neurotic
organizational behavior and work with the behavior.

1. *Separating out, or differentiating, what is happening outside
the organization and for what, through the activities and values
of its members, the organization is responsible.*

Attention must be given to manifestations of the "blaming and
defending game" where personnel in the organization blame problem situations on what "they" on the outside are doing. This can
also be happening within the organization itself between subsystems. However manifested, the projection will likely be used to
disown both power and responsibility for what is going on within
the organization and how that affects the organization. Power and
responsibility will be projected onto external targets. For example,
"The public is stupid! They don't appreciate the utility and aes-
thetic value of our buggy whips. People just don't care anymore.
They have become lazy, want to drive away all closed up in their
adult baby-carriage cars. They close themselves off to nature and
all its beauty. They are burning up our resources instead of, by
having horses and buggies, maintaining the ecology. Just wait!
When all the oil is dried up, they'll need buggies and our buggy
whips." Of course, these statements are farcical. Yet they illustrate
what can happen when personnel in an organization blame the
outside world for not having the same values as they. They maintain a helpless, weak, or powerless position and project power
onto the environment, onto "the others."

In this situation, and in any situation where there is a denial of responsibility through mechanisms such as projection, Gestalt therapy can be used. First, personnel can get in touch with exactly what they are doing. This has to be facilitated by the change agent in a purely descriptive and nonjudgmental way, without didacticism or preaching. Humor helps. The goal of the change agent here is not to judge, but to help personnel perceive what may be an absurd situation.

2. Examining the interaction of these two factors, including the effect of outside forces on the internal pathology.

Continuing the extreme example used in step 1, a television news team visits the buggy whip factory, and in the style of "60 Minutes," makes fun of the obsolete stance of the organization and its members. This can exacerbate a bad situation, making the organization and its membership even more defensive—"circling the wagons" to protect themselves from the bad guys outside. In such cases the change agent can use a Gestalt technique of identification with the object having the projected power, and through role playing or some other technique, have members of the organization become "those outsiders." The change agent will need to help individuals immerse themselves in this role as totally as possible by experiencing the "enemy" and by becoming the "enemy" and having an opportunity to process how it feels to be the "enemy," especially focusing on the feelings of power therein. Some of the projected power can thus begin to be reowned.

3. Describing the "boundary phenomenon" of the organization as the interface between what is outside and inside the organization.

It is important that descriptions come from the experience of the "boundary." Time needs to be spent exploring just where the boundary is; what it feels like; how one knows what is outside and what is inside; how it feels to be inside the boundary and again, by role playing, and so forth, what it is like to be outside the boundary looking in. When using Gestalt techniques such as role playing or projection games, it is important that a climate be established by the change agent that somehow engages those involved in wanting to do whatever Gestalt experiment is being provided. This means that the trainer or change agent has to work from some of the stage one activities proposed earlier. If the Gestalt experiment is structured mechanistically, even when it is used the first or second time, and perfunctorily performed, the appropriate potential use of that Gestalt experiment can be lost. It is important that a Gestalt experiment not be performed for its own sake, but that it fit exactly the situation of the moment. This requires art on the part of the change agent.

Included in examining the boundary phenomenon would be some appreciation of the function the boundary performs, including whether it should be modified, changed, moved in or out, or made more or less permeable. This would be based on examining what is happening at the boundary. Is the organization as a system too open so that the organization is overloaded by input, some of it unnecessary or extraneous? Or is the organization in need of more data, energy, or material from outside? Or is it receiving too much help, as illustrated in the author's research on declining organizations?

Metaphorically speaking, should the office of the CEO subscribe to the *Wall Street Journal, Barrons, Forbes Magazine,* and *Fortune,* or should it subscribe only to the *Buggy Whip Monthly*? Should the buggy whip designer attend the county fair, or travel to Japan to see what they're doing over there to change their buggy whips into gearshift levers?

Of importance in making these decisions has to be a clarity and awareness of both external and internal reality with regard to the organization. Some of the following steps might be involved in this step, or might impinge upon it.

Such decisions are never completely rational or influenced solely by a problem-solving approach. Emotional needs, manifested individually or collectively, are bound to influence these decisions. It is only through an awareness of these and other irrational variables, which Gestalt approaches can facilitate, that decisions can actually become more rational and intelligent.

4. *Describing the nature of the internal pathology in terms of what individuals are doing by themselves, from the CEO down through the hierarchy of management and supervisor levels to the work force.*

When there is pathology that is being manifested through breakdowns or malfunctioning, or even decreased efficiency in terms of tasks of the organization, or when there are communication problems, interrelationship problems, and so forth, with regard to the maintenance function of the organization, these can be described as neurotic organizational behavior. Then the change agent needs to give feedback based on direct observation of what is going on. Whether that feedback is given at the moment or in private, or in a later group process situation, it can be done within the Gestalt mode of simply describing behaviors in terms of what the change agent sees and hears, not what he/she imagines or interprets. Instead of an interpretation of what is happening, Gestalt therapy approaches can provide an appreciation of and respect for how each individual experiences the situation. It is not only salient that the change agent have the opportunity to observe what is going on and give feedback on it, but that the agent help elicit how each individual experiences that particular situation. It is the gestalt of the summation of these individual experiences that makes for the operational reality of what is actually happening in the subsystem or organization.

"Why" not only can be irrelevant, but can interfere with the experience of the individual by moving the individual from the more total experience to a "head trip." Change is less likely to come from the understanding at an intellectual level provided by interpretations. Behavior is essentially not rational. Rather, by making explicit the "how" and "what" of each individual's experience, followed by providing ways to increase opportunities for contact among the personnel involved, (1) these experiences can be shared, and (2) alternative choices may ultimately be realized that provide the promise for real and intrinsic change in the neurotic organizational behavior. Even more important, as this occurs, there will be an increased appreciation of the process of change, itself, which can then open up the system and begin to provide the confidence and knowledge that individuals involved can make necessary changes.

5. *Examining the nature of the internal pathology in terms of the interactions among the individuals when it is supported by the authority or power structure of the organization, formal or informal.*

This is a special case of step 4, where observation and feedback can be used to make explicit how authority and power are being used in interpersonal relationships within the organization. Again, the change agent has to be careful not to give feedback in such a way as to place those to whom it is directed on the defensive. From a Gestalt point of view, feedback should be descriptive. As mentioned earlier, the quality of the voice is crucial here. The change agent can use words that on paper might appear innocuous but, when spoken in judgmental tones might inspire defensiveness and consequently an unwillingness to listen. The important point is that the change agent has to learn to self-process almost instantaneously so that if a judgmental feeling is experienced, it can be dealt with and not allowed to interfere with the professional relationship with members of the organization. It may be helpful for the change agent to request feedback from those with whom the agent is working as to how they are experiencing him/her.

6. *Exploring how the situation is colored by individuals' needs, both real and imagined.*

This step could be explored in two directions.

First, those in the so-called "top-dog" position of having power could be helped to experience (1) how they manifest their power, (2) how they feel as they do this, (3) what needs are being satisfied through these actions and feelings, and (4) without judging themselves, whether these needs can be met in other ways if they interfere with the healthy behavior of the organization.

A CEO who has an unfinished gestalt involving a need to control the universe, perhaps arising out of a vague apprehension of chaos, might believe that by not staying in control, things are going to fall apart. With help to get in touch with this, the CEO could be made aware of how it could directly impinge upon his/her effectiveness with the organization and its personnel. Something so profound and rooted in basic epistimological premises might take time to get at and require therapeutic skills the change agent might not have. Still, if the suspicion that something so deeply rooted is affecting the performance of the CEO exists in the change agent's mind, then he/she may recommend bringing in outside help. One would hope that the change agent's relationship with the CEO would be such that the CEO would be willing to listen to such a possibility and have enough confidence in the change agent to explore it.

A second direction that could be pursued is the underdog situation where personnel respond to demands of superiors. In this case the change agent would be alert to how personnel are directly or indirectly sabotaging the demands of their superiors or the demands of the organization, either perceived as somehow being a top dog. The change agent would explore whether individual personnel have life scripts unfinished with regard to responding to authority figures. Unfinished situations out of the past can strongly influence present behavior. Sometimes the personnel might have and share similar feelings so that the change agent can deal with this in a group setting. Again, humor is important. The light touch, without judgment, can be crucial to dealing with this problem effectively.

7. Carrying out a further exploration of the situation in terms of how it is affected by individuals' perceptions of what the organization needs when these may be colored by individuals' unfinished situations.

This relates specifically to problem situations that may be influenced by the interpersonal relationships described in the preceding step. Problem situations can often be defined on the basis of "unfinished business" of the individuals involved. It is simply a matter of how one sees the world, how one defines oneself in the world, and again, borrowing from stage one, what one hopes and believes is possible when confronting the world. This not only can define a problem situation, but can color the imagined lack of strength for action by personnel. Someone who was originally defined as a "loser" and has internalized that definition is certainly not expecting to have much to contribute to the resolution of some dilemma in the organization. Although perhaps the most competent person available, he/she will let someone else do it. In these cases Gestalt interventions sometimes can provide the biographical shocks necessary to disintegrate the granite "reality" that has been internalized through the primary socialization process in childhood, or perhaps introjected in the secondary socialization process through other experiences in social institutions. If the collective experience of the personnel in the organization has achieved an unhealthy unanimity that does not allow for diversity, and, as a consequence, neurotic organizational behavior seems to be growing, then a biographical shock for the organization itself may be needed. This means that the premises, values, and modes of operation of the organization must first to be experienced, then, dramatically confronted, and then compared with alternatives and the possibilities for change. This will be elaborated in further steps.

8. Enhancing the awareness process within the organization.

Training in the awareness process can be at different levels. There could be training for entire organizations so that all personnel would be provided with certain essential experiences. These might include learning to use descriptive feedback, and to build in opportunities for processing. By processing we mean meta-communication, talking about what is going on as experienced by the individual and the system. Another way to describe this is as communicating about communicating. In Gestalt there is emphasis on process rather than on goals. Goals are incorporated and are important to indicate the direction of the process and nature of the means whereby the process can be facilitated. Preoccupation with goals when tasks are goal oriented may interfere with an awareness of the task process itself. It is through awareness of the task process that improvements can be made, because the task as process is what is happening. Concentrating on where we want to be can take us out of contact with what is actually going on. When workers in a unit with the responsibility for working together to produce certain components become preoccupied with the fact that they need to produce a certain number of units each day, and allow this preoccupation to dominate their thoughts and feelings, they are less likely to meet or exceed their quota. If, instead, they realize the simple fact that though they do have to produce the units, more important is what is going on in the actual production of those units, they will more likely be able to improve the production process.

The second focus of an awareness training process might be on the training of change agents, and possibly the training of management, when roles are different. There is a large repertoire of training possibilities. Priorities would have to be established in terms of the needs of these personnel, influenced, in turn, by the organization's needs. Certainly training could be oriented toward both the avoidance of the development of neurotic organizational behavior and the treatment of neurotic organizational behavior once it were to emerge.

A second aspect of the training of trainers and management would be the establishment of teams that could bring in a variety of intervention skills for dealing with problems. These could include specialists related to various aspects of the organization, specialists with training in various kinds of interventions and those responsible for the processing of the change agent or consulting team, itself, as it performs as a subsystem within the organizational context. The teams would need training in Gestalt work with immediate problems, along with an awareness of the larger gestalts in which the problem situations are emerging. There would be training for looking at the organization as a system, and tending to the interactions, patterns, and relationships that can permeate a system. Perceiving these larger gestalts could involve a combination of what Nevis describes as Colombo and Sherlock Holmes skills. Probably the analytical component should be held in reserve until a larger gestalt has emerged and then be used, not vice versa.

A third aspect of this step would be the designing of a curriculum for training based on increasing risk levels, which, in turn, would be derived from the assessment of readiness of those involved to move into the rather different approach that Gestalt has to offer. The curriculum would probably include certain commonalities from Gestalt therapy such as awareness, personal and emotional expression, and experience-based and choice-making factors. These, when added to more common rational know-how and skill training approaches to change strategies, can provide an ecosystem perspective and procedure for general organizational needs and the special needs of the team or individual.

9. *Using the awareness process to help separate an individual's material from the organization's.*

This is somewhat different from steps 4, 5, and 6 in the sense that the focus is on the contrast between the individual and the organization. This means using Gestalt to help individuals apprehend the nature of the organization itself. In turn, this may necessitate "reowning" factors such as the power to judge or to reward, the power to encourage, the power to open up, the power to provide opportunities, and so on. All these must be "reowned" by the individual when the individual has projected personal capabilities onto the organization. It would be necessary here to separate the projection from the reality. Obviously organizations have powers that the individual does not have, or at least representatives of the organization have these powers. What is important is to focus on any confusion between what is real and what is imagined. The Gestalt technique that would be helpful here would be to separate what one can see from what one imagines, along with an emphasis on how we respond to what we see and what we imagine. Separating seeing, imagining, and responding is the experiment. There is need for clarifying the following: what the individual is able actually to see in terms of reality and what the individual is projecting or imagining; how the individual is responding; the nature of that response and the realization that the individual is the one who is doing the responding, and, in effect, must take responsibility for that response. The confusion in this situation can be exacerbated by organizational myths and delusions. However, this is no way negates the recommended Gestalt seeing, imagining, and responding clarification, for even here myths and delusions can be discerned with help from the change agent by focusing on the separation of these three separate acts.

   10. Using the awareness process to experience what the individual's material is and what some other individual's material is and how this can affect subsystems or the organization.
   Gestalt can be used to improve the communication process that is so essential in the functioning of an organization. Among the problems that contribute to communication failure are the difference between seeing and imagining, mentioned earlier, and separating these from "How I respond." By the latter we mean confusions that arise from projecting one's own values, desires, and needs onto another person, or assuming the other person has the same operational set as the projector. These all relate to contact–boundary functioning. When I imagine how you are responding to me, even though you may not give any external indication of this, I have dissolved the contact boundary and put myself into your position. Thus there is no contact with the "real you," only with my projected self. Perhaps I may have created confluence between you and me. If instead I can learn to see what you are actually doing, check out with you what I do not know, and even those things I imagine I do know, this practice can become invaluable for facilitating relationships and smooth organizational functioning. If I can further (1) make a clear distinction between who I am and what I am doing and who you are and what you are doing, (2) include how I am responding to this, and (3) provide you with opportunities to express how you respond to whatever the situation is, again, we have clarification and improvement in communication.
   This is a further elaboration of the three phases, seeing, imagining, and responding, mentioned in step 9. This sounds simple but is so often neglected that the situation can reach a point of absurdity. The point is that confusions between what I perceive and what I imagine I am and you are become so common that the absurd ceases to be absurd and is, instead, expected, and thus becomes tolerated as part of conventional wisdom.
   The separation of the fantasies we have of one another and the systems we are in from the reality of these can create opportunities to use Gestalt therapeutic interventions for attending to the relationship among resentments, demands, and appreciations, either

explicitly or implicitly expressed. The understanding and experience of these relationships can help clear up many conflict situations. Conflicts are often based on hidden agendas. Resentments are to be experienced. They are not rational, justifiable, or logical, or often even appropriate. They are essentially emotional and, as a consequence, in the "rational" world of organizations are often denied. With every resentment experienced is an implicit demand. "I resent the way you ignore my suggestions" contains the implicit demand of "Pay attention to what I have to say." Connected to every resentment and demand is usually a hidden appreciation. Within Gestalt appreciations are not meant in a conventional sense of "liking." You can appreciate what you don't like. You may appreciate how clever someone is at manipulating, but you may not like it. As a manipulator, the person is a champion. In the situation of being ignored, you could appreciate that the other seems to know what he/she is talking about and has self-confidence. All three—resentments, demands, and appreciations—can exist without any awareness by the individuals who harbor them. The change agent, by bringing them to light to be worked with, can also help bring into awareness how relationships within the organization are consequently affected. Basic to Gestalt for working with individuals in an organizational context is that before one can see others in the organization differently, one must experience oneself differently.

11. Using the awareness process to differentiate between what is said and what is actually done.

The emphasis here is, again without judgment, to make explicit the differences between thinking and talking and acting. The intervention is primarily empirical. This is accomplished by attending to what is happening from moment to moment and using the basic Gestalt questions "What are you doing now?" "What are you experiencing now?" in contrast to "What are you thinking now?" or "Why do you say that?" The confusion between thinking and talking, on the one hand, and acting, on the other, can be eye opening. We tend to give magical powers to words and thoughts and substitute them for action without an awareness that we are doing so. Obviously believing in magic here could interfere with the effectiveness of an organization's processes. Until there is an awareness of what is actually going on, there can be no possibility of choices for change because no need for a change exists in the consciousness of members of the unit. Talking, and thinking it is middle-zone activity, is a comfortable substitute for responsible reaction to the need for action.

12. Learning to use descriptive feedback in contrast to evaluative, assessing, or judgmental feedback.

Gestalt feedback emphasizes the descriptive mode. Feedback is based on actual perception rather than evaluation or judgments. This holds for both consultive feedback and managerial and supervisorial response. Learning to substitute description for evaluation has a number of positive consequences. The evaluative mode cannot help but include biases, values, and goals. This is not to say that these are not sometimes relevant. The question, rather, is when such factors should be introduced. If they are used in feedback situations, they can interfere with or interrupt the learning process of the receiver of the feedback.

What is most important for growth and improvement is knowing, precisely and explicitly, what one is doing at the moment. If we introduce the element of what one *should* be doing before one can appreciate what one actually *is* doing, then confusion can arise out of fear, apprehension, overeagerness to comply, or even defiance. Resentment at being told what to do or feeling depreciated as an individual who has no part in designing his/her own work can interfere with the individual worker's opportunity to take responsibility for what he/she is doing. Furthermore, a pattern of external evaluative feedback can influence the worker to see him/herself as a nonperson, as not existing as a human being but as an object. If instead the feedback is descriptive, the implication is clear: Here are the data, what are you going to do with them? Most important, if feedback is given descriptively consistently, the message is imputed that the worker has the capacity to make decisions based on that feedback, and that these decisions can be worthwhile and constructive.

To do all this, we need to suspend right and wrong or good–bad judgments. We replace these with explicit perceptual descriptions of what is going on *and* emphasize how people are responding to these activities. Furthermore, Gestalt can be used to learn how to reframe what is happening, to use alternative definitions and metaphors. It is often how we define things that makes them so. It is not too difficult to change definitions and escape metaphors by experiencing what we are doing and consciously choosing to replace them. To do this, we must, of course, be aware of how we have defined situations and the nature of the metaphors we have chosen.

Directly related is learning how to "state the obvious." We need to learn the difference between fantasy (which may be the product of imagination and concepts distorted by inappropriate hangings-on to the past, or being caught up with wishes for the future) and the reality of the present moment. As stated earlier, the emphasis within the Gestalt approach is consistently on the "here and now." This is the reality with which we can deal. The rest is conjecture.

13. Examining the structure of the organization, including definitions of what and how things are to be done and values and tasks of the organization that may be in conflict with the external reality of the environment in which the organization functions.

When a person in authority or with power insists that subordinates do things completely that person's way, this imposition of structure, values, and goals *could* be perceived or experienced as leading to the denial of the subordinates' existence. There may be many subordinates who, predisposed to accepting external reality, prefer to have an authority tell them what to do and how to do it. However, those who do have the potential for making their own decisions, for contributing their own ideas, creativity, and actions, could be thwarted from realizing the potential that they do have. Those who are inclined toward an independent style of contributing would be greatly frustrated by an authoritarian stance. Thus the person in authority has to differentiate among those with whom he/she is working so as to fit leadership style to the immediate and long-range needs of the subordinates.

Those who identify with an organization, or with those in authority in the organization, have in effect lost a sense of themselves, individually or collectively. If their identification with the organization has become so frozen, there is no conflict and no frustration, but, at the same time, no growth. When there is no growth, then the potential for contributions to the organization fades away. This can be especially dangerous when those working on the interface with the outside world are responsible for providing information on the marketplace to the organization, and consequently distort their perceptions because of such an identification.

14. *Examining how personnel in the organization may be operationally denying any of the previous 13 steps, influenced by unfinished individual gestalts, and neurotic perceptions and activities, individual or collective, distorted by some construed organizational definitions.*

An example of this may be found in the situation called the trap of "blaming and defending." The blaming and defending syndrome also emerges from a breakdown or communication and contributes to further breakdowns. As a result of some inappropriate organizational decision that, in turn, results in organization breakdowns, or even in some other form of neurotic organizational behavior, there can also be a breakdown in communication. This breakdown in communication can be further exacerbated by "unfinished business" coming out of an individual's process of socialization. From the neurotic organizational behavior or the breakdown, there can be an initial impulse to defend oneself or to blame another person or subsystem, or both. This can be transcended by training in careful attention to an awareness of what we do. We can, instead, learn to share how we respond to the problem situation and listen to the other person express his/her response. Both, again, are done without judgment or evaluation, simply to find out how we are, each of us, so that by taking our own responsibility, we can get on with what needs to be done, instead of becoming entangled in the blaming-defending syndrome.

Other denial mechanisms may be manifesting themselves. These could relate to the five steps in stage one, or as part of a number of the other steps included in this stage.

15. *Exploring the organization to discover whether there is some part or parts of the organization in terms of subsystems or individuals that are responsible for the distortion.*

The point here is not to find the "bad guys," or who is guilty. It is, through a scanning of the organization and its subsystems using the descriptive mode described in step 12, to find out, as precisely and exactly as possible, just what is going on, and to separate this from the blaming mentioned in step 14 or other distortions so that actions based on reality can be taken. Along with this, the distortion process itself could be explored as probably being manifested in the form of one of the defense mechanisms mentioned earlier in the book.

16. *Learning to describe, without evaluation, the immediate*

demands of the environment along with, and in contrast to, demands of a more long-range nature, and using the awareness process for this.

This is simply the separation of an awareness of what needs to be done now and what ultimately will have to be dealt with. The point here is to make clear what the differences are between the two, if such differences exist. The Gestalt technique of "on the one hand," "on the other hand" can be used where those involved can move into the roles of actually being the situation, both immediate and long range, and have a conversation between the two.

"On the one hand, we are the immediate demand. We think we have to find where markets exist for our buggy whips. Are there possible customers we are overlooking? For example, maybe people who don't have buggies would want our buggy whips as interior decorations for their houses. Can we immediately increase our market by switching our advertising from buggy whips as utility to buggy whips as decorations?"

"Well, as long-range plans, we think we need to look into what is happening in Japan. Buggy whip factories there have long ago switched over to gearshift levers. Is there something coming down the pike in terms of the market, where the machinery we have for making our buggy whips can be used for something that is going to be emerging as a need in the marketplace?"

And then we would carry on a dialogue between these two positions to see what emerges and use this in making decisions.

17. Discovering, as part of the awareness process, how individuals in the organization, as individuals or collectively, may have allowed themselves to become immobilized as a consequence of constructing pseudorealities.

This directly relates to the various psychological mechanisms and to a number of the previous steps in terms of separating what is fantasy or delusion or myth from what is real. A number of our earlier suggested interventions could be used. The point here is to separate what is real from what is imagined, and to get in touch with each and discern what the difference is so we can act on a reality base.

18. Mobilizing energy for change.

The technique of using Gestalt to deal with the impasses (being stuck) of individuals might be applied to help focus on what may be blockages in the energy flow process within the organization. Unblocking of the energy flow process can begin to occur through an awareness of how attention is being paid to how things should be, or would be desirable. Such attention is counterproductive. Instead attention and awareness need to be focused on what the actual blocking phenomena are. Care should be given to examining the blockage in explicit and specific terms. Those involved in the blockage may be concentrating instead on goals or ideals, like "wanting to change." Paradoxically the blockage is thus maintained. We mentioned this in stage one.

To the degree that we focus on where we want to be, we cannot attend to what is actually being experienced. It is only through real experience that we can grow and change. The Gestalt experiment here is to facilitate a total immersing of oneself in the impasse situation, comprehensively to explore characteristics and qualities of the impasse, its content, and its boundaries, while at the same time paying no attention whatsoever to wanting to change or evaluating what is happening. There are then possibilities for moving through the impasse. In Gestalt therapy this is described, as we mentioned earlier, as when one experiences "What is," "What is" changes. When one experiences "What is," then that experience is added to the individual's sum of experiences and that sum is changed, not only quantitatively, but qualitatively as well. The personal organization of the individual is inevitably changed. We are describing a disidentification process that can be highlighted by simply attending to a detailed description of what is going on. In other words the individual moves not only within the level of what he/she is doing, but also at a meta-level of observing what the individual is doing, and both at practically the same time. Through this total unjudgmental immersion in and clarification of the structure and the relationships within the impasse, a new perspective and *experience* of the impasse and unblocking of the energies can emerge. The experiment can be applied to individuals as members of subsystems and organizations by staying with impasses within that special context.

There are other techniques in Gestalt that can be used to help mobilize energy. These include exaggeration, which means doing more of what is already being done even to extremes, and the use of polarities, where one does the opposite of what is being done, again to the extreme. The use of exaggeration dramatizes and thus helps the individual or members of the group to become aware of exactly what they are doing. It is, in effect, sticking something right under their individual or collective noses. The polarity intervention helps those with whom the change agent is working become aware of hidden aspects of the personality that are usually projected onto some other person, unit, or institution. What is happening here is denial of parts of the self that, when brought into awareness and reowned, can be utilized in constructive ways. By reowning these projected polarities, the individual or unit becomes more integrated, more of one piece, with more aspects of selves to use when confronting and acting in the world.

19. *On the basis of the awareness process, selecting alternative behaviors to meet actual organizational needs, both immediate and long range.*

This is a matter of combining emotional and rational processes to become aware of alternatives. The salient component here is the addition of emotional and personal dimensions to what is traditionally a rational, or problem-solving, process. Until the emotional and personal factors are dealt with, it is difficult to function in a rational way. Denial of polarities, as mentioned in step 18, is one example of emotional and personal factors interfering with rational and reality-based behavior.

20. *Selecting from these alternatives that which is most appropriate for action.*

An essential Gestalt construct is the concept of responsibility in the Gestalt sense as (1) the ability to respond or the capacity to act and (2) the acceptance or the "owning" of what the individual, the unit, or the organization is or is not doing. This sounds simple, but what we are talking about is an authentic appreciation that I or we are doing this or that I or we are not doing that. Until such an appreciation exists, individuals or groups can avoid taking responsibility for what they are doing. There are many ways to avoid responsibility. This "happening" can be blamed on external circumstances, or can be thought of as some kind of magic situation where things just seem to happen, or can be passed off as bad luck, and so on.

The contact–withdrawal cycle has been described in detail earlier in this work. This is not simply a theoretical construct. It is a form of phenomenon that exists and is usually interfered with. If opportunities for the contact–withdrawal cycles are provided, there is the promise of greatly increased productivity—whatever the nature of that productivity might be. An example from individual Gestalt therapy can demonstrate what we mean. If you are reading a book because you have to, and you force yourself to stay with that book, the learning process is less efficient than if you close your eyes and relax for a few moments, and then return to the book refreshed and ready to go. What happens with the individual certainly happens with individuals within groups, and possibly with the group entity itself.

As for learning to plan productively, we can use Gestalt to differentiate between a planning process that is neurotic in that it is being used as an avoidance to action in the present, and the kind of planning that is healthy because it is used to provide direction, and the means for it, for the actual ongoing moment-to-moment process in terms of the mission of the organization. Planning that is used as an avoidance to action is a special case of the importance of learning the difference between action that takes place solely at the verbal level (talking about) and action in which the organization or any of its subsystems are more totally involved. Here we are learning how to translate information into energy and how to focus this energy into action. There is a fundamental Gestalt construct where the lowest level of action is described as thinking, and the next lowest level is talking about. Action is what is productive. The needs of the organism or the organization are ultimately met through action. The more total is the action involving motoric and sensoric systems, as well as intellectual endeavors, the more satisfaction can be achieved for the organism or the organization.

There is an unusual Gestalt therapy construct that "learning is discovering that something is possible." By this is meant that the discovery that is based on experience, not just intellectual endeavor (although there is obviously an intellectual component in the discovery process) can greatly facilitate any change process. As we stated earlier, "When I believe it, I'll see it." This is what we mean by discovering that something is possible. Choices, alternatives, and fresh approaches to organizational needs can arise from the use of this construct.

21. Building in meta-processes within an open system format.

These allow and encourage continual changes in organizational activities and structures. Within the interaction of the organization and its environment will also be a process emphasis on the avoidance of permanent solutions, which, by becoming fixed, could create new pathologies.

Of great advantage to organizations would be building in, both formally and informally, appropriate opportunities for processing what is happening in the organization as an entity, at each level of the organization, between levels, in a variety of situations, or between key individuals, and so on. When we talk about processing, we mean meta-communication. Being able to communicate about the effectiveness of a communication process is essential to improving that process, and is a basic Gestalt construct. Processing can be appropriate for any organizational functioning. If individuals are provided an opportunity to give feedback on what is happening, not only among themselves but to those in supervisorial roles, supervisors can have a greater appreciation of what is actually going on with the personnel in the organization, and thus be able to do something about it.

To learn how to do processing requires ongoing training at a meta-level. Processing is about experience. Experience can be with either task or maintenance functions. Gestalt emphasis on description instead of evaluation will be an essential part of the process training.

Those who are part of a system will have difficulty in changing that system as long as they act within the paradigm of the system. To create change it may be necessary either to bring someone in from outside the system, or for those in the system to be able to step out and assume a "meta" perspective. They have to be able to look at what is going on, as someone alien to that situation might.

Part of the training of the Gestalt therapist is not to get hooked into a problem, but to stay with the moment-to-moment process, adding, when appropriate, patterns or themes that are emerging from the therapist's experience with the client. Feedback and interventions, like Gestalt experiments, come from the behavior of the client at the moment and are not to be influenced by interpretations of the therapist. Therapists can operate from hypotheses and construct experiments based on these, but always in the context of what happens from moment to moment. They are ever ready to abandon the hypothesis temporarily or forever, depending upon the client's behavior within an existential context. The purpose, then, is not to solve problems per se. If problems are solved, the process involved in the solution is often more important for the client to appreciate and assume. The client then can become increasingly more independent and reality based in behavior. In the organizational context, when the change agent similarly functions, the organization, subsystem, or individuals in the organization can carry out more independent, reality-based decisions and action.

22. Building in an occasional meta-meta-situation systematically to check out processing effectiveness.

This involves first taking a fresh look at what's happening, without emotional entanglements or identification with the system. As personnel are able to do this, they can move to a "meta-meta" level where, having experienced their capability to do the "meta," they can begin to appreciate the value of the process itself and that they have the capacity to carry it out. This means they can function at a meta-meta-level. "If we have done this once, we can do it again. We have the potential for continuing processing." As this appreciation is achieved, the system becomes more open to the "meta" process.

Opportunities for systematic and spontaneous processing can be built into the organization to help avoid the emergence of neurotic organizational behavior, or to work with it when it exists. Meta-processes can counter the creation of internal conditions that lead to declining organizations.

The 22 steps, together and individually, are derived from Gestalt approaches. The steps by themselves, without elaboration, illustrate the kinds of concerns and questions that can evolve from exploring the field from moment to moment as the individual or group interacts with its environment. The interacters and the environment, taken together, are the field. And exploring this field is fundamental in the Gestalt approach.

There are two possible ways to focus Gestalt therapy. The first is concern with an immediate problem or issue. In this case we can work with some pressing item that emerges at the moment and needs "finishing up," the completion of an unresolved or incomplete gestalt that, to the individual, demands attention and resolution. This either can have been brought to a therapy session, or can emerge in the process of the therapy encounter itself. The second focus has a more educational emphasis and is concerned with influencing overall or long-range behavior. Here the therapist attempts to help the client experience what the client is doing, and how, so that the client can discover his/her process—whether it be self-torture, staying stuck, or blaming others. Then upon continuing to do whatever is being done, the client can more quickly become aware of neurotic behavior. The therapist can construct experiments for the client. These enable the client to discover that there is a choice in this matter—either to continue to repeat the disfunctional behavior or to do something different. Most important, not only can the client do something different, but the client can choose alternatives, new ways to be and act. The client learns that, as client, he/she is capable of making choices and following through on them. As a consequence the client can learn new ways to function while engaging in daily activities.

This same statement can be made by substituting organization or subsystems or personnel for "client" and change agent for "therapist."

The Gestalt therapist mainly does two things: the therapist makes what is implicit explicit, and states the obvious. Sometimes these two overlap. These acts of Gestalt therapy may seem simple at first glance. But what should be obvious is often not so obvious because of the noise and confusion we create for ourselves in order not to confront what is obvious. And what is implicit can be carefully buried and smoothed over so that even the remembrance of what is hidden fades away almost completely. We may dread its emergence, as we imagine that the powerlessness and impotency we had at the time it was buried are still with us, and we are still incapable of confronting this material. Even though we know intellectually and rationally that it would be better for us to take care of what often so subtly presses upon us from that burial, we are very clever with our psychological mechanisms of projection, introjection, retroflection, confluence, and disowning.

We can become so accustomed to these mechanisms that they reach the stage of seeming natural and the way to be. When the individual's avoidance is compounded by his/her existing in an organization, where the organization as a system struggles to maintain some balance, we have avoidance compounded by avoidance. Out of a need to maintain balance and evade the possibility of chaos or disintegration, with the attendant stress, organizations can become operationally stuck in the status quo. They may give lip service to growth and change, but individuals in the organization can become comfortable with what they have hidden within themselves, along with how they see themselves as members of the organization. Thus the change agent has to do a dance between working with the individual, with the organization, and with the individual in the organization, an unholy triad, even though at times it may be necessary to work with all three conditions in one individual.

What the change agent hopes to achieve among the individuals, the subsystems, and the organization itself is a more flexible identification process in contrast to a neurotic or frozen character. By character we mean being stuck with only one way to do and see things. A flexible identification process allows for accommodation to changes in context or situation. This in turn encourages a more "here and now" reality base in contrast to being caught in the middle-zone activity of the psychological defense mechanisms, distortions, illusions, fantasies, and mythologies.

It would be hoped that ultimately individuals throughout the organization could be trained in how to use certain Gestalt therapy interventions in order to help one another increase the effectiveness of the subsystem in which they are involved and the organization as a whole. At the same time, this will improve the quality of living in the organizational context. Gestalt therapy could have an immediate and direct impact on what is emphasized by John Naisbitt (1984) in his book *Megatrends* and by others who comment on the increasing importance of the personal growth factor in career and corporation context.

From these suggestions for possible uses of Gestalt therapy, there is indeed the potential for preventing and changing neurotic organizational behavior, and possibly even helping declining organizations. At this point we certainly do not intend to suggest that Gestalt approaches be used exclusively as interventions or strategies in working both from within and externally with the organization. What we do suggest is the potentially rich repertoire of approaches that may be drawn from Gestalt therapy for dealing with what is going on, and possibly even providing a fresh philosophy of operations. As important, and perhaps even more important, there is promise in using a Gestalt therapy perspective to design change strategies for the pathology of an organization and sustaining strategies for its health.

The foregoing is presented only as an introduction and as examples of how Gestalt therapeutic approaches could be used in the organizational context. The reader may be left with questions about some of these. For the reader who would like more specifics and details, we recommend an extensive review of the standard works of Gestalt therapy referred to in the text and other volumes in this series.

A FINAL WORD

This book is a beginning. Obviously some of what has been presented needs more work in the field. We hope we have provided, however, if not always specific "means whereby," at least new directions for action and ways to conceptualize what is going on with organizations. We have attempted to address organizations that are healthy and want to stay that way, and organizations with neurotic behavior that want to do something about rejuvenating their health and productivity. There remains much to be accomplished, but we hope we have opened new doors to exploration toward that end.

BIBLIOGRAPHY

CHAPTER 1

Adams, R. N. *Energy and structure: A theory of social power.* Austin: University of Texas Press, 1975.

Coleman, J. C. *Abnormal psychology and modern life* (4th ed.). Glenville, Ill.: Scott, Foresman, 1972.

De Board, R. *The psychoanalysis of organizations.* London: Tavistock, 1978.

De Greene, K.B. The adaptive organization: Anticipation and mangement of crisis. New York: Wiley, 1982.

Fink, S. L., Beak, J., & Taddeo, K. Organizational crisis and change. *Journal of Applied Behavioral Science,* 1971, 7(1).

Harvey, J. B., & Albertson, D. R. Neurotic organizations: Symptoms, causes and treatment. *Personnel Journal,* Sept., Oct., 1971, L(9, 10), 694–699, 770–777.

Kets de Vries, M., & Miller, D. *Neurotic style and organizational pathology.* Montreal: McGill Faculty of Management (mimeo), 1982.

Levinson, H., with Molinari, J., & Spahn, A. G. *Organizational diagnosis.* Cambridge, Mass.: Harvard University Press, 1972.

Miller, J. G. *Living systems.* New York: McGraw-Hill, 1978.

Perls, F. *The Gestalt approach and eyewitness to therapy.* New York: Bantam, 1980.

Perls, F. S. *Gestalt therapy verbatim.* New York: Bantam, 1976.

Robbins, S. P. *Organization theory: The structure and design of organizations.* Englewood Cliffs, N.J.: Prentice-Hall, 1983.

Smart, C., & Vertinsky, I. Designs for crisis decision units. *Administrative Science Quarterly*, Dec. 1977, *22*, 640–657.

Whetten, D. A. Sources, responses and effects of organizational decline. In J. R. Kimberly, et al. (Eds.), *The organizational life cycle*. San Francisco: Jossey-Bass, 1980.

CHAPTER 2

American College Dictionary. Clarence Bernhart, Editor. New York: Random, 1962.

Argyris, C., & Schon, D. A. *Organizational learning: A theory of action perspective*. Reading, Mass.: Addison-Wesley, 1978.

Boje, D. M., Fedor, D. B., & Rowland, K. M. Myth making: a qualitative step in OD interventions. *Journal of Applied Behavioral Science*, 1982, *18*(1), 17–28.

Boulding, K. E. General systems theory: The skeleton of a science. In W. Buckley (Ed.), *Modern systems research for the behavioral scientist*. Chicago: Aldine, 1968.

Bradford, L. P., & Harvey, J. B. Dealing with dysfunctional organizational myths. *Training and Development Journal*, September 1970, *XXIV*(9), 2–6.

De Greene, K. B. *The adaptive organization: Anticipation and management of crisis*. New York: Wiley, 1982.

Gibson, G. L., Ivancevich, J. M., & Donnelly, J. H. *Organizations: Structure, process and behavior*. Dallas: Business Pub., 1976.

Hannan, M., & Freeman, J. The population ecology of organizations. *American Journal of Sociology*, March 1977, *82*, 929-64.

Harvey, J. B., & Albertson, D. R. Neurotic organizations: Symptoms, causes and treatment. *Personal Journal*, Sept., Oct., 1971, *L*(9, 10), 696–699, 710–777.

Hedberg, B. L. T. How organizations learn and unlearn. In P. C. Nystrom & W. H. Starbuck (Edds.), *Handbook of organizational design* (vol. 1). New York: Oxford University Press, 1981.

Hedberg, B. L. T., & Jonsson, S. A. Strategy formulation as a discontinuous process. *International Studies of Management and Organization*, 1977, (7), 89–109.

Jantsch, E. *Design for evolution: Self-organization and planning in the life of human systems*. New York: Braziller, 1975.

Kets de Vries, M., & Miller, D. *Neurotic style and organizational pathology*. Montreal: McGill, Faculty of Management (mimeo), 1982.

Kriesberg, L. *The sociology of social conflicts*. Englewood Cliffs, N.J.: Prentice-Hall, 1973.

Merry, U., & Arnon, U. *The shell shocked soldier*. (mimeo—Hebrew) Tel-Aviv: Daf Ezer, Hafala, 1973.

Miller, J. G. *Living systems*. New York: McGraw-Hill, 1978.

Perls, F. *The Gestalt approach and eyewitness to therapy.* New York: Bantam, 1980.

Pondy, L.R. & Mitcoff, J.I. Beyond open systems models of organization. In B.M. Staw (Ed.) *Research in organizational behavior.* (Vol. I). Greenwich, Conn.: Ja: Press, 1979.

Scott, R.W. Organization, Rational, natural and open systems. New Jersey: Prentice-Hall, 1981.

CHAPTER 3

Adams, R. N. *Energy and structure: A theory of social power.* Austin: University of Texas Press, 1975.

Aldrich, H. E. *Organizations and environments.* Englewood Cliffs, N.J.: Prentice-Hall, 1979.

Argenti, J. *Organizational collapse.* New York: Halstead Press, 1976.

Berger, P. L., & Luckman, T. *The social construction of reality: A treatise in the sociology of knowledge.* New York: Doubleday, 1966.

Bigelow, J. D. Approaching the organizational navel: An evolutionary perspective in OD. In T. G. Cummings (Ed.), *Systems theory for organization development.* New York: Wiley, 1980.

Carneiro, R. L. Successive reequillibrations as a mechanism of cultural evolution. In W. S. Schieve & P. M. Allen (Eds.), *Self organization in dissipative structures: Applications in the physical and social sciences.* Austin: University of Texas Press, 1982.

Coser, L. A. *The functions of social conflict.* Glencoe, Ill.: Free Press, 1956.

De Greene, K. *The adaptive organization: Anticipation and management of crisis.* New York: Wiley, 1982.

Elgin, D.S. Limits to the management of large complex systems. In *Assessment of future national and international problem areas.* Part iv, Vol. II. Menlo Park, Ca.: Stanford Research International, Center for the Study of Social Policy, 1977.

Glassman, R. Persistence and loose coupling. *Behavioral Science*, 1973, 18, 83–94.

Goffman, E. *Asylums.* New York: Doubleday, 1961.

Kuhn, T. *The structure of scientific revolutions* (2nd ed. enl.). Chicago: University of Chicago Press, 1970.

Levine, C. H. Organizational decline and cutback management. *Public Administration Review*, 1978, 38, 316–325.

Marayuma, M. The second cybernetics: Deviation amplifying mutual causal processes. In W. Buckley (Ed.), *Modern systems research for the behavioral scientist.* Chicago: Aldine, 1968, pp. 304–313.

Miller, J. G. *Living systems.* New York: McGraw-Hill, 1978.

Peters, T., & Waterman, R. *In search of excellence: Lessons from America's best run companies.* New York: Harper & Row, 1982.

Prigogine, I., Allen, P. M., & Herman, R. Long term trends in the evolution of complexity. In E. Laszlo & J. Bierman (Eds.), *Goals in a global community—A report to the Club of Rome,* vol. 1. New York: Pergamon, 1977.

Putney, S. *The conquest of society.* Belmont, Calif.: Wadsworth, 1972.

Rainey, H. G., Backoff, R. W., & Levine, C. H. Comparing public and private organizations. *Public Administration Review,* 1976, 36, 223–234.

Robbins, S. P. *Organization theory: The structure and design of organizations.* Englewood Cliffs, N.J.: Prentice-Hall, 1983.

Vaill, P. The purposing of high performing systems. *Organizational Dynamics,* Autumn 1982.

Weick, K. E. Educational organizations as loosely coupled systems. *Administrative Science Quarterly,* 1976, 21, 1–19.

Whetten, D. A. Sources, responses and effects of organizational decline. In J. R. Kimberly, et al. (Eds.), *The organizational life cycle.* San Francisco: Jossey-Bass, 1980.

CHAPTER 4

Alevras, J. S., & Wepman, B. J. Application of Gestalt therapy principles to organizational consultation. In B. Feder & R. Ronall (Eds.), *Beyond the hot seat, Gestalt approaches to group.* New York: Brunner/Mazel, 1980, pp. 229–238.

Boulding, K. E. General systems theory: The skeleton of science. In W. Buckley (Ed.), *Modern systems research for the behavioral scientist.* Chicago: Aldine, 1968, pp. 3–10.

Bowler, D. T. *General systems thinking: Its scope and applicability.* New York: Elsevier North Holland, 1981.

Burke, W. Warner. Systems theory, Gestalt theory, and organization development. Chapter 9 in G. Cummings (Ed.), *Systems theory for organizational development.* London: Wiley, 1980.

Dubin, R. *Theory building.* New York: Free Press, 1978.

Emery F. E., & Trist, E. L. The causal texture of organizational environments. *Human Relations,* Feb. 1965, XVIII(1), 21–32.

Ennis, K., & Mitchell, S. Staff training for a day care center. In J. Fagan & I. L. Shepherd (Eds.), *Gestalt therapy now.* New York: Harper & Row, 1971, pp. 295–300.

Herman, M. S. The Gestalt orientation to organization development. The shadow of organizational development. In C. Hatcher & P. Himmelstein (Eds.), *The handbook of Gestalt therapy.* New York: Jason Aronson, 1976, pp. 563–600.

Herman, M. S., & Korenich, M. *Authentic management: A Gestalt orientation to organizations and their development.* Reading, Mass.: Addison-Wesley, 1977, pp. 779–795.

James, W. *The will to believe.* New York: Longmans, Green, 1937.

Karp, H. B. A Gestalt approach to collaboration in organizations. In W. J. Pfeiffer & J. E. Jones (Eds.), *The 1976 annual handbook for group facilitators.* San Diego: University Associates, 1976, pp. 203–210.

Katz, D., & Kahn, R. L. *The social psychology of organizations* (2nd ed.). New York: Wiley, 1978.

Kogan, J., & Himmelstein, P. Gestalt therapy resources. In C. Hatcher & P. Himmelstein (Eds.), *The handbook of Gestalt therapy.* New York: Jason Aronson, 1976.

Lawrence, P. R., & Lorsch, J. W. *Organization and environment: Managing differentiation and integration.* Boston: Harvard Business School Research Press, 1967.

Merry, U. *Self done diagnosis.* (Hebrew) Tel-Aviv: Applied Social Research and OD Institute, 1981.

Miller, J. G. *Living systems.* New York: McGraw-Hill, 1978.

Miller, J. G. Living systems: Basic concepts. In W. Gray, F. J. Duhl, & N. D. Rizzo (Eds.), *General systems theory and psychiatry.* Boston: Little, Brown, 1969, pp. 51–134.

Nevis, E. C. *Gestalt awareness process in organizational assessment.* (reprint) Boston: M.I.T., 1980.

Perls, F. S. *Ego, hunger and agression.* New York: Vintage, 1969.

Perls, F. *The Gestalt approach and eyewitness to therapy.* New York: Bantam, 1980.

Perls, F. S. *Gestalt therapy verbatim.* New York: Bantam, 1976.

Perls, F. S., & Goodman, P. The theory of "The removal of inner conflict." In J. O. Stevens (Ed.), *Gestalt is.* Moab, Utah: Real Press, 1975. Reprinted from *Resistance,* 1950, 4, 5–6.

Terreberry, S. The evolution of organizational environments. *Administrative Science Quarterly,* March 1968, XII(4), 590–613.

Von Bertalanffy, L. General systems theory: A critical review. In W. Buckley (Ed.), *Modern systems research for the behavioral scientist.* Chicago: Aldine, 1968.

Zetterberg, H. L. *On theory and verification in sociology* (3rd enl. ed.). New Jersey: Bedminster Press, 1965.

Zinker, J. *Creative process in Gestalt therapy.* New York: Vintage, 1978.

CHAPTER 5

Aldrich, H. E. *Organizations and environments.* Englewood Cliffs, N.J.: Prentice-Hall, 1979.

Argyris, C., & Schon, D. A. *Organizational learning: A theory of action perspective.* Reading, Mass.: Addison-Wesley, 1978.

Birch, A. H. Economic models in political science. The case of "Exit, voice, and loyalty." *British Journal of Political Science*, Jan. 1975, 5, 65–82.

Carroll, S. J., & Tosi, H. L. *Organizational behavior*. Chicago: St. Clair Press, 1977.

Coser, L. A. *The functions of social conflict*. Glencoe, Ill.: Free Press, 1956.

Cyert, R. M., & March, J. G. *A behavioral theory of the firm*. Englewood Cliffs, N.J.: Prentice-Hall, 1963.

De Greene, K. B. *The adaptive organization: Anticipation and management of change*. New York: Wiley, 1982.

Goffman, E. *Asylums*. New York: Doubleday, 1961.

Hamner, C. W., & Organ, D. W. *Organizational behavior: An applied psychological approach*. Dallas: Business Pub., 1978.

Harvey, J. B., & Albertson, D. R. Neurotic organizations: symptoms, causes and treatment. *Personnel Journal*, Sept., Oct., 1971, L(9, 10), 694–699, 770–777.

Hedberg, B. How organizations learn and unlearn. In P. C. Nystrom & W. H. Starbuck (Eds.), *Handbook of organizational design*, vol. 1. New York: Oxford University Press, 1981.

Hedberg, B., Nystrom, P. C., & Starbuck, W. H. Camping on seesaws: Prescriptions for self-designing organization. *Administrative Science Quarterly*, March 1976, 21, 41–65.

Hirschman, A. O. *Exit, voice and loyalty*. Cambridge, Mass.: Harvard University Press, 1972.

Kets de Vries, M., & Miller, D. *Neurotic style and organizational pathology*. Montreal: McGill Faculty of Management (mimeo), 1982.

Kornhauser, A., Dubin, R., & Ross, A. M. *Industrial conflict*. New York: McGraw-Hill, 1954.

Kriesberg, L. *The sociology of social conflicts*. Englewood Cliffs, N.J.: Prentice-Hall, 1973.

Lammers, C. J., & Hickson, D. J. (Eds.). *Organizations alike and unlike*. London: Routledge, Kegan Paul, 1979.

Levinson, H., with Molinari, J., & Spohn, A. G. *Organizational diagnosis*. Cambridge, Mass.: Harvard University Press, 1972.

March, J. G., & Simon, H. A. *Organizations*. New York: Wiley, 1958.

Merton, R. *Social theory and social structure*. New York: Free Press, 1968.

Miller, J. G. *Living systems*. New York: McGraw-Hill, 1978.

Perls, F. *The Gestalt approach and eyewitness to therapy*. New York: Bantam, 1980.

Perls, F. S. *Ego, hunger and aggression*. New York: Vintage, 1969.

Simon, H. A. *The science of the artificial*. Cambridge, Mass.: M.I.T. Press, 1969.

Starbuck, W. H., & Dutton, J. M. Designing adaptive organizations. *Journal of Business Policy*, 1973, 3, 21–28.

Tannenbaum, R. *Of time and the river*. Working Paper #79-7. Los Angeles: Human System Development Study Center, Graduate School of Management, University of California, Los Angeles, 1979.

Thompson, J. D. *Modern organization*. New York: Knopf, 1964.

Watzlawick, P., Weakland, J. H., & Fisch, R. *Change—Principles of problem formation and problem resolution*. New York: Norton, 1974.

CHAPTER 6

Alderfer, C. P. The methodology of diagnosing group and inter group relations in organizations. In H. Meltzer & W. R. Nord (Eds.), *Making organizations humane and productive*. New York: Wiley, 1981.

Alevras, J. S., & Wepman, B. J. Application of Gestalt therapy principles in organizational consultation. In B. Feder & R. Ronall (Eds.), *Beyond the hotseat: Gestalt approaches to group*. New York: Brunner/Mazel, 1980.

Berelson, B., & Steiner, G. A. *Human behavior: An inventory of scientific findings*. New York: Harcourt, Brace & World, 1964.

Bowler, T. D. *General systems thinking*. New York: Elsevier, 1981.

Coser, L. *The functions of social conflict*. Glencoe, Ill.: Free Press, 1956.

De Board, R. *The psychoanalysis of organizations*. London: Tavistock, 1978.

De Greene, K. B. *The adaptive organization: Anticipation and management of crisis*. New York: Wiley, 1982.

Enright, J. *Enlightening Gestalt*. Pro Telos Pub., 1980.

Berelson, B., & Steiner, G. A. *Human behavior: An inventory of scientific findings*. New York: Harcourt, Brace & World, 1964.

Bowler, D. T. *General systems thinking*. New York: Elsevier, 1981.

Coser, L. *The functions of social conflict*. Glencoe, Ill.: Free Press, 1956.

De Board, R. *The psychoanalysis of organizations*. London: Tavistock, 1978.

De Greene, K. B. *The adaptive organization: Anticipation and management of crisis*. New York: Wiley, 1982.

Enright, J. *Enlightening Gestalt*. Pro Telos Pub., 1980.

Galbraith, J. *Designing complex organizations*. Reading, Mass.: Addison-Wesley, 1973.

Goldner, F. H. The division of labor, process and power. In M. N. Zald (Ed.), *Power in organizations*. Nashville, Tenn.: Vanderbilt University Press, 1970. pp. 97–143.

Herman, M. S., & Korenich, M. *Authentic management: A Gestalt orientation to organizations and their management*. Reading, Mass.: Addison-Wesley, 1977.

Kanter, R. M. *Men and women of the organization*. New York: Basic Books, 1977.

Kets de Vries, M., & Miller, D. *Neurotic style and organizational pathology*. Montreal: McGill Faculty of Management (mimeo), 1982.

Levinson, H., with J. Molinari & A. G. Spohn. *Organizational diagnosis*. Cambridge, Mass.: Harvard University Press, 1972.

March, J. G., & Simon, H. A. *Organizations*. New York: Wiley, 1958.

Merton, R. *Social theory and social structure*. New York: Free Press, 1968.

Miller, J. G. *Living systems*. New York: McGraw-Hill, 1978.

Miller, J. G., & Miller, J. L. General living systems theory and small groups. In H. I. Kaplan & B. J. Sadock (Eds.), *Comprehensive group psychotherapy* (2nd ed.). Baltimore: Williams & Wilkins, 1983.

Parsons, T. *The social system*. Glencoe, Ill.: Free Press, 1951.

Perls, F. *The Gestalt approach and eyewitness to therapy*. New York: Bantam, 1980.

Perls, F. S. *Ego, hunger and aggression.* New York: Vintage, 1969.

Perls, F. S. *Gestalt therapy verbatim.* New York: Bantam, 1976.

Perls, F. S., Hefferline, R. J., & Goodman, P. *Gestalt therapy: Excitement and growth in the human personality.* New York: The Julian Press, 1951.

Polster, E., & Polster, M. *Gestalt therapy integrated.* New York: Vintage Books, 1974.

Westerlund, G., & Sjostrand, S. E. *Organizational myths.* New York: Harper, 1979.

CHAPTER 7

Ackoff, R. L. *Creating the corporate future.* New York: Wiley, 1981.

Argyris, C., & Schon, D. A. *Organizational learning: A theory of action perspective.* Reading, Mass.: Addison-Wesley, 1978.

Bateson, G. *Steps to an ecology of the mind.* New York: Ballantine, 1972.

Beer, M. A social systems model for OD. In T. G. Cummings (Ed.), *Systems theory for organizational development.* Chichester: Wiley, 1981, pp. 73–116.

Berelson, B., & Steiner, G. A. *Human behavior: An inventory of scientific findings.* New York: Harcourt, Brace & World, 1964.

Berrien, K.F. *General and social systems.* New Brunswick, N.J.: Rutgers University Press, 1968.

Bibeault, D. B. *Corporate turnaround.* New York: McGraw-Hill, 1982.

Bowler, T. D. *General systems thinking.* New York: Elsevier, 1981.

Bradford, L. P., & Harvey, J. B. Dealing with dysfunctional organizational myths. *Training and Development Journal,* Sept. 1970, XXIV(9), 2–6.

De Board, R. *The psychoanalysis of organizations.* London: Tavistock, 1978.

Harvey, J. B., & Albertson, D. R. Neurotic organizations. *Personnel Journal,* Sept., Oct. 1971, L(9, 10), pp. 694–699, 770–777.

Hedberg, B. How organizations learn and unlearn. In P. C. Nystrom & W. H. Starbuck (Eds.), *The handbook of organization design: Adapting organizations to their environment,* vol. 1. New York: Oxford University Press, 1981, pp. 3–27.

Kets de Vries, M., & Miller, D. *Neurotic style and organizational pathology.* Montreal: McGill Faculty of Management (Mimeo), 1982.

Levinson, H., et al. *Organizational diagnosis.* Cambridge, Mass.: Harvard University Press, 1972.

Luthans, F. *Organizational behavior* (3rd ed.). New York: McGraw-Hill, 1981.

Marquis, H. H. *The changing corporate image.* New York: American Managerial Association, 1970.

Miller, J. G., & Miller, J. L. The earth as a system. *Behavioral Science,* vol. 27, 1982, pp. 303–322.

Perls, F. The Gestalt approach and eyewitness to therapy. New York: Bantam, 1980.

Perls, F. S. Ego, hunger and aggression. New York: Vintage, 1969.

Perls, F. S. Gestalt therapy verbatim. New York: Bantam, 1976.

Toffler, A. Future shock. New York: Bantam, 1971.

Villere, M. F. Transactional analysis at work. Englewood Cliffs, N.J.: Prentice-Hall, 1981.

Westerlund, G., & Sjostrand, S. E. Organizational myths. New York: Harper & Row, 1979.

CHAPTER 8

Ashby, W. R. Design for a brain. New York: Wiley, 1960.

Bales, R. F. How people interact. In A. W. Gouldner & H. P. Gouldner (Eds.), Modern sociology. New York: Harcourt, Brace & World, 1963, pp. 70–76.

Berelson, B., & Steiner, G. A. Human behavior: An inventory of scientific findings. New York: Harcourt, Brace & World, 1964.

Blake, R. R., & Mouton, J. S. The new managerial grid. Houston: Gulf Publishing, 1978.

Bowers, D. G., & Seashore, S. E. Protecting organizational effectiveness with a four factor theory of leadership. Administrative Science Quarterly, 1966, 11, 238–263.

Buckley, W. Sociology and modern systems theory. Englewood Cliffs, N.J.: Prentice-Hall, 1967.

Cannon, Walter B. The wisdom of the body (rev. ed.). New York: Norton, 1939.

Cohen, A. R., & Gadon, H. Alternative work schedules: Integrating individual and organizational needs. Reading, Mass.: Addison-Wesley, 1978.

Cummings, T. G. Socio-technical systems: An intervention strategy. In W. W. Burke (Ed.), Current issues and strategies in OD. New York: Human Sciences Press, 1976, pp. 187–213.

Cummings, T. G. (Ed.) Systems theory and organizational development. London: Wiley, 1980.

Jantsch, E. Design for evolution: Self organization and planning in the life of human systems. New York: Braziller, 1975.

Katz, D., & Kahn, R. L. The social psychology of organizations (2nd ed.). New York: Wiley, 1978.

Kimberly, J. R., Miles, R. H., et al. The organizational life cycle: Issues in the creation, transformation and decline of organizations. San Francisco: Jossey-Bass, 1980.

Klapp, O. E. Opening and closing in open systems. Behavioral Science, 1975, 20, 251–257.

Lippitt, G. L. Organizational renewal (2nd ed.). Englewood Cliffs, N.J.: Prentice-Hall, 1982.

Miller, J. G. The nature of liiving systems. In F. Baker (Ed.), *The nature of organizational systems*. Illinois: Irwin, 1978.

Perls, F. *The Gestalt approach and eyewitness to therapy*. New York: Bantam, 1980.

Perls, F. S., Hefferline, R. F., & Goodman, P. *Gestalt therapy: Excitement and growth in the human personality*. New York: Julian Press, 1951.

Polster, E., & Polster, M. *Gestalt therapy integrated*. New York: Random House, 1974.

Prigogine, I. *From being to becoming: Time and complexity in the physical sciences*. San Francisco: Freeman, 1980.

Reddin, W. J. *Effective management by objectives*. New York: McGraw-Hill, 1970.

Thompson J. D. *Organization in action*. New York: McGraw-Hill, 1967.

Von Bertalanffy, L. General system theory: A critical review. In W. Buckley (Ed.), *Modern systems research for the behavioral scientist*. Chicago: Aldine, 1968.

CHAPTER 9

Alderfer, C. P. The methodology of diagnosing group and intergroup relations in organizations. In H. Mellzer and W. R. Nord (Eds.), *Making organizations humane and productive*. New York: Wiley, 1981, pp. 355–371.

Berrien, K. F. *General and social systems*. New Brunswick, N.J.: Rutgers University Press, 1968.

Bowler, T. D. *General systems thinking: Its scope and applicability*. New York: Elsevier-North Holland, 1981.

Burke, W. W. Systems theory, Gestalt therapy, and organization development. In T. G. Cummings (Ed.), *Systems theory for organization development*. London: Wiley, 1980.

De Board, R. *The psychoanalysis of organizations*. London: Tavistock, 1978.

Goffman, E. *Asylums*. Doubleday, 1961.

Jantsch, E. *Design for evolution: Organization and planning in the life of human systems*. New York: Braziller, 1975.

Klapp, O. E. Opening and closing in open systems. *Behavioral Science*, 1975, *20*, 251–257.

Levinson, H. *Organizational diagnosis*. Cambridge, Mass.: Harvard University Press, 1972.

Litterer, J. A. *The analysis of organizations*. New York: Wiley, 1973.

Merry, U., & Allerhand, M. *Developing teams and organizations*. Reading, Mass.: Addison-Wesley, 1977.

Miller, J. G. *Living systems*. New York: McGraw-Hill, 1978.

Niv, A. Organizational disintegration: Roots, processes and types. In J. R. Kimberly et al. (Eds.), *The organizational life cycle*. San Francisco: Jossey-Bass, 1980.

Perls, F. *The Gestalt approach and eyewitness to therapy*. New York: Bantam, 1980.

Perls, F. S. *Gestalt therapy verbatim*. New York: Bantam, 1976.

Perls, F. S., Hefferline, R. F., & Goodman, P. *Gestalt therapy: Excitement and growth in the human personality*. New York: Julian Press, 1951.

Thompson, J. D. *Organization in action*. New York: McGraw-Hill, 1967.

CHAPTER 10

Angynis, C., & Schon, D. A. *Organizational learning: A theory of achon perspective*. Reading, Mass.: Addison-Wesley,, 1978.

Beckhard, R. The confrontation meeting. *Harvard Business Review*, March–April 1967, LXV(2), 149–154.

Beer, M. A social systems model for OD. In T.G. Cummings (Ed.), *Systems theory for organizational development*. Chichester: Wiley, 1981, pp. 73-116.

Berrien, K. F. *General and social systems*. New Brunswick, N.J.: Rutgers University Press, 1968.

Blake, R. R., & Mouton, J. S. *The new management grid*. Houston: Gulf Publishing, 1978.

Blau, P. *The dynamics of bureaucracy*. Chicago: University of Chicago Press, 1963.

Bowers, D. G., & Seashore, S. E. Protecting organizational effectiveness with a four-factor theory of leadership. *Administrative Science Quarterly*, 1966, 11, 238–63.

Bowler, T. D. *General systems thinking*. New York: Elsevier, 1981.

Clapp, N. W. *Work group norms: Leverage for organizational change, I: Theory; II: Application*. BPA Organization Development Reading Series, no. 2. Plainfield, N.J.: Block-Petrella-Weisbord Associates, Inc.

De Greene, K. *The adaptive organization: Anticipation and management of crisis*. New York: John Wiley, 1982.

Emery, F. *Democracy at work*. Leiden: Martinus Nijhoff, 1975.

Gibb, J. R. Defensive communication. *Journal of Communication*, Sept. 1961, XI(3), 141–148.

Gouldner, A. W. *Patterns of industrial democracy*. Glencoe: Free Press, 1954.

Gouldner, A. W., & Gouldner, H. P. *Modern sociology*. New York: Harcourt, Brace & World, 1963.

Harrison, R. Role negotiations. In W. W. Burke & H. A. Hornstein (Eds.), *The social technology of OD*. Fairfax, Va.: NTL Learning Resources, 1972, pp. 84–96.

Jantsch, E. *Design for evolution: Self organization and planning in the life of human systems.* New York: Braziller, 1975.

Jayuram, G. K. Open systems planning. In W. G. Bennis, D. Benne, R. Chin, & K. E. Corey (Eds.), The planning of change, (3rd ed.). New York: Holt, Rinehart & Winston, 1976.

Katzel, R. A. Attitudes and motivation. In H. Meltzer & W. R. Nord (Eds.), *Making organizations humane and productive.* New York: Wiley, 1981.

Kepner, E.H., & Tregoe, B. The Rational Man. New York: McGraw-Hill, 1965.

Levinson, H. *Organizational diagnosis.* Cambridge, Mass.: Harvard University Press, 1972.

Likert, R. *The human organization: Its management and value.* New York: McGraw-Hill, 1967.

Lippitt, G., & Lippitt, R. *The consulting process in action.* La Jolla: University Associates, 1978.

Luthans, F. *Organizational behavior.* New York: McGraw-Hill, 1981.

McGregor, D. M. The human side of enterprise. In W. G. Bennis, D. Benne, & R. Chin (Eds.) *The planning of change.* New York: Holt, Rinehart & Winston, 1964.

Merry, U., & Allerhand, M. *Developing teams and organizations.* Reading, Mass.: Addison-Wesley, 1977.

Merton, R. *Social theory and social structure.* New York: Free Press, 1968.

Miller, J. G. *Living systems.* New York: McGraw-Hill, 1978.

Miller, J. G. The earth as a system. *Behavioral Science,* 1982, vol. 27.

Perls, F. *The Gestalt approach and eyewitness to therapy.* New York: Bantam, 1980.

Perls, F. S. *Ego, hunger and agression.* New York: Vintage, 1969.

Perls, F. S. *Gestalt therapy verbatim.* New York: Bantam, 1976.

Roethlisberger, F. J., & Dickson, W. J. *Management and the worker.* Cambridge, Mass.: Harvard University Press, 1939.

Schein, E. H. *Process consultation: Its role in organization development.* Reading, Mass.: Addison-Wesley, 1969.

Selznick, P. *TVA and the grass roots.* Berkeley: University of California Press, 1949.

Steele, F., & Jenks, S. *The feel of the work place.* Reading, Mass.: Addison-Wesley, 1977.

Vaill, P. Towards a behavioral description of high-performing systems. In M. W. McCall & M. M. Lombardo (Eds.), *Leadership: Where else can we go?* Durham, N.C.: Duke University Press, 1978.

Walton. R.E. How to counter alienation in the plant. In W.A. Passmove & J.J. Sherwood (Eds.), *Socio technical systems: A source book.* La Jolla, Ca.: University Associates, 1978.

Zinker, J. *Creative process in Gestalt therapy.* New York: Random House, 1977.

CHAPTER 11

Alevras, J. S., & Wepman, B. J. Application of Gestalt therapy principles to organizational consultation. In B. Feder & R. Ronall (Eds.), *Beyond the hot seat, Gestalt approaches to group*. New York: Brunner/Mazel, 1980, pp. 229–238.

Burke, W. Warner. Systems theory, Gestalt theory, and Organization development. Chapter 9. G. Cummings (Ed.) *Systems theory for organizational development*. London: Wiley, 1980.

Enright, J. *Therapy without resistance*. Richmond, Calif.: ARC Associates.

Herman, M. S. Notes on freedom. In W. J. Pfeiffer & J. E. Jones (Eds.), *The 1972 Annual hardbook for group facilitators*. San Diego: University Associates, 1972, pp. 211–224.

Herman, M. S. The Gestalt orientation to organization development. In C. Hatcher & P. Hamelstein (Eds.), *The handbook of Gestalt therapy*. New York: Jason Aronson, 1976, pp. 563–600.

Herman, M. S., & Korenich, M. *Authentic management: A Gestalt orientation to organizations and their management*. Reading, Mass.: Addison-Wesley, 1977.

Karp, H. B. A Gestalt approach to collaboration in organizations. In W. J. Pfeiffer and J. E. Jones (Eds.), *The 1976 annual handbook for group facilitators*. San Diego: University Associates, 1976, pp. 203–210.

Naisbitt, J. *Megatrends*. New York: Warner Books, 1984.

Nevis, E. C. *Gestalt awareness process in organizational assessment*. (mimeo) Sloan School of Management, 1980.

Nevis, E. C. A Gestalt approach to organizational consulting. New York: Gestalt Institute of Cleveland Press, 1986.

Subject Index

Amana villages, 212
American College Dictionary, 27
Anti-Tuberculosis League, 219
Applied Social Research Institute, 4
Authentic Management, 80

Bader-Meynhoff, 173
Barron's, 268
Behavior, as Gestalt concept
  dysfunctional, in organizations, 82
  healthy, 76, 80
  neurotic, 76, 77, 86
Blocking
  action in organizations, 239-244
  awareness of needs, 224-226
  energy mobilization, 226-239
  in Gestalt Therapy, 226-229
  task/maintenance cycle, 222-224
Boeing, 43
Boredom, 236-239

Caterpillar, 43
Chrysler, 58
Climate, 46, 47
Collaboration, 81
Communication, 47, 48, 80, 224
Conflict,
  paralyzing, 92-94, 96
Confluence, 80, 137
  as neurotic mechanism, 116, 118,
    285
  at organizational level, 138-148
  in Gestalt therapy, 137, 138

Contact/withdrawal
  as input and output, 190-193
  at the organizational level, 188-198
  cycle, *figure* 223
  disruption of, 200-220
  in Gestalt therapy, 180-182, 184-
    188, 196
  meaning of, *table* 187
  "opening and closing," 193, 194,
    212, *figure* 213
  task and maintenance cycle, 194,
    195, *table* 197
  work cycle, 195, 196, *table* 197
Context, 119

Darkness at Noon, 127
Decline, of organizations
  change, 51, 52
  climate, 46, 47
  communication, 47, 48
  comparison, *table,* 44, 45
  criteria, 43
  dynamics of, 54-59
  fantasy, 43, 46
  functioning, 49, 50
  goals, 48, 49
  summary, 52-54
  trends, 50, 51
Delusions, 119
Delusions, organizational; see organizational delusions
Diagnosis,
  self-done, 84

301

Author Index